Financial Accounting

Financial Accounting

Lawrence Mueller

Willford Press
www.willfordpress.com

Published by Willford Press,
118-35 Queens Blvd., Suite 400,
Forest Hills, NY 11375, USA

ISBN: 978-1-68285-974-2

Cataloging-in-Publication Data

Financial accounting / Lawrence Mueller.
p. cm.
Includes bibliographical references and index.
ISBN 978-1-68285-974-2
1. Accounting. 2. Financial statements. 3. Bookkeeping. 4. Finance. I. Mueller, Lawrence.
HF5636 .F56 2022
657--dc23

For information on all Willford Press publications
visit our website at www.willfordpress.com

Willford Press

Table of Contents

Preface

This book has been written, keeping in view that students want more practical information. Thus, my aim has been to make it as comprehensive as possible for the readers. I would like to extend my thanks to my family and co-workers for their knowledge, support and encouragement all along.

The field of accounting that deals with the summary, analysis and reporting of financial transactions related to a business is known as financial accounting. It includes the preparation of financial statements that are available for public use. There are three major components of financial statements, namely, statement of cash flows, statement of profit and loss, and statement of financial position. Some of the objectives of this field are the systematic recording of transactions, providing information to users in order to facilitate informed decision making, and knowing solvency position. Fundamental qualities of financial accounting include relevance, materiality, reliability, understandability and comparability. This book provides comprehensive insights into the field of financial accounting. The topics included herein are of utmost significance and bound to provide incredible insights to readers. It aims to serve as a resource guide for students and experts alike and contribute to the growth of the discipline of financial accounting.

A brief description of the chapters is provided below for further understanding:

Chapter - What is Financial Accounting?

The field of accounting which is concerned with the summary, analysis and reporting of the business-related financial transactions is referred to as financial accounting. It plays a key role in recording transactions, communicating information externally or internally, and analyzing competitors. The topics elaborated in this chapter will help in gaining a better perspective about financial accounting.

Chapter - Principles and Concepts in Financial Accounting

The standards and rules which are used to regulate the field of accounting are known as accounting principles. Some of the key principles and concepts in financial accounting are principle of regularity, principle of sincerity, entity concept, money measurement concept, bookkeeping and realization concept. This chapter closely examines these key concepts and principles of financial accounting.

Chapter - Financial Mathematics and Ratios

The application of mathematical methods to financial problems is known as financial mathematics. The relative magnitude of two selected numerical values that are taken from the financial statements of an enterprise is termed as financial ratio. This chapter discusses in detail the concepts and application related to financial mathematics and ratios such as accounting liquidity and bias ratio.

Chapter - Financial Capital

The money which is used to acquire items and equipment that are needed to offer services and build products is termed as financial capital. Some of the key types of financial capital are capital expenditure, working capital, share capital, fixed capital, etc. The diverse applications of these types of financial capital have been thoroughly discussed in this chapter.

Chapter - Financial Statements

The formal records of the financial activities and positions of a business, entity or person are referred to as financial statements. The four basic financial statements are balance sheet, income statement, cash flow statement and statement of changes in equity. The topics elaborated in this chapter will help in gaining a better perspective about these types of financial statements.

Chapter - Financial Statement Analysis

The process of analyzing and reviewing an organization's financial statements in order to make better economic decisions for earning income in future is referred to as financial statement analysis. The most common methods of financial statement analysis are horizontal analysis and vertical analysis. This chapter has been carefully written to provide an easy understanding of these methods of financial statement analysis.

Lawrence Mueller

1

What is Financial Accounting?

The field of accounting which is concerned with the summary, analysis and reporting of the business-related financial transactions is referred to as financial accounting. It plays a key role in recording transactions, communicating information externally or internally, and analyzing competitors. The topics elaborated in this chapter will help in gaining a better perspective about financial accounting.

ACCOUNTING

Accounting is the language of finance. It conveys the financial position of the firm or business to anyone who wants to know. It helps to translate the workings of a firm into tangible reports that can be compared.

Accounting is all about the process that helps to record, summarize, analyze, and report data that concerns financial transactions. Let's understand the components a little better to understand the true meaning of accounting.

Recording

The first and foremost function that accounting looks forward to achieving is the recording of the different transactions that are made within the firm. This can also be referred to as book-keeping which is a process of recognizing the transactions and setting them up as records.

Book-keeping is only concerned with the recording segment and nothing else. Accounting maintains a few books for the cause of recording. The maintenance of the procedure happens in a systematic manner.

The three different ways of recording are:

- Putting up a system that will help in maintaining the records.
- Tracking financial transactions.
- Aggregating the reports to present a final set of financial reports.

Summarizing

Raw data is generally the result of recording transactions. However, these raw data are not of much significance to the organization. They have no part to play in the decision-making process. As a result of this, the accountants divide these raw data into several categories. So the recording of the transactions is then followed up by summarizing.

Reporting

The affairs in any company are the responsibility of the management. The owners must know about the various operations happening within the firm using their money. Therefore, to take care of this, owners receive reports. They receive these reports quarterly and at the end, they receive an annual report that summarizes all their performances.

Analyzing

Finally, there is an analysis of all the results so far. After recording and summary, it is very important to draw conclusions. It is the responsibility of the management to check for the positive and negative points.

Therefore, to analyze all of this, accounting introduces the concept of comparison. Comparing profits, sales, equity, and so on with one another to determine and analyze the performance and growth of an organization.

Basic Fundamentals of Accounting

Accounting is all about the term ALOE. Do not confuse it with the plant! ALOE is a term that has an important role to play in the accounting world and the understanding of the meaning of accounting. Here is what the acronym, “A-L-O-E” means.

- A – Assets.
- L – Liabilities.
- OE – Owner’s Equity.

This is one of the basic concepts of accounting. The equation for the same goes like this:

Assets = Liabilities + Owner’s Equity

Here is the meaning of every term that ALOE stands for:

- Assets: Assets are the items that belong to you and you are the owner of it. These items correspond to a "value" and can serve you cash in exchange for it. Examples of Assets are Car, House, etc.
- Liabilities: Whatever you own is a liability. Even a loan that you take from a bank to buy any sort of asset is a liability.
- Owner's Equity: The total amount of cash someone (anyone) invests in an organization is Owner's Equity. The investment done is not necessarily money always. It can be in the form of stocks too.

Objectives of Accounting

Maintaining Records

As we mentioned, accounting is the spoken language of transactions. The human brain cannot store endless information. And so accounting takes the charge of keeping the records of all the transactions made within a firm.

Profit and Loss

Business is directly proportional to profits. It is all about earning profits. The accounting chart of profit and loss determines whether there is a profit or loss made in the business. The income and expenditure decide profit and loss.

Utility of Resources

Resources are a very crucial part of any organization and for a firm to function smoothly, they play a significant role. The records hold the responsibility to report to the firm about the different activities along with its timing. Hence, it becomes easy for the management to take note of the details before putting in the money.

Estimation of Financial Position

A business person is not only interested in knowing the Profit and Losses of his business but he also wants to know how much he owes to his creditors and how much he has to pay to his debtors. For this purpose, he prepares a statement in which all such details are recorded. This statement is known as Balance sheet. With the help of Balance sheet Financial position of the business can be understood.

Helps in Decision Making

With the help of all the records that have been maintained by following Accounting Procedures, Decisions can be made with all those information which eventually helps in the smooth functioning of the organisation.

FINANCIAL ACCOUNTING

Financial accounting is a specialized branch of accounting that keeps track of a company's financial transactions. Using standardized guidelines, the transactions are recorded, summarized, and presented in a financial report or financial statement such as an income statement or a balance sheet.

Companies issue financial statements on a routine schedule. The statements are considered external because they are given to people outside of the company, with the primary recipients being owners/stockholders, as well as certain lenders. If a corporation's stock is publicly traded, however, its financial statements (and other financial reportings) tend to be widely circulated, and information will likely reach secondary recipients such as competitors, customers, employees, labor organizations, and investment analysts.

It's important to point out that the purpose of financial accounting is not to report the value of a company. Rather, its purpose is to provide enough information for others to assess the value of a company for themselves.

Because external financial statements are used by a variety of people in a variety of ways, financial accounting has common rules known as accounting standards and as generally accepted accounting principles (GAAP). In the U.S., the Financial Accounting Standards Board (FASB) is the organization that develops the accounting standards and principles. Corporations whose stock is publicly traded must also comply with the reporting requirements of the Securities and Exchange Commission (SEC), an agency of the U.S. government.

Double Entry and the Accrual Basis of Accounting

At the heart of financial accounting is the system known as double entry bookkeeping (or "double entry accounting"). Each financial transaction that a company makes is recorded by using this system.

The term "double entry" means that every transaction affects at least two accounts. For example, if a company borrows $50,000 from its bank, the company's Cash account increases, and the company's Notes Payable account increases. Double entry also means that one of the accounts must have an amount entered as a debit, and one of the accounts must have an amount entered as a credit. For any given transaction, the debit amount must equal the credit amount.

The advantage of double entry accounting is this: at any given time, the balance of a company's asset accounts will equal the balance of its liability and stockholders' (or owner's) equity accounts.

Financial accounting is required to follow the accrual basis of accounting (as opposed to the "cash basis" of accounting). Under the accrual basis, revenues are reported when they are earned, not when the money is received. Similarly, expenses are reported when they are incurred, not when they are paid. For example, although a magazine publisher receives a $24 check from a customer for an annual subscription, the publisher reports as revenue a monthly amount of $2 (one-twelfth of the annual subscription amount). In the same way, it reports its property tax expense each month as one-twelfth of the annual property tax bill.

By following the accrual basis of accounting, a company's profitability, assets, liabilities and other financial information is more in line with economic reality.

Accounting Principles

If financial accounting is going to be useful, a company's reports need to be credible, easy to understand, and comparable to those of other companies. To this end, financial accounting follows a set of common rules known as accounting standards or generally accepted accounting principles.

GAAP is based on some basic underlying principles and concepts such as the cost principle, matching principle, full disclosure, going concern, economic entity, conservatism, relevance, and reliability.

GAAP, however, is not static. It includes some very complex standards that were issued in response to some very complicated business transactions. GAAP also addresses accounting practices that may be unique to particular industries, such as utility, banking, and insurance. Often these practices are a response to changes in government regulations of the industry.

GAAP includes many specific pronouncements as issued by the Financial Accounting Standards Board. The FASB is a non-government group that researches current needs and develops accounting rules to meet those needs.

In addition to following the provisions of GAAP, any corporation whose stock is publicly traded is also subject to the reporting requirements of the Securities and Exchange Commission (SEC), an agency of the U.S. government. These requirements mandate an annual report to stockholders as well as an annual report to the SEC. The annual report to the SEC requires that independent certified public accountants audit a company's financial statements, thus giving assurance that the company has followed GAAP.

Financial Statements

Financial accounting generates the following general-purpose, external, financial statements:

- Income statement (sometimes referred to as "results of operations" or "earnings statement" or "profit and loss [P&L] statement").
- Balance sheet (sometimes referred to as "statement of financial position").
- Statement of cash flows (sometimes referred to as "cash flow statement").
- Statement of stockholders' equity.

Income Statement

The income statement reports a company's profitability during a specified period of time. The period of time could be one year, one month, three months, 13 weeks, or any other time interval chosen by the company.

The main components of the income statement are revenues, expenses, gains, and losses. Revenues include such things as sales, service revenues, and interest revenue. Expenses include the cost of goods sold, operating expenses (such as salaries, rent, utilities, advertising), and nonoperating expenses (such as interest expense). If a corporation's stock is publicly traded, the earnings per share of its common stock are reported on the income statement.

Balance Sheet

The balance sheet is organized into three parts: (1) assets, (2) liabilities, and (3) stockholders' equity at a specified date (typically, this date is the last day of an accounting period).

The first section of the balance sheet reports the company's assets and includes such things as cash, accounts receivable, inventory, prepaid insurance, buildings, and equipment. The next section reports the company's liabilities; these are obligations that are due at the date of the balance sheet and often include the word "payable" in their title (Notes Payable, Accounts Payable, Wages Payable, and Interest Payable). The final section is stockholders' equity, defined as the difference between the amount of assets and the amount of liabilities.

Statement of Cash Flows

The statement of cash flows explains the change in a company's cash (and cash equivalents) during the time interval indicated in the heading of the statement. The change is divided into three parts: (1) operating activities, (2) investing activities, and (3) financing activities.

The operating activities section explains how a company's cash (and cash equivalents) have changed due to operations. Investing activities refer to amounts spent or received in transactions involving long-term assets. The financing activities section reports such things as cash received through the issuance of long-term debt, the issuance of stock, or money spent to retire long-term liabilities.

Statement of Stockholders' Equity

The statement of stockholders' (or shareholders') equity lists the changes in stockholders' equity for the same period as the income statement and the cash flow statement. The changes will include items such as net income, other comprehensive income, dividends, the repurchase of common stock, and the exercise of stock options.

Financial Reporting

Financial reporting is a broader concept than financial statements. In addition to the financial statements, financial reporting includes the company's annual report to stockholders, its annual report to the Securities and Exchange Commission (Form 10-K), its proxy statement, and other financial information reported by the company.

Financial Accounting vs. other Accounting

Financial accounting represents just one sector in the field of business accounting. Another sector, managerial accounting, is so named because it provides financial information to a company's management. This information is generally internal (not distributed outside of the company) and is primarily used by management to make decisions. Other sectors of the accounting field include cost accounting, tax accounting, and auditing.

Importance of Financial Accounting

Financial accounting, which some call "the language of business," is important to companies of any size. For small-business owners, the importance of financial accounting sometimes is overlooked. By understanding how useful financial accounting can be to the success of a small business, you can focus on the qualities that can take your business the furthest.

Recording Transactions

A major use of financial accounting is for the recording of transactions. This function of accounting is also known as bookkeeping. Small-business owners use financial accounting to record business activity in the company's ledger. Because financial accounting uses the double-entry system, each transaction affects two accounts, representing the two sides to a transaction. For example, if a business owner purchases land for cash, he would record a debit to the land account to represent the receipt of land, and a credit to the cash account to represent the outflow of cash. This use of accounting is important to small-business owners because it provides a methodological approach to describing the activities of business.

Communicating Information Externally

Small-business owners use financial accounting to communicate information to external parties. People and organizations that use the financial information of a company, but are not part of the company, are known as external users of financial statements. Owners communicate the financial health and well-being of a company to external users through the financial statements, which are the end result of recording financial accounting transactions. External users will examine the financial statements and compare the results to their own expectations, forming an assessment of the company. Common external users include banks, suppliers and leasing companies.

Communicating Information Internally

While managerial accounting is more geared towards internal users, financial accounting is also used for internal information communication. Internal users of financial accounting information include the finance team and employees who may be interested in profit-sharing or stock-based compensation agreements. Small-business owners can use financial accounting information to share company strengths and weaknesses with employees. For small public companies, a common metric is the company's share price. Owners may tie bonus and compensation amounts to share price and encourage employee productivity accordingly.

Analysis and Comparison

Small-business owners may use financial accounting information to analyze competitors and evaluate investment opportunities. Because financial accounting is governed by generally accepted accounting principles, the financial statements of different companies are comparable to one another. This basis for comparability provides a standard method of analysis. Small-business owners can compute financial ratios using the company's financial statements, and compare the ratios to benchmarks or other competitors. While financial statements are comparable, small-business owners should exercise some caution, as non-financial measures can provide insight into a company's health as well.

ASSET

An asset is anything of monetary value owned by a person or business. Assets are classed as capital/fixed, current, tangible or intangible and expressed in terms of their cash value on financial statements. Tangible assets include money, land, buildings, investments, inventory, cars, trucks, boats, or other valuables. Intangibles such as goodwill are also considered to be assets.

Capital Assets

Also known as Fixed Assets, capital assets are those tangible physical assets acquired to carry on the business of a company with a life exceeding one year. Examples include:

- Land,
- Buildings,
- Vehicles,
- Boats,
- Aircraft,
- Tools,
- Machinery,
- Computer hardware, mobile phones, etc.,
- Equipment.

Businesses that have a high ratio of capital costs to labor costs are known as Capital Intensive businesses; that is, they require a large financial investment in capital assets to produce goods or services. Examples of capital intensive industries include:

- Mining,
- Farming,
- Transportation - Airlines, railroads, trucking, etc.,
- Oil and gas,
- Fishing,
- Construction.

Aside from being used to generate income, capital assets are important for businesses in that they can be sold if the business is in financial difficulty or used as collateral for business loans. In this case the lender will normally issue a lien against the asset so it can be seized if the loan is not repaid.

Given that most capital assets decline in value over time, in financial records capital assets are usually expressed as the cost of the asset minus depreciation. Capital assets depreciate at different rates depending on the asset class. The annual depreciation is a tax write off (In Canada this is known is the Capital Cost Allowance or CCA).

Non-capital intensive businesses create wealth in ways that do not require plants, machinery, or expensive equipment, rather they rely on "intellectual capital". Non-capital businesses have much lower barriers to entry given the minimal startup costs. Examples include:

- Software development firms,
- Consultants,
- Writers,
- Accountants,
- Lawyers.

Current Assets

Items that are currently cash or expected to be turned into cash within one year are known as current assets. This includes:

- Cash,
- Inventory,
- Accounts receivable.

Intangible Assets

Examples of intangible assets include items such as:

- Client lists,
- Franchise agreements,
- Favorable finance or lease agreements,
- Brand names,
- Distribution networks,
- Patents,
- Proprietary processes or technology (or anything protected by copyright),
- Supplier contracts,
- Skilled employees.

Intangible assets do not appear on balance sheets but (depending on the business) may make up a substantial part of the asset value of a business.

Classification of assets as tangible or intangible is not necessarily a straightforward process. For example, the oil and gas industry has special accounting rules for classifying petroleum reserves as either tangible or intangible depending on the stage of development, as does the mining industry (e.g. an oil field or ore body does not become a tangible asset until it becomes commercially viable and begins producing oil and gas or ore).

Because the underlying commodity can be subject to large fluctuations in price, the value of assets in commodity-based industries such as oil and gas and mining can vary enormously in a relatively short period of time - the huge drop in oil prices in 2015, for instance, forced many oil and gas companies to take major write downs on assets due to the decline in the value of reserves. On the other hand, a factory owned by a manufacturing business is typically a long term core asset that slowly depreciates in value over time.

LIABILITY

Liabilities are legally binding obligations that are payable to another person or entity. Settlement of a liability can be accomplished through the transfer of money, goods, or services. A liability is increased in the accounting records with a credit and decreased with a debit. A liability can be considered a source of funds, since an amount owed to a third party is essentially borrowed cash that can then be used to support the asset base of a business. Examples of liabilities are:

- Accounts payable,
- Accrued liabilities,
- Deferred revenue,
- Interest payable,
- Notes payable,
- Taxes payable,
- Wages payable.

Liabilities are aggregated on the balance sheet within two general classifications, which are current liabilities and long-term liabilities. You would classify a liability as a current liability if you expect to liquidate the obligation within one year. All other liabilities are classified as long-term liabilities. If you have a long-term note or bond payable, that portion of it due for payment within the next year is classified as a current liability. Most types of liabilities are classified as current liabilities, including accounts payable, accrued liabilities, and wages payable.

It is possible to have a negative liability, which arises when a company pays more than the amount of a liability, thereby theoretically creating an asset in the amount of the overpayment. Negative liabilities tend to be quite small.

A contingent liability is a potential liability that will only be confirmed as a liability when an uncertain event has been resolved at some point in the future. You should only record a contingent liability if it is probable that the liability will occur, and if you can reasonably estimate its amount. The outcome of a lawsuit is a typical contingent liability.

A provision is a liability or reduction in the value of an asset that an entity elects to recognize now, before it has exact information about the amount involved. For example, an entity routinely records provisions for bad debts, sales allowances, and inventory obsolescence. Less common provisions are for severance payments, asset impairments, and reorganization costs.

ASSET LIABILITY MANAGEMENT

Asset Liability Management (ALM) can be defined as a mechanism to address the risk faced by a bank due to a mismatch between assets and liabilities either due to liquidity or changes in interest rates. Liquidity is an institution's ability to meet its liabilities either by borrowing or converting assets. Apart from liquidity, a bank may also have a mismatch due to changes in interest rates as banks typically tend to borrow short term (fixed or floating) and lend long term (fixed or floating).

A comprehensive ALM policy framework focuses on bank profitability and longterm viability by targeting the net interest margin (NIM) ratio and Net Economic Value (NEV), subject to balance sheet constraints. Significant among these constraints are maintaining credit quality, meeting liquidity needs and obtaining sufficient capital.

An insightful view of ALM is that it simply combines portfolio management techniques (that is, asset, liability and spread management) into a coordinated process. Thus, the central theme of ALM is the coordinated – and not piecemeal – management of a bank's entire balance sheet.

Although ALM is not a relatively new planning tool, it has evolved from the simple idea of maturity-matching of assets and liabilities across various time horizons into a framework that includes sophisticated concepts such as duration matching, variablerate pricing, and the use of static and dynamic simulation.

Measuring Risk

The function of ALM is not just protection from risk. The safety achieved through ALM also opens up opportunities for enhancing net worth. Interest rate risk (IRR) largely poses a problem to a bank's net interest income and hence profitability. Changes in interest rates can significantly alter a bank's net interest income (NII), depending on the extent of mismatch between the asset and liability interest rate reset times. Changes in interest rates also affect the market value of a bank's equity. Methods of managing IRR first require a bank to specify goals for either the book value or the market value of NII. In the former case, the focus will be on the current value of NII and in the latter, the focus will be on the market value of equity. In either case, though, the bank has to measure the risk exposure and formulate strategies to minimise or mitigate risk.

The immediate focus of ALM is interest-rate risk and return as measured by a bank's net interest margin.

NIM = (Interest income – Interest expense) / Earning assets.

A bank's NIM, in turn, is a function of the interest-rate sensitivity, volume, and mix of its earning assets and liabilities. That is,

NIM = f (Rate, Volume, Mix).

Sources of Interest Rate Risk

The primary forms of interest rate risk include repricing risk, yield curve risk, basis risk and optionality.

Effects of Interest Rate Risk

Changes in interest rates can have adverse effects both on a bank's earnings and its economic value.

The Earnings Perspective

From the earnings perspective, the focus of analyses is the impact of changes in interest rates on accrual or reported earnings. Variation in earnings (NII) is an important focal point for IRR analysis because reduced interest earnings will threaten the financial performance of an institution.

Economic Value Perspective

Variation in market interest rates can also affect the economic value of a bank's assets, liabilities, and Off Balance Sheet (OBS) positions. Since the economic value perspective considers the potential impact of interest rate changes on the present value of all future cash flows, it provides a more comprehensive view of the potential long-term effects of changes in interest rates than is offered by the earnings perspective.

Interest Rate Sensitivity and Gap Management

This model measures the direction and extent of asset-liability mismatch through a funding or maturity GAP (or, simply, GAP). Assets and liabilities are grouped in this method into time buckets according to maturity or the time until the first possible resetting of interest rates. For each time bucket the GAP equals the difference between the interest rate sensitive assets (RSAs) and the interest rate sensitive liabilities (RSLs). In symbols:

Sl. No.	Sl. No. Type of GAP	Change in Interest Rates (Δr)	Change in Net Interest Income (ΔNII)
1	RSA = RSLs	Increase	No change
2	RSA = RSLs	Decrease	No change
3	RSAs ≥ RSLs	Increase	NII increases
4	RSAs ≥ RSLs	Decrease	NII decreases
5	RSAs ≤ RSLs	Increase	NII decreases
6	RSAs ≤ RSLs	Decrease	NII increases

$$GAP = RSAs - RSLs$$

When interest rates change, the bank's NII changes based on the following interrelationships:

$$\Delta NII = (RSAs - RSLs)$$

$$\Delta r \, \Delta NII = GAP \times \Delta r$$

A zero GAP will be the best choice either if the bank is unable to speculate interest rates accurately or if its capacity to absorb risk is close to zero. With a zero GAP, the bank is fully protected against both increases and decreases in interest rates as its NII will not change in both cases.

As a tool for managing IRR, GAP management suffers from three limitations:

- Financial institutions in the normal course are incapable of out-predicting the markets, hence maintain the zero GAP.
- It assumes that banks can flexibly adjust assets and liabilities to attain the desired GAP.
- It focuses only on the current interest sensitivity of the assets and liabilities, and ignores the effect of interest rate movements on the value of bank assets and liabilities.

Cumulative GAP Model

In this model, the sum of the periodic GAPs is equal to the cumulative GAP measured by the maturity GAP model. While the periodic GAP model corrects many of the deficiencies of the GAP model, it does not explicitly account for the influence of multiple market rates on the interest income.

Duration GAP Model (DAGAP)

Duration is defined as the average life of a financial instrument. It also provides an approximate measure of market value interest elasticity. Duration analysis begins by computing the individual duration of each asset and liability and weighting the individual durations by the percentage of the asset or liability in the balance sheet to obtain the combined asset and liability duration.

$$DURgap = DURassets - Kliabilities \; DURliabilities$$

Where,

Kliabilities = Percentage of assets funded by liabilities

DGAP directly indicates the effect of interest rate changes on the net worth of the institution. The funding GAP technique matches cash flows by structuring the short-term maturity buckets. On the other hand, the DGAP hedges against IRR by structuring the portfolios of assets and liabilities to change equally in value whenever the interest rate changes. If DGAP is close to zero, the market value of the bank's equity will not change and, accordingly, become immunised to any changes in interest rates.

DGAP analysis improves upon the maturity and cumulative GAP models by taking into account the timing and market value of cash flows rather than the horizon maturity. It gives a single index measure of interest rate risk exposure.

The application of duration analysis requires extensive data on the specific characteristics and current market pricing schedules of financial instruments. However, for institutions which have a high proportion of assets and liabilities with embedded options, sensitivity analysis conducted using duration as the sole measure of price elasticity is likely to lead to erroneous results due to the existence of convexity in such instruments. Apart from this, duration analysis makes an assumption of parallel shifts in the yield curve, which is not always true. To take care of this, a high degree of analytical approach to yield curve dynamics is required. However, immunisation through duration eliminates the possibility of unexpected gains or losses when there is a parallel shift in the yield curve. In other words, it is a hedging or risk-minimisation strategy; not a profit-maximisation strategy.

Simulation Analysis

Simulations serve to construct the risk-return profile of the banking portfolio. Scenario analysis addresses the issue of uncertainty associated with the future direction of interest rates by allowing the analysis of isolated attributes with the use of 'what if' simulations. However, it is debatable if simulation analysis, with its attendant controls and ratification methods, can effectively capture the dynamics of yield curve evolution and interest rate sensitivity of key financial variables.

Managing Interest Rate Risk

Depending upon the risk propensity of an institution, risk can be controlled using a variety of techniques that can be classified into direct and synthetic methods. The direct method of restructuring the balance sheet relies on changing the contractual characteristics of assets and liabilities to achieve a particular duration or maturity GAP. On the other hand, the synthetic method relies on the use of instruments such as interest rate swaps, futures, options and customised agreements to alter the balance sheet risk exposure. Since direct restructuring may not always be possible, the availability of synthetic methods adds a certain degree of flexibility to the assetliability GAP management process. In addition, the process of securitisation and financial engineering can also be used to create assets with wide investor appeal in order to adjust asset-liability GAPs.

Using Interest Rate Swaps to Hedge Interest Rate Risk

Interest rate swaps (IRS) represent a contractual agreement between a financial institution and a counterparty to exchange cash flows at periodic intervals, based on a notional amount. The purpose of an interest rate swap is to hedge interest rate risk. By arranging for another party to assume its interest payments, a bank can put in place such a hedge. Financial institutions can use such swaps to synthetically convert floating rate liabilities to fixed rate liabilities. The arbitrage potential associated with different comparative financing advantages (spreads) enables both parties to benefit through lower borrowing costs.

In case of a falling interest rate scenario, prepayment will increase with an attendant shortening of the asset's average life. The financial institution may have to continue exchanging swap cash flows for a period longer than the average life of the asset. In order to protect such situations, options on swaps or 'swaptions' may be used. Call options on swaps allow the financial institution to call the swap, while put options on swaps allow the institution to activate or put the swap after a specific period.

Using Financial Futures to Hedge Interest Rate Risk

A futures contract is an agreement between a buyer and seller to exchange a fixed quantity of a financial asset at an agreed price on a specified date. Interest rate futures (IRF) can be used to control the risk associated with the asset/liability GAP either at the macro-level or at the micro-level. A macro-hedge is used to protect the entire balance sheet, whereas a micro-hedge is applied to individual assets or transactions. A buyer, holding a long position, would purchase a futures contract when interest rates are expected to fall. The seller of a futures contract, on the other hand, would take a short position in anticipation of rising rates. The protection provided by financial futures is symmetric in that losses (or gains) in the value of the cash position are offset by gains (or losses) in the value of the futures position. Forward contracts are also available to hedge against exchange rate risk.

Futures contracts are not without their own risks. Among the most important is basis risk, especially prevalent in cross hedging. Financial institutions must also pay close attention to the hedging ratio, and managements must be careful to follow regulatory and accounting rules governing the use of futures contracts.

Using Options to Hedge Interest Rate Risk

Options can be used to create a myriad risk-return profiles using two essential ingredients: calls and puts. Call option strategies are profitable in bullish interest rate scenarios. With respect to the ALM process, options can be used for reducing risk and enhancing yield. Put options can be used to provide insurance against price declines, with limited risk if the opposite occurs. Similarly, call options can be used to enhance profits if the market rallies, with the maximum loss restricted to the upfront premium.

Customised Interest Rate Agreements

'Customised interest rate agreements' is the general term used to classify instruments such as interest rate caps and floors. In return for the protection against rising liability costs, the cap buyer pays a premium to the cap seller. The pay-off profile of the cap buyer is asymmetric in nature, in that if interest rates do not rise, the maximum loss is restricted to the cap premium. Since the cap buyer gains when interest rates rise, the purchase of a cap is comparable to buying a strip of put options. Similarly, in return for the protection against falling asset returns, the floor buyer pays a premium to the seller of the floor. The pay-off profile of the floor buyer is also asymmetric in nature since the maximum loss is restricted to the floor premium. As interest rates fall, the pay-off to the buyer of the floor increases in proportion to the fall in rates. In this respect, the purchase of a floor is comparable to the purchase of a strip of call options.

By buying an interest rate cap and selling an interest rate floor to offset the cap premium, financial institutions can also limit the cost of liabilities to a band of interest rate constraints. This strategy, known as an interest rate 'collar,' has the effect of capping liability costs in rising rate scenarios.

Role of Securitisation in ALM

By using securitisation, financial institutions can create securities suitable for resale in capital markets from assets which otherwise would have been held to maturity. In addition to providing an alternative route for asset/liability restructuring, securitisation may also be viewed as a form of direct financing in which savers are directly lending to borrowers. Securitisation also provides the additional advantage of cleansing the balance sheet of complex and highly illiquid assets as long as the transformations required to enhance marketability are available on a cost-effective basis. Securitisation transfers risks such as interest rate risk, credit risk (unless the loans are securitised with full or partial recourse to the originator) and pre-payment risk to the ultimate investors of the securitised assets.

Besides increasing the liquidity and diversification of the loans portfolio, securitisation allows a financial institution to recapture some part of the profits of lending and permits reduction in the cost of intermediation.

References

- Meaning-of-accounting, meaning-and-scope-of-accounting, principles-and-practice-of-accounting, guides: toppr.com, Retrieved 12 July 2019
- Explanation, financial-accounting: accountingcoach.com, Retrieved 29 March 2019
- Financial-accounting-important-company-4945: azcentral.com, Retrieved 11 January 2019
- Assets-definition-2947887: thebalancesmb.com, Retrieved 1 August 2019
- What-are-liabilities: accountingtools.com, Retrieved 5 March 2019
- Financial-services, industries: oracle.com, Retrieved 15 February 2019

2

Principles and Concepts in Financial Accounting

The standards and rules which are used to regulate the field of accounting are known as accounting principles. Some of the key principles and concepts in financial accounting are principle of regularity, principle of sincerity, entity concept, money measurement concept, bookkeeping and realization concept. This chapter closely examines these key concepts and principles of financial accounting.

ACCOUNTING PRINCIPLES

There are general rules and concepts that govern the field of accounting. These general rules–referred to as basic accounting principles and guidelines–form the groundwork on which more detailed, complicated, and legalistic accounting rules are based. For example, the Financial Accounting Standards Board (FASB) uses the basic accounting principles and guidelines as a basis for their own detailed and comprehensive set of accounting rules and standards.

The phrase "generally accepted accounting principles" (or "GAAP") consists of three important sets of rules: (1) the basic accounting principles and guidelines, (2) the detailed rules and standards issued by FASB and its predecessor the Accounting Principles Board (APB), and (3) the generally accepted industry practices.

If a company distributes its financial statements to the public, it is required to follow generally accepted accounting principles in the preparation of those statements. Further, if a company's stock is publicly traded, federal law requires the company's financial statements be audited by independent public accountants. Both the company's management and the independent accountants must certify that the financial statements and the related notes to the financial statements have been prepared in accordance with GAAP.

GAAP is exceedingly useful because it attempts to standardize and regulate accounting definitions, assumptions, and methods. Because of generally accepted accounting principles we are able to assume that there is consistency from year to year in the methods used to prepare a company's financial statements. And although variations may exist, we can make reasonably confident conclusions when comparing one company to another, or comparing one company's financial statistics to the statistics for its industry. Over the years the generally accepted accounting principles have become more complex because financial transactions have become more complex.

Basic Accounting Principles and Guidelines

Since GAAP is founded on the basic accounting principles and guidelines, we can better understand GAAP if we understand those accounting principles. The following is a list of the ten main accounting principles and guidelines together with a highly condensed explanation of each.

Economic Entity Assumption

The accountant keeps all of the business transactions of a sole proprietorship separate from the business owner's personal transactions. For legal purposes, a sole proprietorship and its owner are considered to be one entity, but for accounting purposes they are considered to be two separate entities.

Monetary Unit Assumption

Economic activity is measured in U.S. dollars, and only transactions that can be expressed in U.S. dollars are recorded. Because of this basic accounting principle, it is assumed that the dollar's purchasing power has not changed over time. As a result accountants ignore the effect of inflation on recorded amounts. For example, dollars from a 1960 transaction are combined (or shown) with dollars from a 2018 transaction.

Time Period Assumption

This accounting principle assumes that it is possible to report the complex and ongoing activities of a business in relatively short, distinct time intervals such as the five months ended May 31, 2018, or the 5 weeks ended May 1, 2018. The shorter the time interval, the more likely the need for the accountant to estimate amounts relevant to that period. For example, the property tax bill is received on December 15 of each year. On the income statement for the year ended December 31, 2017, the amount is known; but for the income statement for the three months ended March 31, 2018, the amount was not known and an estimate had to be used.

It is imperative that the time interval (or period of time) be shown in the heading of each income statement, statement of stockholders' equity, and statement of cash flows. Labeling one of these financial statements with "December 31" is not good enough–the reader needs to know if the statement covers the one week ended December 31, 2018 the month ended December 31, 2018 the three months ended December 31, 2018 or the year ended December 31, 2018.

Cost Principle

From an accountant's point of view, the term "cost" refers to the amount spent (cash or the cash equivalent) when an item was originally obtained, whether that purchase happened last year or thirty years ago. For this reason, the amounts shown on financial statements are referred to as historical cost amounts.

Because of this accounting principle asset amounts are not adjusted upward for inflation. In fact, as a general rule, asset amounts are not adjusted to reflect any type of increase in value. Hence, an asset amount does not reflect the amount of money a company would receive if it were to sell the asset at today's market value. (An exception is certain investments in stocks and bonds that are actively traded on a stock exchange.) If you want to know the current value of a company's long-term assets, you will not get this information from a company's financial statements–you need to look elsewhere, perhaps to a third-party appraiser.

Full Disclosure Principle

If certain information is important to an investor or lender using the financial statements, that information should be disclosed within the statement or in the notes to the statement. It is because of this basic accounting principle that numerous pages of "footnotes" are often attached to financial statements. As an example, let's say a company is named in a lawsuit that demands a significant amount of money. When the financial statements are prepared it is not clear whether the company will be able to defend itself or whether it might lose the lawsuit. As a result of these conditions and because of the full disclosure principle the lawsuit will be described in the notes to the financial statements. A company usually lists its significant accounting policies as the first note to its financial statements.

Going Concern Principle

This accounting principle assumes that a company will continue to exist long enough to carry out its objectives and commitments and will not liquidate in the foreseeable future. If the company's financial situation is such that the accountant believes the company will not be able to continue on, the accountant is required to disclose this assessment. The going concern principle allows the company to defer some of its prepaid expenses until future accounting periods.

Matching Principle

This accounting principle requires companies to use the accrual basis of accounting. The matching principle requires that expenses be matched with revenues. For example, sales commissions expense should be reported in the period when the sales were made (and not reported in the period when the commissions were paid). Wages to employees are reported as an expense in the week when the employees worked and not in the week when the employees are paid. If a company agrees to give its employees 1% of its 2018 revenues as a bonus on January 15, 2019, the company should report the bonus as an expense in 2018 and the amount unpaid at December 31, 2018 as a liability. The expense is occurring as the sales are occurring.

Because we cannot measure the future economic benefit of things such as advertisements (and thereby we cannot match the ad expense with related future revenues), the accountant charges the ad amount to expense in the period that the ad is run.

Revenue Recognition Principle

Under the accrual basis of accounting (as opposed to the cash basis of accounting), revenues are recognized as soon as a product has been sold or a service has been performed, regardless of when the money is actually received. Under this basic accounting principle, a company could earn and report $20,000 of revenue in its first month of operation but receive $0 in actual cash in that month. For example, if ABC Consulting completes its service at an agreed price of $1,000, ABC should recognize $1,000 of revenue as soon as its work is done—it does not matter whether the client pays the $1,000 immediately or in 30 days. Do not confuse revenue with a cash receipt.

Materiality

Because of this basic accounting principle or guideline, an accountant might be allowed to violate another accounting principle if an amount is insignificant. Professional judgement is needed to decide whether an amount is insignificant or immaterial. An example of an obviously immaterial item is the purchase of a $150 printer by a highly profitable multi-million dollar company. Because the printer will be used for five years, the matching principle directs the accountant to expense the cost over the five-year period. The materiality guideline allows this company to violate the matching principle and to expense the entire cost of $150 in the year it is purchased. The justification is that no one would consider it misleading if $150 is expensed in the first year instead of $30 being expensed in each of the five years that it is used. Because of materiality, financial statements usually show amounts rounded to the nearest dollar, to the nearest thousand, or to the nearest million dollars depending on the size of the company.

Conservatism

If a situation arises where there are two acceptable alternatives for reporting an item, conservatism directs the accountant to choose the alternative that will result in less net income and less asset amount. Conservatism helps the accountant to "break a tie." It does not direct accountants to be conservative. Accountants are expected to be unbiased and objective. The basic accounting principle of conservatism leads accountants to anticipate or disclose losses, but it does not allow a similar action for gains. For example, potential losses from lawsuits will be reported on the financial statements or in the notes, but potential gains will not be reported. Also, an accountant may write inventory down to an amount that is lower than the original cost, but will not write inventory up to an amount higher than the original cost.

GENERALLY ACCEPTED ACCOUNTING PRINCIPLES

Generally accepted accounting principles (GAAP) refer to a common set of accepted accounting principles, standards, and procedures that companies and their accountants must follow when they compile their financial statements. GAAP is a combination of authoritative standards (set by policy boards) and the commonly accepted ways of recording and reporting accounting information. GAAP improves the clarity of the communication of financial information.

GAAP may be contrasted with pro forma accounting and with the IFRS standards, which are both considered to be non-GAAP.

GAAP is meant to ensure a minimum level of consistency in a company's financial statements, which makes it easier for investors to analyze and extract useful information. GAAP also facilitates the cross-comparison of financial information across different companies.

These 10 general principles can help you remember the main mission and direction of the GAAP system:

- Principle of Regularity: The accountant has adhered to GAAP rules and regulations as a standard.

- Principle of Consistency: Professionals commit to applying the same standards throughout the reporting process to prevent errors or discrepancies. Accountants are expected to fully disclose and explain the reasons behind any changed or updated standards.
- Principle of Sincerity: The accountant strives to provide an accurate depiction of a company's financial situation.
- Principle of Permanence of Methods: The procedures used in financial reporting should be consistent.
- Principle of Non-compensation: Both negatives and positives should be fully reported with transparency and without the expectation of debt compensation.
- Principle of Prudence: Emphasizing fact-based financial data representation that is not clouded by speculation.
- Principle of Continuity: While valuing assets, it should be assumed the business will continue to operate.
- Principle of Periodicity: Entries should be distributed across the appropriate periods of time. For example, revenue should be divided by its relevant periods.
- Principle of Materiality/Good Faith: Accountants must strive for full disclosure in financial reports.
- Principle of Utmost Good Faith: It is used within the insurance industry. It presupposes that parties remain honest in transactions.

Compliance

GAAP must be followed when a company distributes its financial statements outside of the company. If a corporation's stock is publicly traded, the financial statements must also adhere to rules established by the U.S. Securities and Exchange Commission (SEC).

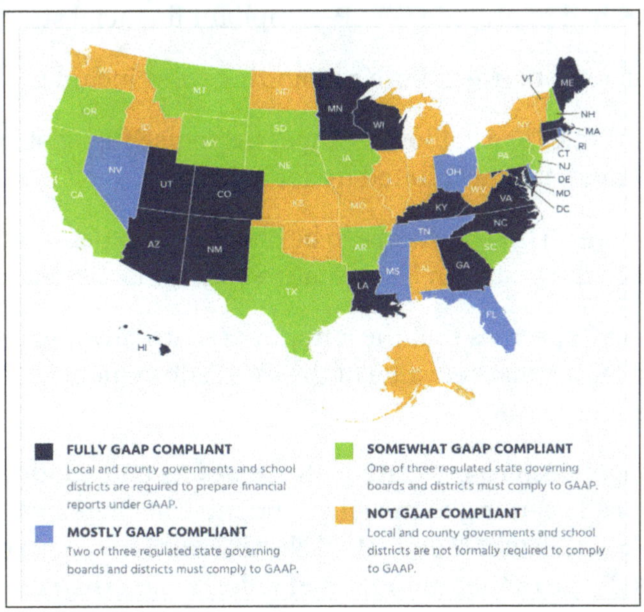

GAAP covers such things as revenue recognition, balance sheet item classification and outstanding share measurements. If a financial statement is not prepared using GAAP, investors should be cautious. Also, some companies may use both GAAP and non-GAAP compliant measures when reporting financial results. GAAP regulations require that non-GAAP measures are identified in financial statements and other public disclosures, such as press releases.

The hierarchy of GAAP is designed to improve financial reporting. It consists of a framework for selecting the principles that public accountants should use in preparing financial statements in line with U.S. GAAP. At the top of the GAAP hierarchy are statements by the Financial Accounting Standards Board (FASB) and opinions by American Institute of Certified Public Accountants (AICPA). The next level consists of FASB Technical Bulletins and AICPA Industry Audit and Accounting Guides and Statements of Position. On the third level are AICPA Accounting Standards Executive Committee Practice Bulletins and positions of the FASB Emerging Issues Task Force (EITF). On the lowest level are FASB implementation guides, AICPA Accounting Interpretations, AICPA Industry Audit and Accounting Guides and Statements of Position not cleared by the FASB. Also included are practices that are widely recognized.

Accountants are directed to first consult sources at the top of the hierarchy and then proceed to lower levels only if there is no relevant pronouncement at a higher level. The FASB's Statement of Accounting Standards No. 162 provides a detailed explanation of the hierarchy.

GAAP vs. IFRS

GAAP is focused on the practices of U.S. companies. The Financial Accounting Standards Board (FASB) issues GAAP. The international alternative to GAAP is the International Financial Reporting Standards (IFRS) set by the International Accounting Standards Board (IASB). The IASB and the FASB have been working on the convergence of IFRS and GAAP since 2002. Due to the progress achieved in this partnership, the SEC, in 2007, removed the requirement for non-U.S. companies registered in America to reconcile their financial reports with GAAP if their accounts already complied with IFRS. This was a big achievement, because prior to the ruling, non-U.S. companies trading on U.S. exchanges had to provide GAAP-compliant financial statements.

Some differences that still exist between both accounting rules include:

- LIFO Inventory - While GAAP allows companies to use the Last In First Out (LIFO) as an inventory cost method, it is prohibited under IFRS.
- Costs of Development - These costs are to be charged to expense as they are incurred under GAAP. Under IFRS, the costs can be capitalized and amortized over multiple periods.
- Write-Downs - GAAP specifies that the amount of write-down of an inventory or fixed asset cannot be reversed if the market value of the asset subsequently increases. The write-down can be reversed under IFRS.

As corporations increasingly need to navigate global markets and conduct operations worldwide, international standards are becoming increasingly popular at the expense of GAAP, even in the U.S. As the chart below shows, in 2004, almost all North American companies reported their earnings using GAAP metrics. By 2016 that number had fallen to less than half.

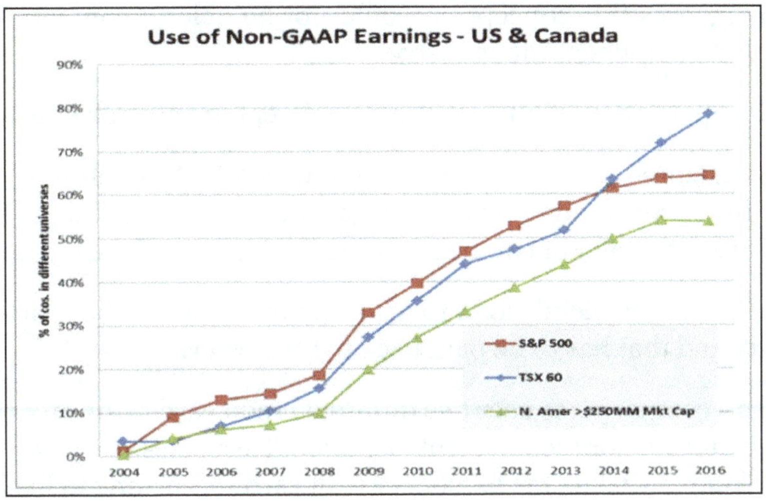

ENTITY CONCEPT

The business entity concept (also known as separate entity and economic entity concept) states that the transactions related to a business must be recorded separately from those of its owners and any other business. In other words, while recording transactions in a business, we take into account only those events that affect that particular business; the events that affect anyone else other than the business entity are not relevant and are therefore not included in the accounting records of the business.

This concept is very important because if transactions of a business are mixed up with that of its owners or other businesses, the accounting information would lose its usability.

The business entity concept of accounting is applicable to all types of business organizations (i.e., sole proprietorship, partnership and corporation) even if a law does not recognize a business and its owner as the separate entities.

Need of Business Entity Concept

The business entity concept of accounting is of great importance because of the following reasons:

1. The business entity concept is essential to separately measure the performance of a particular business in terms of profitability and cash flows etc.
2. It helps in assessing the financial position of each and every business separately on a particular date.
3. It becomes difficult and impossible to audit the records of a business if they are intermingled with those of different entities/individuals.
4. The concept ensures that each and every business entity is taxed separately.
5. The employment of business entity concept is very general among business organizations.

If a company ignores this concept, it would not be able to compare its financial performance with that of others in the industry.

Some examples of the application of business entity concept are given below:

1. Mr. John has acquired a floor of a building having 3 halls for $1,500 per month. He uses two halls for his business and one for personal purpose. According to business entity concept, only $1,000 (the rent of two halls) is a valid expense of the business.
2. The owner of a company lends loan to his company. It would be strictly recorded as company's liability and that has to be paid back to the owner.
3. Mr. Sam owns a company. He uses two different credit cards – one for the payment of business expenses and one for the payment of personal expenses. He pays $200 as the electricity bill of his company using his personal credit card. According to business entity concept of accounting, the electricity bill of the business should have been paid using company's credit card. The payment of $200 using personal credit card would therefore be considered as the contribution of additional capital by Sam.

MONEY MEASUREMENT CONCEPT

Money Measurement Concept in accounting, also known as Measurability Concept, means that only transactions and events that are capable of being measured in monetary terms are recognized in the financial statements.

All transactions and events recorded in the financial statements must be reduced to a unit of monetary currency. Where it is not possible to assign a reliable monetary value to a transaction or event, it shall not be recorded in the financial statements.

However, any material transactions and events that are not recorded for failing to meet the measurability criteria might need be disclosed in the supplementary notes of financial statements to assist the users in gaining a better understanding of the financial performance and position of the entity.

Recognition Criteria

The recognition criteria defined by IASB and FASB require that the elements of financial statements (i.e. assets, liabilities, income and expense) must only be recognized in the financial statements if its cost or value can be measured with sufficient reliability. Therefore, an entity shall not recognize an element of financial statement unless a reliable value can be assigned to it.

In many cases however the preparers of financial statements are unable to arrive at a precise amount to be recognized in the financial statements and must resort to the use of reasonable estimates in arriving at an approximate value. The use of reasonable estimates is a very important component in the preparation of financial statements and as long as forming estimates do not involve a high degree of subjectivity and uncertainty they do not undermine the reliability of financial information.

Where a significant element of financial statement is not recognized because of the inability to measure its monetary value with sufficient reliability, it may be disclosed in the supplementary notes of financial statements to enhance the users' understandability and completeness of the presented financial information.

Examples of Application

- Skills and competence of employees cannot be attributed an objective monetary value and should therefore not be recognized as assets in the balance sheet. However, those transactions related to employees that can be measured reliably such as salaries expense and pension obligations are recognized in the financial statements.
- Where it is not possible to measure reliably the amount of settlement of a legal claim against the company, no liability is recognized in the financial statements. Instead, the nature and circumstances surrounding the lawsuit are disclosed in the supplementary notes to the financial statements if considered material.
- IAS 38 Intangible Assets and ASC 350 Intangibles - Goodwill and Other require that internally generated goodwill shall not be recognized as an asset in the balance sheet. This is due to the difficulty in identifying and measuring the cost of internally generated goodwill as distinct from the cost of running the day to day operations of the business.

However, IFRS 3 Business Combinations and ASC 805 Business Combinations permit purchased goodwill to be recognized as an asset in the financial statements since the cost of purchased goodwill is usually determinable objectively as the amount of consideration paid in excess of the value of other identifiable assets of the acquired business.

FINANCIAL AUDIT

A financial audit is conducted to provide an opinion whether "financial statements" (the information being verified) are stated in accordance with specified criteria. Normally, the criteria are international accounting standards, although auditors may conduct audits of financial statements prepared using the cash basis or some other basis of accounting appropriate for the organisation. In providing an opinion whether financial statements are fairly stated in accordance with accounting standards, the auditor gathers evidence to determine whether the statements contain material errors or other misstatements.

The audit opinion is intended to provide reasonable assurance, but not absolute assurance, that the financial statements are presented fairly, in all material respects, and give a true and fair view in accordance with the financial reporting framework. The purpose of an audit is to provide an objective independent examination of the financial statements, which increases the value and credibility of the financial statements produced by management, thus increase user confidence in the financial statement, reduce investor risk and consequently reduce the cost of capital of the preparer of the financial statements.

In accordance with the US GAAP, auditors must release an opinion of the overall financial statements in the auditor's report. Auditors can release three types of statements other than an unqualified/unmodified opinion. The unqualified auditor's opinion is the opinion that the financial statements are presented fairly. A qualified opinion is that the financial statements are presented fairly in all material respects in accordance with US GAAP, except for a material misstatement that does not however pervasively affect the user's ability to rely on the financial statements. A qualified opinion can also be issued for a scope limitation that is of limited significance. Further the auditor can instead issue a disclaimer, because there is insufficient and appropriate evidence to form an opinion or because of lack of independence. In a disclaimer the auditor explains the reasons for withholding an opinion and explicitly indicates that no opinion is expressed. Finally, an adverse audit opinion is issued when the financial statements do not present fairly due to departure from US GAAP and the departure materially affects the financial statements overall. In an adverse auditor's report the auditor must explain the nature and size of the misstatement and must state the opinion that the financial statements do not present fairly in accordance with US GAAP.

Financial audits are typically performed by firms of practicing accountants who are experts in financial reporting. The financial audit is one of many assurance functions provided by accounting firms. Many organizations separately employ or hire internal auditors, who do not attest to financial reports but focus mainly on the internal controls of the organization. External auditors may choose to place limited reliance on the work of internal auditors. Auditing promotes transparency and accuracy in the financial disclosures made by an organization, therefore would likely reduce such corporations concealmeant of unscrupulous dealings.

Internationally, the International Standards on Auditing (ISA) issued by the International Auditing and Assurance Standards Board (IAASB) is considered as the benchmark for audit process. Almost all jurisdictions require auditors to follow the ISA or a local variation of the ISA.

Financial audits exist to add credibility to the implied assertion by an organisation's management that its financial statements fairly represent the organisation's position and performance to the firm's stakeholders. The principal stakeholders of a company are typically its shareholders, but other parties such as tax authorities, banks, regulators, suppliers, customers and employees may also have an interest in knowing that the financial statements are presented fairly, in all material aspects. An audit is not designed to provide absolute assurance, being based on sampling and not the testing of all transactions and balances; rather it is designed to reduce the risk of a material financial statement misstatement whether caused by fraud or error. A misstatement is defined in ISA 450 as an error, omitted disclosure or inappropriate accounting policy. "Material" is an error or omission that would affect the users decision. Audits exist because they add value through easing the cost of information asymmetry and reducing information risk, not because they are required by law (note: audits are obligatory in many EU-member states and in many jurisdictions are obligatory for companies listed on public stock exchanges). For collection and accumulation of audit evidence, certain methods and means generally adopted by auditors are:

1. Posting checking,
2. Testing the existence and effectiveness of management controls that prevent financial statement misstatement,
3. Casting checking,

4. Physical examination and count,
5. Confirmation,
6. Inquiry,
7. Observation,
8. Inspection,
9. Year-end scrutiny,
10. Re-computation,
11. Tracing in subsequent period,
12. Bank reconciliation,
13. Vouching,
14. Verification of existence, ownership, title and value of assets and determination of the extent and nature of liabilities.

Financial audit is a profession known for its male dominance. According to the latest survey, it found that 70%-80% of the financial auditors are male, with 2% being female and the rest being a mixture of both.

Big Four

Greenwood et al. defined the audit firm as professional partnership which has a decentralized organization relationship between the national head office and local offices. Local offices can make most decision except for the drawing up professional standard and maintaining it.

The Big Four are the four largest international professional services networks, offering audit, assurance, tax, consulting, advisory, actuarial, corporate finance, and legal services. They handle the vast majority of audits for publicly traded companies as well as many private companies, creating an oligopoly in auditing large companies. It is reported that the Big Four audit 99% of the companies in the FTSE 100, and 96% of the companies in the FTSE 250 Index, an index of the leading mid-cap listing companies. The Big Four firms are shown below, with their latest publicly available data. None of the Big Four firms is a single firm; rather, they are professional services networks. Each is a network of firms, owned and managed independently, which have entered into agreements with other member firms in the network to share a common name, brand and quality standards. Each network has established an entity to co-ordinate the activities of the network. In one case (KPMG), the co-ordinating entity is Swiss, and in three cases (Deloitte Touche Tohmatsu, PricewaterhouseCoopers and Ernst & Young) the co-ordinating entity is a UK limited company. Those entities do not themselves perform external professional services, and do not own or control the member firms. They are similar to law firm networks found in the legal profession. In many cases each member firm practises in a single country, and is structured to comply with the regulatory environment in that country. In 2007 KPMG announced a merger of four member firms (in the United Kingdom, Germany, Switzerland and

Liechtenstein) to form a single firm. Ernst & Young also includes separate legal entities which manage three of its four areas: Americas, EMEIA (Europe, The Middle East, India and Africa), and Asia-Pacific. (Note: the Japan area does not have a separate area management entity). These firms coordinate services performed by local firms within their respective areas but do not perform services or hold ownership in the local entities. This group was once known as the "Big Eight", and was reduced to the "Big Six" and then "Big Five" by a series of mergers. The Big Five became the Big Four after the demise of Arthur Andersen in 2002, following its involvement in the Enron scandal.

Costs

Costs of audit services can vary greatly dependent upon the nature of the entity, its transactions, industry, the condition of the financial records and financial statements, and the fee rates of the CPA firm. A commercial decision such as the setting of audit fees is handled by companies and their auditors. Directors are responsible for setting the overall fee as well as the audit committee. The fees are set at a level that could not lead to audit quality being compromised. The scarcity of staffs and the lower audit fee lead to very low billing realization rates. As a result, accounting firms, such as KPMG, PricewaterhouseCoopers and Deloitte who used to have very low technical inefficiency, have started to use AI tools. Research has found that annual reports that convey optimistic tone are associated with lower audit fees, suggesting that annual report tone reflects factors that auditors consider in assessing audit risk.

Audit of Government Expenditure

The earliest surviving mention of a public official charged with auditing government expenditure is a reference to the Auditor of the Exchequer in England in 1314. The Auditors of the Imprest were established under Queen Elizabeth I in 1559 with formal responsibility for auditing Exchequer payments. This system gradually lapsed and in 1780, Commissioners for Auditing the Public Accounts were appointed by statute. From 1834, the Commissioners worked in tandem with the Comptroller of the Exchequer, who was charged with controlling the issuance of funds to the government.

As Chancellor of the Exchequer, William Ewart Gladstone initiated major reforms of public finance and Parliamentary accountability. His 1866 Exchequer and Audit Departments Act required all departments, for the first time, to produce annual accounts, known as appropriation accounts. The Act also established the position of Comptroller and Auditor General (C&AG) and an Exchequer and Audit Department (E&AD) to provide supporting staff from within the civil service. The C&AG was given two main functions – to authorise the issue of public money to government from the Bank of England, having satisfied himself that this was within the limits Parliament had voted – and to audit the accounts of all Government departments and report to Parliament accordingly.

Auditing of UK government expenditure is now carried out by the National Audit Office. The Australian National Audit Office conducts all financial statement audits for entities controlled by the Australian Government.

Governance and Oversight

Seal of the United States Government Accountability Office.

In the United States, the SEC has generally deferred to the accounting industry (acting through various organisations throughout the years) as to the accounting standards for financial reporting, and the U.S. Congress has deferred to the SEC.

This is also typically the case in other developed economies. In the UK, auditing guidelines are set by the institutes (including ACCA, ICAEW, ICAS and ICAI) of which auditing firms and individual auditors are members. While in Australia, the rules and professional code of ethics are set by The Institute of Chartered Accountants Australia (ICAA), CPA Australia (CPA) and The National Institute of Accountants (NIA).

Accordingly, financial auditing standards and methods have tended to change significantly only after auditing failures. The most recent and familiar case is that of Enron. The company succeeded in hiding some important facts, such as off-book liabilities, from banks and shareholders. Eventually, Enron filed for bankruptcy, and (as of 2006) is in the process of being dissolved. One result of this scandal was that Arthur Andersen, then one of the five largest accountancy firms worldwide, lost their ability to audit public companies, essentially killing off the firm.

A recent trend in audits (spurred on by such accounting scandals as Enron and Worldcom) has been an increased focus on internal control procedures, which aim to ensure the completeness, accuracy and validity of items in the accounts, and restricted access to financial systems. This emphasis on the internal control environment is now a mandatory part of the audit of SEC-listed companies, under the auditing standards of the Public Company Accounting Oversight Board (PCAOB) set up by the Sarbanes-Oxley Act.

Many countries have government sponsored or mandated organizations who develop and maintain auditing standards, commonly referred to generally accepted auditing standards or GAAS. These standards prescribe different aspects of auditing such as the opinion, stages of an audit, and controls over work product (*i.e.*, working papers).

Some oversight organisations require auditors and audit firms to undergo a third-party quality review periodically to ensure the applicable GAAS is followed.

Stages of an Audit

The following are the stages of a typical audit:

Plan and Design an Audit Approach

- Accept Client and Perform Initial Planning.
- Understand the Client's Business and Industry.
    - What should auditors understand?
        - The relevant industry, regulatory, and other external factors including the applicable financial reporting framework.
        - The nature of the entity.
        - The entity's selection and application of accounting policies.
        - The entity's objectives and strategies, and the related business risks that may result in material misstatement of the financial statements.
        - The measurement and review of the entity's financial performance.
        - Internal control relevant to the audit.
- Assess Client's Business Risk.
- Set Materiality and Assess Accepted Audit Risk (AAR) and Inherent Risk (IR).
- Understand Internal Control and Assess Control Risk (CR).
- Develop Overall Audit Plan and Audit Program.

Phase II: Perform Test of Controls and Substantive Test of Transactions

- Test of Control: if the auditor plans to reduce the determined control risk, then the auditor should perform the test of control, to assess the operating effectiveness of internal controls (e.g. authorisation of transactions, account reconciliations, segregation of duties) including IT General Controls. If internal controls are assessed as effective, this will reduce (but not entirely eliminate) the amount of 'substantive' work the auditor needs to do.
- Substantive test of transactions: evaluate the client's recording of transactions by verifying the monetary amounts of transactions, a process called substantive tests of transactions. For example, the auditor might use computer software to compare the unit selling price on duplicate sales invoices with an electronic file of approved prices as a test of the accuracy objective for sales transactions. Like the test of control in the preceding paragraph, this test satisfies the accuracy transaction-related audit objective for sales. For the sake of efficiency, auditors often perform tests of controls and substantive tests of transactions at the same time.

- Assess Likelihood of Misstatement in Financial Statement.
- At this stage, if the auditor accept the CR that has been set at the phase I and does not want to reduce the controls risk, then the auditor may not perform test of control. If so, then the auditor perform substantive test of transactions.
- This test determines the amount of work to be performed i.e. substantive testing or test of details.

Phase III: Perform Analytical Procedures and Tests of Details of Balances

- Where internal controls are strong, auditors typically rely more on substantive analytical procedures (the comparison of sets of financial information, and financial with non-financial information, to see if the numbers 'make sense' and that unexpected movements can be explained).
- Where internal controls are weak, auditors typically rely more on Substantive Tests of Detail of Balance (selecting a sample of items from the major account balances, and finding hard evidence (e.g. invoices, bank statements) for those items).
- Some audits involve a 'hard close' or 'fast close' whereby certain substantive procedures can be performed before year-end. For example, if the year-end is 31 December, the hard close may provide the auditors with figures as at 30 November. The auditors would audit income/expense movements between 1 January and 30 November, so that after year end, it is only necessary for them to audit the December income/expense movements and 31 December balance sheet. In some countries and accountancy firms these are known as 'rollforward' procedures.

Phase IV: Complete the Audit and Issue an Audit Report

After the auditor has completed all procedures for each audit objective and for each financial statement account and related disclosures, it is necessary to combine the information obtained to reach an overall conclusion as to whether the financial statements are fairly presented. This highly subjective process relies heavily on the auditor's professional judgment. When the audit is completed, the CPA must issue an audit report to accompany the client's published financial statements.

Responsibilities of an Auditor

Corporations Act 2001 requires the auditor to:

- Gives a true and fair view about whether the financial report complies with the accounting standards.
- Conduct their audit in accordance with auditing standards.
- Give the directors and auditor's independence declaration and meet independence requirements.
- Report certain suspected contraventions to ASIC.

Commercial Relationships versus Objectivity

One of the major issues faced by private auditing firms is the need to provide independent auditing services while maintaining a business relationship with the audited company.

The auditing firm's responsibility to check and confirm the reliability of financial statements may be limited by pressure from the audited company, who pays the auditing firm for the service. The auditing firm's need to maintain a viable business through auditing revenue may be weighed against its duty to examine and verify the accuracy, relevancy, and completeness of the company's financial statements. This is done by auditor.

Numerous proposals are made to revise the current system to provide better economic incentives to auditors to perform the auditing function without having their commercial interests compromised by client relationships. Examples are more direct incentive compensation awards and financial statement insurance approaches.

- There are several related professional qualifications in the field of financial audit including Certified Internal Auditor, Certified General Accountant, Chartered Certified Accountant, Chartered Accountant and Certified Public Accountant.

Auditors and Technology

Currently, many entities being audited are using information systems, which generate information electronically. For the audit evidences, auditors get dynamic information generated from the information systems in real time. There are less paper documents and pre-numbered audit evidences available, which leads a revolution to audit mythology.

BOOKKEEPING

Bookkeeping is the recording of financial transactions, and is part of the process of accounting in business. Transactions include purchases, sales, receipts, and payments by an individual person or an organization/corporation. There are several standard methods of bookkeeping, including the single-entry and double-entry bookkeeping systems. While these may be viewed as "real" bookkeeping, any process for recording financial transactions is a bookkeeping process.

Bookkeeping is the work of a bookkeeper (or book-keeper), who records the day-to-day financial transactions of a business. They usually write the daybooks (which contain records of sales, purchases, receipts, and payments), and document each financial transaction, whether cash or credit, into the correct daybook—that is, petty cash book, suppliers ledger, customer ledger, etc.—and the general ledger. Thereafter, an accountant can create financial reports from the information recorded by the bookkeeper.

Bookkeeping refers mainly to the record-keeping aspects of financial accounting, and involves preparing source documents for all transactions, operations, and other events of a business.

The bookkeeper brings the books to the trial balance stage: an accountant may prepare the income statement and balance sheet using the trial balance and ledgers prepared by the bookkeeper.

The origin of book-keeping is lost in obscurity, but recent researches indicate that methods of keeping accounts have existed from the remotest times of human life in cities. Babylonian records written with styli on small slabs of clay have been found dating to 2600 BCE. The term "waste book" was used in colonial America, referring to the documenting of daily transactions of receipts and expenditures. Records were made in chronological order, and for temporary use only. Daily records were then transferred to a daybook or account ledger to balance the accounts and to create a permanent journal; then the waste book could be discarded, hence the name.

Process

The bookkeeping process primarily records the financial effects of transactions. An important difference between a manual and an electronic accounting system is the former's latency between the recording of a financial transaction and its posting in the relevant account. This delay, which is absent in electronic accounting systems due to nearly instantaneous posting to relevant accounts, is characteristic of manual systems, and gave rise to the primary books of accounts—cash book, purchase book, sales book, etc.—for immediately documenting a financial transaction.

In the normal course of business, a document is produced each time a transaction occurs. Sales and purchases usually have invoices or receipts. Deposit slips are produced when lodgements (deposits) are made to a bank account. Checks (spelled "cheques" in the UK and several other countries) are written to pay money out of the account. Bookkeeping first involves recording the details of all of these source documents into multi-column journals (also known as books of first entry or daybooks). For example, all credit sales are recorded in the sales journal; all cash payments are recorded in the cash payments journal. Each column in a journal normally corresponds to an account. In the single entry system, each transaction is recorded only once. Most individuals who balance their check-book each month are using such a system, and most personal-finance software follows this approach.

After a certain period, typically a month, each column in each journal is totalled to give a summary for that period. Using the rules of double-entry, these journal summaries are then transferred to their respective accounts in the ledger, or account book. For example, the entries in the Sales Journal are taken and a debit entry is made in each customer's account (showing that the customer now owes us money), and a credit entry might be made in the account for "Sale of class 2 widgets" (showing that this activity has generated revenue for us). This process of transferring summaries or individual transactions to the ledger is called posting. Once the posting process is complete, accounts kept using the "T" format undergo balancing, which is simply a process to arrive at the balance of the account.

As a partial check that the posting process was done correctly, a working document called an unadjusted trial balance is created. In its simplest form, this is a three-column list. Column One contains the names of those accounts in the ledger which have a non-zero balance. If an account has a debit balance, the balance amount is copied into Column Two (the debit column); if an account has a credit balance, the amount is copied into Column Three (the credit column). The debit column is then totalled, and then the credit column is totalled. The two totals must agree—which is not by chance—because under the double-entry rules, whenever there is a posting, the debits of the posting equal the credits of the posting. If the two totals do not agree, an error has been made, either in the journals or during the posting process. The error must be located and rectified, and the totals of the debit column and the credit column recalculated to check for agreement before any further processing can take place.

Once the accounts balance, the accountant makes a number of adjustments and changes the balance amounts of some of the accounts. These adjustments must still obey the double-entry rule: for example, the inventory account and asset account might be changed to bring them into line with the actual numbers counted during a stocktake. At the same time, the expense account associated with usage of inventory is adjusted by an equal and opposite amount. Other adjustments such as posting depreciation and prepayments are also done at this time. This results in a listing called the adjusted trial balance. It is the accounts in this list, and their corresponding debit or credit balances, that are used to prepare the financial statements.

Finally financial statements are drawn from the trial balance, which may include:

- The income statement, also known as the statement of financial results, profit and loss account, or P&L.
- The balance sheet, also known as the statement of financial position.
- The cash flow statement.
- The statement of changes in equity, also known as the statement of total recognised gains and losses.

Entry Systems

Single-entry System

The primary bookkeeping record in single-entry bookkeeping is the *cash book*, which is similar to a checking account register (in UK: cheque account, current account), except all entries are allocated among several categories of income and expense accounts. Separate account records are maintained for petty cash, accounts payable and receivable, and other relevant transactions such as inventory and travel expenses. To save time and avoid the errors of manual calculations, single-entry bookkeeping can be done today with do-it-yourself bookkeeping software.

Double-entry System

A double-entry bookkeeping system is a set of rules for recording financial information in a financial accounting system in which every transaction or event changes at least two different nominal ledger accounts.

Daybooks

A daybook is a descriptive and chronological (diary-like) record of day-to-day financial transactions; it is also called a book of original entry. The daybook's details must be transcribed formally into journals to enable posting to ledgers. Daybooks include:

- Sales daybook, for recording sales invoices.
- Sales credits daybook, for recording sales credit notes.
- Purchases daybook, for recording purchase invoices.
- Purchases debits daybook, for recording purchase debit notes.

- Cash daybook, usually known as the cash book, for recording all monies received and all monies paid out. It may be split into two daybooks: a receipts daybook documenting every money-amount received, and a payments daybook recording every payment made.
- General Journal daybook, for recording journal entries.

Petty Cash Book

A petty cash book is a record of small-value purchases before they are later transferred to the ledger and final accounts; it is maintained by a petty or junior cashier. This type of cash book usually uses the imprest system: a certain amount of money is provided to the petty cashier by the senior cashier. This money is to cater for minor expenditures (hospitality, minor stationery, casual postage, and so on) and is reimbursed periodically on satisfactory explanation of how it was spent.

Journals

Journals are recorded in the general journal daybook. A journal is a formal and chronological record of financial transactions before their values are accounted for in the general ledger as debits and credits. A company can maintain one journal for all transactions, or keep several journals based on similar activity (e.g., sales, cash receipts, revenue, etc.), making transactions easier to summarize and reference later. For every debit journal entry recorded, there must be an equivalent credit journal entry to maintain a balanced accounting equation.

Ledgers

A ledger is a record of accounts.The ledger is a permanent summary of all amounts entered in supporting Journals which list individual transactions by date. These accounts are recorded separately, showing their beginning/ending balance. A journal lists financial transactions in chronological order, without showing their balance but showing how much is going to be charged in each account. A ledger takes each financial transaction from the journal and records it into the corresponding account for every transaction listed. The ledger also sums up the total of every account, which is transferred into the balance sheet and the income statement. There are three different kinds of ledgers that deal with book-keeping:

- Sales ledger, which deals mostly with the accounts receivable account. This ledger consists of the records of the financial transactions made by customers to the business.
- Purchase ledger is the record of the purchasing transactions a company does; it goes hand in hand with the Accounts Payable account.

Chart of Accounts

A chart of accounts is a list of the accounts codes that can be identified with numeric, alphabetical, or alphanumeric codes allowing the account to be located in the general ledger. The equity section of the chart of accounts is based on the fact that the legal structure of the entity is of a particular legal type. Possibilities include *sole trader*, *partnership*, *trust*, and *company*.

Computerized Book Keeping

Computerized bookkeeping removes many of the paper "books" that are used to record the financial transactions of a business entity; instead, relational databases are used today, but typically, these still enforce the norms of bookkeeping methodology including the single-entry and double-entry bookkeeping systems. CPAs supervise the internal controls for computerized bookkeeping systems, which serve to minimize errors in documenting the numerous activities a business entity may initiate or complete over an accounting period.

VALUATION

In finance, valuation is the process of determining the present value (PV) of an asset. Valuations can be done on assets (for example, investments in marketable securities such as stocks, options, business enterprises, or intangible assets such as patents and trademarks) or on liabilities (e.g., bonds issued by a company). Valuations are needed for many reasons such as investment analysis, capital budgeting, merger and acquisition transactions, financial reporting, taxable events to determine the proper tax liability, and in litigation.

Common terms for the value of an asset or liability are market value, fair value, and intrinsic value. The meanings of these terms differ. For instance, when an analyst believes a stock's intrinsic value is greater (or less) than its market price, an analyst makes a "buy" (or "sell") recommendation. Moreover, an asset's intrinsic value may be subject to personal opinion and vary among analysts. The International Valuation Standards include definitions for common bases of value and generally accepted practice procedures for valuing assets of all types. Regardless, the valuation itself is done generally using one or more of the following approaches:

1. Absolute value models ("Intrinsic valuation") that determine the present value of an asset's expected future cash flows. These models take two general forms: multi-period models such as discounted cash flow models, or single-period models such as the Gordon model (which, in fact, often "telescope" the former). These models rely on mathematics rather than price observation.

2. Relative value models determine value based on the observation of market prices of 'comparable' assets, relative to a common variable like earnings, cashflows, book value or sales. This result, will often be used to complement/assess the intrinsic valuation.

3. Option pricing models, in this context, are used to value specific balance-sheet items, or the asset itself, when these have option-like characteristics. Examples of the first type are warrants, employee stock options, and investments with embedded options such as callable bonds; the second type are usually real options. The most common option pricing models employed here are the Black–Scholes-Merton models and lattice models. This approach is sometimes referred to as contingent claim valuation, in that the value will be contingent on some other asset.

Usage

In finance, valuation analysis is required for many reasons including tax assessment, wills and estates, divorce settlements, business analysis, and basic bookkeeping and accounting. Since the value of things fluctuates over time, valuations are as of a specific date like the end of the accounting quarter or year. They may alternatively be mark-to-market estimates of the current value of assets or liabilities as of this minute or this day for the purposes of managing portfolios and associated financial risk (for example, within large financial firms including investment banks and stockbrokers).

Some balance sheet items are much easier to value than others. Publicly traded stocks and bonds have prices that are quoted frequently and readily available. Other assets are harder to value. For instance, private firms that have no frequently quoted price. Additionally, financial instruments that have prices that are partly dependent on theoretical models of one kind or another are difficult to value. For example, options are generally valued using the Black–Scholes model while the liabilities of life assurance firms are valued using the theory of present value. Intangible business assets, like goodwill and intellectual property, are open to a wide range of value interpretations.

It is possible and conventional for financial professionals to make their own estimates of the valuations of assets or liabilities that they are interested in. Their calculations are of various kinds including analyses of companies that focus on price-to-book, price-to-earnings, price-to-cash-flow and present value calculations, and analyses of bonds that focus on credit ratings, assessments of default risk, risk premia, and levels of real interest rates. All of these approaches may be thought of as creating estimates of value that compete for credibility with the prevailing share or bond prices, where applicable, and may or may not result in buying or selling by market participants. Where the valuation is for the purpose of a merger or acquisition the respective businesses make available further detailed financial information, usually on the completion of a non-disclosure agreement.

It is important to note that valuation requires judgment and assumptions:

- There are different circumstances and purposes to value an asset (e.g., distressed firm, tax purposes, mergers and acquisitions, financial reporting). Such differences can lead to different valuation methods or different interpretations of the method results.
- All valuation models and methods have limitations (e.g., degree of complexity, relevance of observations, mathematical form).
- Model inputs can vary significantly because of necessary judgment and differing assumptions.

Users of valuations benefit when key information, assumptions, and limitations are disclosed to them. Then they can weigh the degree of reliability of the result and make their decision.

Business Valuation

Businesses or fractional interests in businesses may be valued for various purposes such as mergers and acquisitions, sale of securities, and taxable events. An accurate valuation of privately owned companies largely depends on the reliability of the firm's historic financial information. Public company financial statements are audited by Certified Public Accountants (USA), Chartered

Certified Accountants (ACCA) or Chartered Accountants (UK and Canada) and overseen by a government regulator. Alternatively, private firms do not have government oversight—unless operating in a regulated industry—and are usually not required to have their financial statements audited. Moreover, managers of private firms often prepare their financial statements to minimize profits and, therefore, taxes. Alternatively, managers of public firms tend to want higher profits to increase their stock price. Therefore, a firm's historic financial information may not be accurate and can lead to over- and undervaluation. In an acquisition, a buyer often performs due diligence to verify the seller's information.

Financial statements prepared in accordance with generally accepted accounting principles (GAAP) show many assets based on their historic costs rather than at their current market values. For instance, a firm's balance sheet will usually show the value of land it owns at what the firm paid for it rather than at its current market value. But under GAAP requirements, a firm must show the fair values (which usually approximates market value) of some types of assets such as financial instruments that are held for sale rather than at their original cost. When a firm is required to show some of its assets at fair value, some call this process "mark-to-market". But reporting asset values on financial statements at fair values gives managers ample opportunity to slant asset values upward to artificially increase profits and their stock prices. Managers may be motivated to alter earnings upward so they can earn bonuses. Despite the risk of manager bias, equity investors and creditors prefer to know the market values of a firm's assets—rather than their historical costs—because current values give them better information to make decisions.

There are commonly three pillars to valuing business entities: comparable company analyses, discounted cash flow analysis, and precedent transaction analysis.

Discounted Cash Flow Method

This method estimates the value of an asset based on its expected future cash flows, which are discounted to the present (i.e., the present value). This concept of discounting future money is commonly known as the time value of money. For instance, an asset that matures and pays $1 in one year is worth less than $1 today. The size of the discount is based on an opportunity cost of capital and it is expressed as a percentage or discount rate.

In finance theory, the amount of the opportunity cost is based on a relation between the risk and return of some sort of investment. Classic economic theory maintains that people are rational and averse to risk. They, therefore, need an incentive to accept risk. The incentive in finance comes in the form of higher expected returns after buying a risky asset. In other words, the more risky the investment, the more return investors want from that investment. Using the same example as above, assume the first investment opportunity is a government bond that will pay interest of 5% per year and the principal and interest payments are guaranteed by the government. Alternatively, the second investment opportunity is a bond issued by small company and that bond also pays annual interest of 5%. If given a choice between the two bonds, virtually all investors would buy the government bond rather than the small-firm bond because the first is less risky while paying the same interest rate as the riskier second bond. In this case, an investor has no incentive to buy the riskier second bond. Furthermore, in order to attract capital from investors, the small firm issuing the second bond must pay an interest rate higher than 5% that the government bond pays. Otherwise, no investor is likely to buy that bond and, therefore, the firm will be unable to raise capital.

But by offering to pay an interest rate more than 5% the firm gives investors an incentive to buy a riskier bond.

For a valuation using the discounted cash flow method, one first estimates the future cash flows from the investment and then estimates a reasonable discount rate after considering the riskiness of those cash flows and interest rates in the capital markets. Next, one makes a calculation to compute the present value of the future cash flows.

Guideline Companies Method

This method determines the value of a firm by observing the prices of similar companies (called "guideline companies") that sold in the market. Those sales could be shares of stock or sales of entire firms. The observed prices serve as valuation benchmarks. From the prices, one calculates price multiples such as the price-to-earnings or price-to-book ratios—one or more of which used to value the firm. For example, the average price-to-earnings multiple of the guideline companies is applied to the subject firm's earnings to estimate its value.

Many price multiples can be calculated. Most are based on a financial statement element such as a firm's earnings (price-to-earnings) or book value (price-to-book value) but multiples can be based on other factors such as price-per-subscriber.

Net Asset Value Method

The third-most common method of estimating the value of a company looks to the assets and liabilities of the business. At a minimum, a solvent company could shut down operations, sell off the assets, and pay the creditors. Any cash that would remain establishes a floor value for the company. This method is known as the net asset value or cost method. In general the discounted cash flows of a well-performing company exceed this floor value. Some companies, however, are worth more "dead than alive", like weakly performing companies that own many tangible assets. This method can also be used to value heterogeneous portfolios of investments, as well as nonprofits, for which discounted cash flow analysis is not relevant. The valuation premise normally used is that of an orderly liquidation of the assets, although some valuation scenarios (e.g., purchase price allocation) imply an "in-use" valuation such as depreciated replacement cost new.

An alternative approach to the net asset value method is the excess earnings method. The excess earnings method has the appraiser identify the value of tangible assets, estimate an appropriate return on those tangible assets, and subtract that return from the total return for the business, leaving the "excess" return, which is presumed to come from the intangible assets. An appropriate capitalization rate is applied to the excess return, resulting in the value of those intangible assets. That value is added to the value of the tangible assets and any non-operating assets, and the total is the value estimate for the business as a whole.

Specialised Cases

In the below cases, depending on context, Real options valuation techniques are also sometimes employed.

Valuation of a Suffering Company

When valuing "distressed securities", various adjustments are typically made to the valuation result; this would be true whether market-, income-, or asset-based. These adjustments consider:

- Lack of marketability discount of shares.
- Control premium or lack of control discount.
- Excess or restricted cash.
- Other non-operating assets and liabilities.
- Above- or below-market leases.
- Excess salaries in the case of private companies.

The financial statements here are similarly recast, including adjustments to working capital, deferred capital expenditures, cost of goods sold, Non-recurring professional fees and costs, and certain non-operating income/expense items.

In many of these cases, the company in question is valued using real options analysis - This value serves to complement (or sometimes replace) the above value.

Valuation of a Startup company

Startup companies such as Uber, which was valued at $50 billion in early 2015, are assigned post-money valuations based on the price at which their most recent investor put money into the company. The price reflects what investors, for the most part venture capital firms, are willing to pay for a share of the firm. They are not listed on any stock market, nor is the valuation based on their assets or profits, but on their potential for success, growth, and eventually, possible profits. Many startup companies use internal growth factors to show their potential growth which may attribute to their valuation. The professional investors who fund startups are experts, but hardly infallible.

Valuation of Intangible Assets

Valuation models can be used to value intangible assets such as for patent valuation, but also in copyrights, software, trade secrets, and customer relationships. Since few sales of benchmark intangible assets can ever be observed, one often values these sorts of assets using either a present value model or estimating the costs to recreate it. Regardless of the method, the process is often time-consuming and costly.

Valuations of intangible assets are often necessary for financial reporting and intellectual property transactions.

Stock markets give indirectly an estimate of a corporation's intangible asset value. It can be reckoned as the difference between its market capitalisation and its book value (by including only hard assets in it).

Valuation of Mining Projects

In mining, valuation is the process of determining the value or worth of a mining property. Mining valuations are sometimes required for IPOs, fairness opinions, litigation, mergers and acquisitions, and shareholder-related matters. In valuation of a mining project or mining property, fair market value is the standard of value to be used.

The CIMVal Standards ("Canadian Institute of Mining, Metallurgy and Petroleum on Valuation of Mineral Properties") are a recognised standard for valuation of mining projects and is also recognised by the Toronto Stock Exchange. The standards stress the use of the cost approach, market approach, and the income approach, depending on the stage of development of the mining property or project.

ACCOUNTING IDENTITY

An accounting identity is an equality that must be true regardless of the value of its variables, or a statement that by definition (or construction) must be true. Where an accounting identity applies, any deviation from numerical equality signifies an error in formulation, calculation or measurement.

The term accounting identity may be used to distinguish between propositions that are theories (which may or may not be true, or relationships that may or may not always hold) and statements that are by definition true. Despite the fact that the statements are by definition true, the underlying figures as measured or estimated may not add up due to measurement error, particularly for certain identities in macroeconomics.

The most basic identity in accounting is that the balance sheet must balance, that is, that assets must equal the sum of liabilities (debts) and equity (the value of the firm to the owner). In its most common formulation it is known as the accounting equation:

Assets = Liabilities + Equity

where debt includes non-financial liabilities. Balance sheets are commonly presented as two parallel columns, each summing to the same total, with the assets on the left, and liabilities and owners' equity on the right. The parallel columns of Assets and Equities are, in effect, two views of the same set of business facts.

The balance of the balance sheet reflects the conventions of double-entry bookkeeping, by which business transactions are recorded. In double-entry bookkeeping, every transaction is recorded by paired entries, and typically a transaction will result in two or more pairs of entries. The sale of product, for example, would record both a receipt of cash (or the creation of a trade receivable in the case of an extension of credit to the buyer) and a reduction in the inventory of goods for sale; the receipt of cash or a trade receivable is an addition to revenue, and the reduction in goods inventory is an addition to expense. In this case, an "expense" is the "expending" of an asset. Thus, there are two pairs of entries: an addition to revenue balanced by an addition to cash; a subtraction from inventory balanced by an addition to expense. The cash and inventory accounts are asset accounts; the revenue and expense accounts will close at the end of the accounting period to affect equity.

Double-entry bookkeeping conventions are employed as well for the National Accounts. Economic concepts such as national product, aggregate income, investment and savings, as well as the balance of payments and balance of trade, involve accounting identities. The application of double-entry bookkeeping conventions in measuring aggregate economic activity derives from the recognition that: every purchase is also a sale, every payment made translates income received, and every act of lending also an act of borrowing.

Here the term *identity* is a mathematical identity or a logical tautology, since it defines an equivalence which does not depend on the particular values of the variables.

Identities in Accounting

Accounting has a number of identities in common usage, and since many identities can be decomposed into others, no comprehensive listing is possible.

Inter-period Identities

Accounting identities also apply between accounting periods, such as changes in cash balances. For example:

Cash at beginning of period + Changes in cash during period = Cash at end of period.

Value of an Asset

Any asset recorded in a firm's balance sheet will have a carrying value. By definition, the carrying value must equal the historic cost (or acquisition cost) of the asset, plus (or minus) any subsequent adjustments in the value of the asset, such as depreciation.

Carrying value = Historic cost + Change in value.

Economics

In economics, there are numerous accounting identities.

Balance of Payments

One of the most commonly known is the balance of payments identity, where:

Current Account Surplus + Capital Account Surplus = Increase in Official Reserve Account.

A common problem with the balance of payments identity is that, due to measurement error, the balance of payments may not total correctly. For example, in the context of the identity that the sum of all countries' current accounts must be zero, *The Economist* magazine has noted that "In theory, individual countries' current-account deficits and surpluses should cancel each other out. But because of statistical errors and omissions they never do."

Gross Domestic Product

The basic equation for gross domestic product is also an identity, and is sometimes referred to as the National Income Identity:

GDP = consumption + investment + government spending + (exports – imports).

This identity holds because investment refers to the sum of intended and unintended investment, the latter being unintended accumulations of inventories; unintended inventory accumulation necessarily equals output produced (GDP) minus intended uses of that output—consumption, intended investment in machinery, inventories, etc., government spending, and net exports.

Investment

Investment = Fixed investment + Inventory investment.

Gross investment – Depreciation = Net investment.

Banking

A key identity that is used in explaining the multiple expansion of the money supply is:

Bank assets = Bank liabilities + Owners' equity.

Here the liabilities include deposits of customers, against which reserves often must be held.

BIG BATH

Big Bath in accounting is an earnings management technique whereby a one-time charge is taken against income in order to reduce assets, which results in lower expenses in the future. The write-off removes or reduces the asset from the financial books and results in lower net income for that year. The objective is to 'take one big bath' in a single year so future years will show increased net income.

This technique is often employed in a year when sales are down from other external factors and the company would report a loss in any event. For example, inventory valued on the books at $100 per item is written down to $50 per item resulting in a net loss of $50 per item in the current year. Note there is no cash impact to this write-down. When that same inventory is sold in later years for $75 per item, the company reports an income of $25 per item in the future period. This process takes an inventory loss and turns it into a 'profit'. Corporations will often wait until a bad year to employ this 'big bath' technique to 'clean up' the balance sheet. Although the process is discouraged by auditors, it is still used. In recent times, General Motors and other US Corporations have taken huge write downs on balance sheet assets resulting in massive losses. The same result can be achieved by recording in one year the future cash costs of expected plant closing or employee layoffs. The objective is to take these losses all at once, so future periods can show positive net income.

Incentives

The incentives behind this earnings management technique varies. A widespread belief of why companies utilize this technique is to improve external reputation and appeal to investors and creditors. In most large corporations, managers are in charge of financial reporting. This gives managers the incentive of bias reporting to increase the reputation of their company and to attribute those gains to their own ability. Other possible reasons why some managers have the incentive to tamper with their company financial reporting is for higher salary and recognition of their abilities to increase profit. It is often believed that earning management activities are common before and after management changes. Thus, other incentives may possibly be led by management turnovers.

Earnings Management

Often time Managers use reporting strategies regardless if the external users are naive and ignore management's ability to manipulate earnings or if users are sophisticated and can accurately deduce the management's disclosure strategy. When times are bad for the corporations financially, as a financial reporting strategy, managers will under-report earnings by the maximum they can in the current period, in order to report higher future earnings. On the other hand, in both academic and business press, earnings management has negative connotations because it suggests the tampering of earnings by management at the disadvantage of investors and other external users. Furthermore, biased financial reporting goes against GAAP regulations.

Accounting Standards

One source finds that aside from manager's and auditor's incentives, accounting standards has a huge impact on earnings management behavior. Moreover, some have argued that the market rewards management for smoother earnings as well. International Accounting Reporting Standards (IFRS) restrict revised earning reports of companies who rely on big bath provisions to maintain their increase in income, even if they are only gaining a very minimal amount of earnings. IFRS is a global set of accounting standards that require companies to report accurate annual earnings. The standards are an accurate measurement of earnings because there is only a single standard rather than multiple standards that could present opportunity to Big Bath strategies.

Applications

In 2016, Samsung reported to have battery issues in the newest Note 7 release. The defective batteries accrued substantial financial costs of approximately three billion dollars from Samsung's reported four billion dollars of net profit. Some predict Samsung will implement the Big Bath technique to have a lower net income in 2016, then will increase in the following years. The Big Bath technique will allow Samsung to wash away bad debts.

In a 2014 Wall Street Journal article, emerging banking CEOs are most likely to take Big Baths to increase banking performance and net profits in the following years. New CEOs attribute decrease in income in the first year to former CEOs. Initial artificial decrease in net income provides the illusion of an increased income in the next year.

CONSOLIDATION

In business, consolidation or amalgamation is the merger and acquisition of many smaller companies into a few much larger ones. In the context of financial accounting, *consolidation* refers to the aggregation of financial statements of a group company as consolidated financial statements. The taxation term of consolidation refers to the treatment of a group of companies and other entities as one entity for tax purposes. Under the Halsbury's Laws of England, 'amalgamation' is defined as "a blending together of two or more undertakings into one undertaking, the shareholders of each blending company, becoming, substantially, the shareholders of the blended undertakings. There may be amalgamations, either by transfer of two or more undertakings to a new company, or to the transfer of one or more companies to an existing company".

Consolidation is the practice, in business, of legally combining two or more organizations into a single new one. Upon consolidation, the original organizations cease to exist and are supplanted by a new entity.

Economic Motivation

- Access to new technologies/techniques.
- Access to new clients.
- Access to new geographies.
- Cheaper financing for a bigger company.
- Seeking for hidden or nonperforming assets belonging to a target company (e.g. real estate).
- Bigger companies tend to have superior bargaining power over their suppliers and clients (e.g. Walmart).
- Synergies.

Types of Business Amalgamations

There are three forms of business combinations:

- Statutory Merger: a business combination that results in the liquidation of the acquired company's assets and the survival of the purchasing company.
- Statutory Consolidation: a business combination that creates a new company in which none of the previous companies survive.
- Stock Acquisition: a business combination in which the purchasing company acquires the majority, more than 50%, of the Common stock of the acquired company and both companies survive.
- Variable interest entity.

Accounting Treatment (US GAAP)

A parent company can acquire another company by purchasing its net assets or by purchasing a majority share of its common stock. Regardless of the method of acquisition; direct costs, costs of issuing securities and indirect costs are treated as follows:

- Direct costs, Indirect and general costs: the acquiring company expenses all acquisition related costs as they are incurred.
- Costs of issuing securities: these costs reduce the issuing price of the stock.

Purchase of Net Assets

Treatment to the acquiring company: When purchasing the net assets the acquiring company records in its books the receipt of the net assets and the disbursement of cash, the creation of a liability or the issuance of stock as a form of payment for the transfer.

Treatment to the acquired company: The acquired company records in its books the elimination of its net assets and the receipt of cash, receivables or investment in the acquiring company (if what was received from the transfer included common stock from the purchasing company). If the acquired company is liquidated then the company needs an additional entry to distribute the remaining assets to its shareholders.

Purchase of Common Stock

Treatment to the purchasing company: When the purchasing company acquires the subsidiary through the purchase of its common stock, it records in its books the investment in the acquired company and the disbursement of the payment for the stock acquired.

Treatment to the acquired company: The acquired company records in its books the receipt of the payment from the acquiring company and the issuance of stock.

FASB 141 Disclosure Requirements: FASB 141 requires disclosures in the notes of the financial statements when business combinations occur. Such disclosures are:

- The name and description of the acquired entity and the percentage of the voting equity interest acquired.
- The primary reasons for acquisition and descriptions of factors that contributed to recognition of goodwill.
- The period for which results of operations of acquired entity are included in the income statement of the combining entity.
- The cost of the acquired entity and if it applies the number of shares of equity interest issued, the value assigned to those interests and the basis for determining that value.
- Any contingent payments, options or commitments.
- The purchase and development assets acquired and written off.

Treatment of goodwill impairments:

- If Non-Controlling Interest (NCI) based on fair value of identifiable assets: impairment taken against parent's income & R/E.

- If NCI based on fair value of purchase price: impairment taken against subsidiary's income & R/E.

Reporting Intercorporate Interest—Investments in Common Stock

20% Ownership or Less—Investment

When a company purchases 20% or less of the outstanding common stock, the purchasing company's influence over the acquired company is not significant. (APB 18 specifies conditions where ownership is less than 20% but there is significant influence).

The purchasing company uses the cost method to account for this type of investment. Under the cost method, the investment is recorded at cost at the time of purchase. The company does not need any entries to adjust this account balance unless the investment is considered impaired or there are liquidating dividends, both of which reduce the investment account.

Liquidating dividends : Liquidating dividends occur when there is an excess of dividends declared over earnings of the acquired company since the date of acquisition. Regular dividends are recorded as dividend income whenever they are declared.

Impairment loss : An impairment loss occurs when there is a decline in the value of the investment other than temporary.

20% to 50% Ownership—Associate Company

When the amount of stock purchased is between 20% and 50% of the common stock outstanding, the purchasing company's influence over the acquired company is often significant. The deciding factor, however, is significant influence. If other factors exist that reduce the influence or if significant influence is gained at an ownership of less than 20%, the equity method may be appropriate (FASB interpretation 35 (FIN 35) underlines the circumstances where the investor is unable to exercise significant influence).

To account for this type of investment, the purchasing company uses the equity method. Under the equity method, the purchaser records its investment at original cost. This balance increases with income and decreases for dividends from the subsidiary that accrue to the purchaser.

Treatment of Purchase Differentials: At the time of purchase, purchase differentials arise from the difference between the cost of the investment and the book value of the underlying assets.

Purchase differentials have two components:

- The difference between the fair market value of the underlying assets and their book value.
- Goodwill: The difference between the cost of the investment and the fair market value of the underlying assets.

Purchase differentials need to be amortized over their useful life; however, new accounting guidance states that goodwill is not amortized or reduced until it is permanently impaired, or the underlying asset is sold.

More than 50% Ownership—Subsidiary

When the amount of stock purchased is more than 50% of the outstanding common stock, the purchasing company has control over the acquired company. Control in this context is defined as ability to direct policies and management. In this type of relationship the controlling company is the parent and the controlled company is the subsidiary. The parent company needs to issue consolidated financial statements at the end of the year to reflect this relationship.

Consolidated financial statements show the parent and the subsidiary as one single entity. During the year, the parent company can use the equity or the cost method to account for its investment in the subsidiary. Each company keeps separate books. However, at the end of the year, a consolidation working paper is prepared to combine the separate balances and to eliminate the intercompany transactions, the subsidiary's stockholder equity and the parent's investment account. The result is one set of financial statements that reflect the financial results of the consolidated entity. There are three forms of combination: 1. horizontal integration:is the combination of firms in the same business lines and markets. 2. vertical integration: is the combination of firms with operations in different but successive stages of production or distribution or both. 3. Conglomeration: is the combination of firms with unrelated and diverse products or services functions, or both.

GOING CONCERN CONCEPT

Continuation of an entity as a going concern is presumed as the basis for financial reporting unless and until the entity's liquidation becomes imminent. Preparation of financial statements under this presumption is commonly referred to as the going concern basis of accounting. If and when an entity's liquidation becomes imminent, financial statements are prepared under the liquidation basis of accounting (Financial Accounting Standards Board, 2014).

The going concern assumption is universally understood and accepted by accounting professionals; however, it has never been formally incorporated into U.S GAAP. In October 2008, FASB issued an Exposure Draft called "Going Concern." It discusses the following possible pronouncements for the going concern:

- Reconsideration of defining and incorporating the terms going concern and substantial doubt into U.S. GAAP.
- The time horizon over which management would evaluate the entity's ability to meet its obligations.
- The type of information that management should consider in evaluating the entity's ability to meet its obligations.
- The effect of subsequent events on management's evaluation of the entity's ability to meet its obligations.
- Whether to provide guidance on the liquidation basis of accounting.

A current definition of the going concern assumption can be found in the AICPA Statement on Auditing Standards No.1 Codification of Auditing Standards and Procedures, Section 341, " The Auditor's Consideration of an Entity's Ability to Continue as a Going Concern"(AU Section 341). The 'going concern' concept assumes that the business will remain in existence long enough for all the assets of the business to be fully utilized. Utilized assets means obtaining the complete benefit from their earning potential. (i.e. if you recently purchased equipment costing $5,000 that had 5 years of productive/useful life, then under the going concern assumption, the accountant would only write off one year's value $1,000 (1/5th) this year, leaving $4,000 to be treated as a fixed asset with future economic value for the business).

Accounting

This accounting principle assumes that, a company will continue to exist long enough to carry out its objectives and commitments and will not liquidate in the foreseeable future. If the company's financial situation is such that the accountant believes the company will not be able to continue on, the accountant is required to disclose this assessment.

The going concern principle allows the company to defer some of its prepaid expenses until future accounting periods. The going concern assumption is a fundamental assumption in the preparation of financial statements. Under the going concern assumption, an entity is ordinarily viewed as continuing in business for the foreseeable future with neither the intention nor the necessity of liquidation, ceasing trading or seeking protection from creditors pursuant to laws or regulations. Accordingly, unless the going concern assumption is inappropriate in the circumstances of the entity, assets and liabilities are recorded on the basis that the entity will be able to realize its assets, discharge its liabilities, and obtain refinancing (if necessary) in the normal course of business.

An entity is assumed to be a going concern in the absence of significant information to the contrary. An example of such contrary information is an entity's inability to meet its obligations as they come due without substantial asset sales or debt restructurings. If such were not the case, an entity would essentially be acquiring assets with the intention of closing its operations and reselling the assets to another party.

If the accountant believes that an entity may no longer be a going concern, then this brings up the issue of whether its assets are impaired, which may call for the write-down of their carrying amount to their liquidation value, and the recognition of liabilities that arise on account of the entity's imminent closure (which may not arise otherwise). Thus, the value of an entity that is assumed to be a going concern is higher than its breakup value, since a going concern can potentially continue to earn profits.

The going concern concept is not clearly defined anywhere in generally accepted accounting principles, and so is subject to a considerable amount of interpretation regarding when an entity should report it. However, generally accepted auditing standards (GAAS) do instruct an auditor regarding the consideration of an entity's ability to continue as a going concern.

The auditor evaluates an entity's ability to continue as a going concern for a period not less than one year following the date of the financial statements being audited (a longer period may be considered if the auditor believes such extended period to be relevant). The auditor considers such items as negative trends in operating results, loan defaults, denial of trade credit from suppliers uneconomical long-term commitments, and legal proceedings in deciding if there is a substantial doubt about an entity's ability to continue as a going concern. If so, the auditor must draw attention to the uncertainty regarding the entity's ability to continue as a going concern, in their auditor's report. On the other hand, inappropriate use of the going concern assumption by an entity may cause the auditor to issue an adverse opinion on the financial statements. This Guidance provides a framework to assist directors, audit committees and finance teams in determining whether it is appropriate to adopt the going concern basis for preparing financial statements and in making balanced, proportionate and clear disclosures. Separate standards and guidance have been issued by the Auditing Practices Board to address the work of auditors in relation to going concern.

Assumption

Under the going concern assumption, an entity is viewed as continuing in business for the foreseeable future. General purpose financial statements are prepared on a going concern basis, unless management either intends to liquidate the entity or to cease operations, or has no realistic alternative but to do so. Special purpose financial statements may or may not be prepared in accordance with a financial reporting framework for which the going concern basis is relevant (for example, the going concern basis is not relevant for some financial statements prepared on a tax basis in particular jurisdictions). When the use of the going concern assumption is appropriate, assets and liabilities are recorded on the basis that the entity will be able to realize its assets and discharge its liabilities in the normal course of business.

Auditing

Continuation of an entity as a going concern is assumed in financial reporting in the absence of significant information to the contrary. Ordinarily, information that significantly contradicts the going concern assumption relates to the entity's inability to continue to meet its obligations as they become due without substantial disposition of assets outside the ordinary course of business, restructuring of debt, externally forced revisions of its operations, or similar actions.

Responsibilities

The auditor has a responsibility to evaluate whether there is substantial doubt about the entity's ability to continue as a going concern for a reasonable period of time, not to exceed one year beyond the date of the financial statements being audited (hereinafter referred to as a reasonable period of time). The auditor's evaluation is based on his or her knowledge of relevant conditions and events that exist at or have occurred prior to the date of the auditor's report. Information about such conditions or events is obtained from the application of auditing procedures planned and performed to achieve audit objectives that are related to management's assertions embodied in the financial statements being audited, as described in Auditing Standard No. 15, Audit Evidence.

The auditor should evaluate whether there is substantial doubt about the entity's ability to continue as a going concern for a reasonable period of time in the following manner:

The auditor considers whether the results of his procedures performed in planning, gathering evidential matter relative to the various audit objectives, and completing the audit identify conditions and events that, when considered in the aggregate, indicate there could be substantial doubt about the entity's ability to continue as a going concern for a reasonable period of time. It may be necessary to obtain additional information about such conditions and events, as well as the appropriate evidential matter to support information that mitigates the auditor's doubt.

If the auditor believes there is substantial doubt about the entity's ability to continue as a going concern for a reasonable period of time, he should obtain information about management's plans that are intended to mitigate the effect of such conditions or events, and assess the likelihood that such plans can be effectively implemented.

After the auditor has evaluated management's plans, he concludes whether he has substantial doubt about the entity's ability to continue as a going concern for a reasonable period of time. If the auditor concludes there is substantial doubt, he should consider the adequacy of disclosure about the entity's possible inability to continue as a going concern for a reasonable period of time, and include an explanatory paragraph (following the opinion paragraph) in his audit report to reflect his conclusion. If the auditor concludes that substantial doubt does not exist, he should consider the need for disclosure.

The auditor is not responsible for predicting future conditions or events. The fact that the entity may cease to exist as a going concern subsequent to receiving a report from the auditor that does not refer to substantial doubt, even within one year following the date of the financial statements, does not, in itself, indicate inadequate performance by the auditor. Accordingly, the absence of reference to substantial doubt in an auditor's report should not be viewed as providing assurance as to an entity's ability to continue as a going concern.

Procedures

It is not necessary to design audit procedures solely to identify conditions and events that, when considered in the aggregate, indicate there could be substantial doubt about the entity's ability to continue as a going concern for a reasonable period of time. The results of auditing procedures designed and performed to achieve other audit objectives should be sufficient for that purpose. The following are examples of procedures that may identify such conditions and events:

- Analytical procedures.
- Review of subsequent events.
- Review of compliance with the terms of debt and loan agreements.
- Reading of minutes of meetings of stockholders, board of directors, and important committees of the board.
- Inquiry of an entity's legal counsel about litigation, claims, and assessments.
- Confirmation with related and third parties of the details of arrangements to provide or maintain financial support.

Conditions and Events

In performing audit procedures such as those presented in paragraph .05, the auditor may identify information about certain conditions or events that, when considered in the aggregate, indicate there could be substantial doubt about the entity's ability to continue as a going concern for a reasonable period of time. The significance of such conditions and events will depend on the circumstances, and some may have significance only when viewed in conjunction with others. The following are examples of such conditions and events:

- Negative trends—for example, recurring operating losses, working capital deficiencies, negative cash flows from operating activities, adverse key financial ratios.
- Other indications of possible financial difficulties—for example, default on loan or similar agreements, arrearages in dividends, denial of usual trade credit from suppliers, restructuring of debt, noncompliance with statutory capital requirements, need to seek new sources or methods of financing or to dispose of substantial assets.
- Internal matters—for example, work stoppages or other labor difficulties, substantial dependence on the success of a particular project, uneconomic long-term commitments, need to significantly revise operations.
- External matters that have occurred—for example, legal proceedings, legislation, or similar matters that might jeopardize an entity's ability to operate; loss of a key franchise, license, or patent; loss of a principal customer or supplier; uninsured or underinsured catastrophe such as a drought, earthquake, or flood.

Managements Plans

If, after considering the identified conditions and events in the aggregate, the auditor believes there is substantial doubt about the ability of the entity to continue as a going concern for a reasonable period of time, he should consider management's plans for dealing with the adverse effects of the conditions and events. The auditor should obtain information about the plans and consider whether it is likely the adverse effects will be mitigated for a reasonable period of time and that such plans can be effectively implemented. The auditor's considerations relating to management plans may include the following:

Plans to dispose of assets:

- Restrictions on disposal of assets, such as covenants limiting such transactions in loan or similar agreements or encumbrances against assets.
- Apparent marketability of assets that management plans to sell.
- Possible direct or indirect effects of disposal of assets.

Plans to borrow money or restructure debt:

- Availability of debt financing, including existing or committed credit arrangements, such as lines of credit or arrangements for factoring receivables or sale-leaseback of assets.

- Existing or committed arrangements to restructure or subordinate debt or to guarantee loans to the entity.
- Possible effects on management's borrowing plans of existing restrictions on additional borrowing or the sufficiency of available collateral.

Plans to reduce or delay expenditures:

- Apparent feasibility of plans to reduce overhead or administrative expenditures, to postpone maintenance or research and development projects, or to lease rather than purchase assets.
- Possible direct or indirect effects of reduced or delayed expenditures.

Plans to increase ownership equity:

- Apparent feasibility of plans to increase ownership equity, including existing or committed arrangements to raise additional capital.
- Existing or committed arrangements to reduce current dividend requirements or to accelerate cash distributions from affiliates or other investors.

When evaluating management's plans, the auditor should identify those elements that are particularly significant to overcoming the adverse effects of the conditions and events and should plan and perform auditing procedures to obtain evidential matter about them. For example, the auditor should consider the adequacy of support regarding the ability to obtain additional financing or the planned disposal of assets.

When prospective financial information is particularly significant to management's plans, the auditor should request management to provide that information and should consider the adequacy of support for significant assumptions underlying that information. The auditor should give particular attention to assumptions that are:

- Material to the prospective financial information.
- Especially sensitive or susceptible to change.
- Inconsistent with historical trends.

The auditor's consideration should be based on knowledge of the entity, its business, and its management and should include (a) reading of the prospective financial information and the underlying assumptions and (b) comparing prospective financial information in prior periods with actual results and comparing prospective information for the current period with results achieved to date. If the auditor becomes aware of factors, the effects of which are not reflected in such prospective financial information, he should discuss those factors with management and, if necessary, request revision of the prospective financial information.

Financial Statement Effects

When, after considering management's plans, the auditor concludes there is substantial doubt about the entity's ability to continue as a going concern for a reasonable period of time, the auditor should consider the possible effects on the financial statements and the adequacy of the related disclosure. Some of the information that might be disclosed includes:

- Pertinent conditions and events giving rise to the assessment of substantial doubt about the entity's ability to continue as a going concern for a reasonable period of time.
- The possible effects of such conditions and events.
- Management's evaluation of the significance of those conditions and events and any mitigating factors.
- Possible discontinuance of operations.
- Management's plans (including relevant prospective financial information).
- Information about the recoverability or classification of recorded asset amounts or the amounts or classification of liabilities.

When, primarily because of the auditor's consideration of management's plans, he concludes that substantial doubt about the entity's ability to continue as a going concern for a reasonable period of time is alleviated, he should consider the need for disclosure of the principal conditions and events that initially caused him to believe there was substantial doubt. The auditor's consideration of disclosure should include the possible effects of such conditions and events, and any mitigating factors, including management's plans.

Effects on the Auditor's Report

If, after considering identified conditions and events and management's plans, the auditor concludes that substantial doubt about the entity's ability to continue as a going concern for a reasonable period of time remains, the audit report should include an explanatory paragraph (following the opinion paragraph) to reflect that conclusion. The auditor's conclusion about the entity's ability to continue as a going concern should be expressed through the use of the phrase "substantial doubt about its (the entity's) ability to continue as a going concern" [or similar wording that includes the terms substantial doubt and going concern] as illustrated in paragraph.

An example follows of an explanatory paragraph (following the opinion paragraph) in the auditor's report describing an uncertainty about the entity's ability to continue as a going concern for a reasonable period of time.

The accompanying financial statements have been prepared assuming that the Company will continue as a going concern. As discussed in Note X to the financial statements, the Company has suffered recurring losses from operations and has a net capital deficiency that raise substantial doubt about its ability to continue as a going concern. Management's plans in regard to these matters are also described in Note X. The financial statements do not include any adjustments that might result from the outcome of this uncertainty.

If the auditor concludes that the entity's disclosures with respect to the entity's ability to continue as a going concern for a reasonable period of time are inadequate, a departure from generally accepted accounting principles exists. This may result in either a qualified (except for) or an adverse opinion. Reporting guidance for such situations is provided in section 508, Reports on Audited Financial Statements.

Substantial doubt about the entity's ability to continue as a going concern for a reasonable period of time that arose in the current period does not imply that a basis for such doubt existed in the prior period and, therefore, should not affect the auditor's report on the financial statements of the prior period that are presented on a comparative basis. When financial statements of one or more prior periods are presented on a comparative basis with financial statements of the current period, reporting guidance is provided in section 508.

If substantial doubt about the entity's ability to continue as a going concern for a reasonable period of time existed at the date of prior period financial statements that are presented on a comparative basis, and that doubt has been removed in the current period, the explanatory paragraph included in the auditor's report on the financial statements of the prior period should not be repeated.

Exceptions

Because the issuance of a going-concern opinion is feared to be a self-fulfilling prophecy, auditors may be reluctant to issue one. A going-concern opinion may lower stockholders' and creditors' confidence in the company; ratings agencies may then downgrade the debt, leading to an inability to obtain new capital and an increase in the cost of existing capital. In 1978, the AICPA formed an independent commission (the Cohen Commission) that issued a report expressing this sentiment.

Creditors often regard a subject to qualification as a separate reason for not granting a loan, a reason in addition to the circumstances creating the uncertainty that caused the qualification. This frequently puts the auditor in the position, in effect, of deciding whether a company is able to obtain the funds it needs to continue operating. Thus, the auditor's qualification tends to be a self-fulfilling prophecy. The auditor's expression of uncertainty about the company's ability to continue may contribute to making it a certainty.

The fear is that a going-concern opinion can hasten the demise of an already troubled company, reduce a loan officer's willingness to grant a line of credit to that troubled company, or increase the point spread that would be charged if that company were granted a loan. Auditors are placed at the center of a moral and ethical dilemma: whether to issue a going-concern opinion and risk escalating the financial distress of their client, or not issue a going-concern opinion and risk not informing interested parties of the possible failure of the company. The hope is that issuing a going-concern opinion might promote timelier rescue activity.

Another, more troubling reason that auditors might fail to issue a going-concern opinion has been alluded to by the mainstream media in the WorldCom and Enron business failures: lack of auditor independence. Management determines the auditor's tenure and remuneration. The threat of receiving a going-concern modification may send management to another auditor, in a phenomenon referred to as "opinion shopping." Moreover, in an extreme case of a self-fulfilling prophecy, if the client does go bankrupt, the auditor loses future audit fees. This fear of losing future fees could compromise the auditor's ability to render an unbiased opinion on a client's financial statements.

The Private Securities Litigation Reform Act of 1995 made it much more difficult for a plaintiff to bring suit successfully against a company's auditors. While the act did codify as law the reporting requirements of SAS 59, it also made it more difficult for a plaintiff's attorneys to successfully pursue class-action litigation against auditors. Furthermore, in cases where auditors did fail to modify their audit opinions in accordance with SAS 59, the damage awards were limited to proportionate liability. When comparing the potential costs of issuing a going-concern opinion (hastening the demise of the client; losing audit fees) to the costs of not issuing a going-concern opinion (litigation), the result of the act was essentially to tip the scales in favor of not issuing a going-concern opinion. Since the act was passed, high-profile litigation citing the auditors' failure to issue a going-concern opinion, such as the class-action lawsuits by Kmart's shareholders against PricewaterhouseCoopers, and Adelphia's against Deloitte & Touche, has been drastically reduced.

The most critical reason that auditors might fail to issue a going-concern opinion, however, could be a fundamental misunderstanding of the assumption itself.

Use in Risk Management

If a public or private company reports that its auditors have doubts about its ability to continue as a going concern, investors may take that as a sign of increased risk, although an emphasis of matter paragraph in an audit report does not necessarily indicate that a company is on the verge of insolvency. Despite this, some fund managers may be required to sell the stock to maintain an appropriate level of risk in their portfolios. A negative judgment may also result in the breach of bank loan covenants or lead a debt rating firm to lower the rating on the company's debt, making the cost of existing debt increase and preventing the company from obtaining additional debt financing. Because of such responses to expressed concerns by auditors, in the 1970s, the American Institute of Certified Public Accountants' Cohen commission concluded that an auditor's expression of uncertainty about the entity's ability to continue as a going concern "tends to be a self-fulfilling prophecy. The auditor's expression of uncertainty about the company's ability to continue may contribute to making its failure a certainty." Businesses should also communicate with business advisors as well as their auditors in the time of trouble. Communication can let advisors and auditors help when needed. They can help business review their internal risk management along with other internal controls.

REALISATION CONCEPT

Realization Concept of Accounting states that revenue is only recognized when goods or services are delivered or rendered to the buyer.

Conservatism concept suggests the period when revenue should be recognized. However realization concept indicates that the amount of revenue that should be recognized from a given sale. Realization basically refers to the inflows of cash or claims to cash arising from the sale of goods or services.

It furthers states that the amount recognized as revenue is the amount that is reasonably certain to be realized. In other words, customers are reasonably certain to pay. But of course, there is room for differences in judgement as to how certain 'reasonably certain' is.

However, the concept does clearly allow for the amount of revenue recognized to be less than the selling price of the goods and services sold. One obvious situation is the sale of merchandise at a discount at an amount less than its normal selling price. In these types of cases, revenue is recorded at the lower amount, not the normal price.

Example of Realization Concept

Suppose a customer buys 5000 worth of items from a store, paying cash, store realizes 5000 from the sale. Now suppose, the same store sells a suit for 20,000. However the purchaser agrees to pay within 30 days, the store realizes 20,000 from the sale in the form of receivables. Provides that the purchaser has good credit record so that payment is reasonably certain.

A less obvious situation arises with the sale of merchandise on credit. When a company makes a credit sale, it expects that the customers will pay the bill. Experience may indicate, however, that not all customers do pay their bill. In measuring the revenue for a period, the amount of sales made on credit should be reduced by estimated amount of credit sales that will never be realized that is by the estimated amount of bad debts.

For example, If a store makes credit sale of 1,00,000 during a period and if experience indicates that 3 percent of credit sales will eventually became bad debts, the amount of revenue for the period is 97,000 not 1,00,000.

ACCRUAL CONCEPT

Accrual (*accumulation*) of something is, in finance, the adding together of interest or different investments over a period of time. It holds specific meanings in accounting, where it can refer to accounts on a balance sheet that represent liabilities and non-cash-based assets used in accrual-based accounting. These types of accounts include, among others, accounts payable, accounts receivable, goodwill, deferred tax liability and future interest expense.

Accruals in Accounting

For example, a company delivers a product to a customer who will pay for it 30 days later in the next fiscal year, which starts a week after the delivery. The company recognizes the proceeds as a revenue in its current income statement still for the fiscal year of the delivery, even though it will not get paid until the following accounting period. The proceeds are also an accrued income (asset) on the balance sheet for the delivery fiscal year, but not for the next fiscal year when cash is received.

Similarly, a salesperson, who sold the product, earned a commission at the moment of sale (or delivery). The company will recognize the commission as an expense in its current income statement, even though the salesperson will actually get paid at the end of the following week in the next accounting period. The commission is also an accrued liability on the balance sheet for the delivery period, but not for the next period when the commission (cash) is paid out to the salesperson.

The term *accrual* is also often used as an abbreviation for the terms accrued expense and accrued revenue that share the common name word, but they have the opposite economic/accounting characteristics.

- Accrued revenue: revenue is recognized before cash is received.
- Accrued expense: expense is recognized before cash is paid out.

Accrued Revenue

Accrued revenue (or accrued assets) is an asset, such as unpaid proceeds from a delivery of goods or services, when such income is earned and a related revenue item is recognized, while cash is to be received in a later period, when the amount is deducted from *accrued revenues.*

In the rental industry, there are specialized revenue accruals for rental income which crosses month end boundaries. These are normally utilized by rental companies who charge in arrears, based on an anniversary of a contract date. For example, a rental contract which began on 15 January, being invoiced on a recurring monthly basis will not generate its first invoice until 14 February. Therefore, at the end of the January financial period an accrual must be raised for sixteen days' worth of the monthly charge. This may be a simple pro-rate basis (e.g. 16/31 of the monthly charge) or may be more complex if only week days are being charged or a standardized month is being used (e.g. 28 days, 30 days etc.)

Accrued Expense

Accrued expense is a liability whose timing or amount is uncertain by virtue of the fact that an invoice has not yet been received. The uncertainty of the accrued expense is not significant enough to qualify it as a provision. An example of an accrued expense is a pending obligation to pay for goods or services received from a counterpart, while cash is to be paid out in a later accounting period when the amount is deducted from *accrued expenses.*

Under International Financial Reporting Standards, this difference is best summarized by IAS 37 which states:

11 Provisions can be distinguished from other liabilities such as trade payables and accruals because there is uncertainty about the timing or amount of the future expenditure required in settlement. By contrast:

- Trade payables are liabilities to pay for goods or services that have been received or supplied and have been invoiced or formally agreed with the supplier.
- Accruals are liabilities to pay for goods or services that have been received or supplied but have not been paid, invoiced or formally agreed with the supplier, including amounts due to employees (for example, amounts relating to accrued vacation pay). Although it is sometimes necessary to estimate the amount or timing of accruals, the uncertainty is generally much less than for provisions.

"Accruals are often reported as part of trade and other payables, whereas provisions are reported separately.

To add to the confusion, some legalistic accounting systems take a simplistic view of 'accrued revenue' and 'accrued expenses", defining each as revenue or expense that has not been formally invoiced. This is primarily due to tax considerations, since in some countries, the act of issuing an invoice creates taxable revenue, even if the customer does not ultimately pay and the related receivable becomes non-collectable.

Accruals in Payroll

In payroll, a common benefit that an employer will provide for employees is a vacation or sick accrual. This means that as time passes, an employee accumulates additional sick leave or vacation time and this time is placed into a bank. Once the time is accumulated, the employer or the employer's payroll provider will track the amount of time used for sick or vacation.

Length of Service

For most employers, a time-off policy is published and followed with regard to benefit accruals. These guidelines ensure that all employees are treated fairly with regard to the distribution and use of sick and vacation time.

Within these guidelines, the rate at which the employee will accumulate the vacation or sick time is often determined by length of service (the amount of time the employee has worked for the employers).

Trial Period

In many cases, these guidelines indicate there is a trial period (usually 30 to 90 days) where no time is awarded to the employee. This does not prevent an employee from calling in sick immediately after being hired, but it does mean that they will not get paid for this time off. However, it does prevent an employee, for example, scheduling a vacation for the second week of work. After this trial period, the award of time may begin or it may be retroactive, back to the date of hire.

Rollover/Carry over

Some accrual policies have the ability to carry over or roll over some or all unused time that has been accrued into the next year. If the accrual policy does not have any type of rollover, any accrued time that is in the bank is usually lost at the end of the employer's calendar year.

Other uses

When referring to clinical trials, the definition of "accrual" is either the process of recruiting patients into a trial, or the number of patients in a trial.

MATCHING CONCEPT

The matching concept is an accounting principle that requires the identification and recording of expenses associated with revenue earned and recognized during the same accounting period.

Accordingly, under the matching concept the expenses of a particular accounting period are the costs of the assets used to earn the revenue that is recognized in that period. It follows, therefore, that when expenses in a period are matched with the revenues generated for the same period, the result is the net income or loss for that period.

While in everyday vernacular, the terms "cost," "expenditure," and "expense" are used almost interchangeably; in discussing accounting principles, these terms have distinctly different meanings. A cost is the amount of money, or other resources, used for a specific purpose. When a cost is incurred, it is associated with an expenditure; expenditures can either result in the decrease of an asset, such as cash, or the increase of a liability, such as accounts payable. Thus, expenditures result in either assets or expenses. If the expenditure will benefit future periods, such as the purchase of office equipment, it is an asset. If it will benefit the current period, such as the purchase of supplies needed to fill immediate manufacturing needs, it is an expense of that period. Logically, then, it follows that an expense is a cost item that is specifically applicable to the current accounting period used during that period to earn revenue.

The Conservatism Concept

Oftentimes, when deciding which revenues and expenses to match in a given accounting period, accountants have a difficult time recognizing which revenues and expenses are certain for that period. Like many people, accountants and other business professionals tend to be overly optimistic concerning the revenues that their companies generate but tend to be more realistic concerning the associated expenses. Thus, certain accounting principles have been developed to offset the tendency toward optimism. These principles recognize that increases in reported net income require stronger proof than do increases in expenses. Therefore, when deciding which expenses and revenues to acknowledge during a given accounting period, accountants are supposed to apply the conservatism concept. This concept has two conditions associated with it—firms can recognize expenses as soon as they are reasonably possible, and firms can recognize revenues as soon as they are reasonably certain.

Usually, a company applies the matching concept by being reasonably certain which items will generate revenue and matching them with any possible expenses for those items. To illustrate, if a company produces an item costing $100 that it later sells for $150, the company must decide the accounting period in which it is reasonably certain to receive the $150. When this is decided, the company must match the $100 cost with the $150 revenue as an expense, resulting in $50 income from sales. Interestingly, not all companies take these steps in the same order; sometimes expenses are first identified and later revenues are matched to them.

Revenue and Expense Recognition

The best matching of revenues and expenses occurs under the accrual basis of accounting. Under the accrual basis, revenue (as well as expenses, and other changes in assets, liabilities, and equity) is generally recognized in the period in which the economic event takes place, usually at the point of sale—not when the cash actually changes hands. Revenue recognition occurs at this time because the earnings process is complete and there is evidence supporting the sale price. Earnings, however, can be identified at other times, such as during an item's production, at the end of an item's production but prior to its sale, or when the money is collected, as with payments made on installments. Costs are recognized as expenses in a particular period if (1) there is a direct association between costs and revenues for the period or (2) the costs cannot be assigned to the generation of revenues of any period in the future.

The recognition of revenues and expenses can become more complicated, however, because companies often spend money or assume liabilities for non-monetary assets affecting more than one accounting period. Examples of transactions affecting more than one period are: (1) supplies purchased in a prior accounting period but used for several later periods; (2) insurance premiums paid that cover more than one period; (3) buildings and equipment; and (4) expenses—such as salaries—paid after a service has been rendered. Initially, these expenses are recorded at their original amounts, which represents the future benefit that the company anticipates receiving from these items. As they are used, the related costs must be matched against the revenues earned for the particular period. For example, for equipment and buildings, accountants gradually expense the costs of these assets over their estimated service life, a concept known as depreciation.

In accounting, adjusting entries are completed at the end of the accounting period to update the accounts for internal business transactions. Adjusting entries are commonly used to effect the matching of revenues and expenses. For example, the amount of materials used during a particular accounting period would be recorded by an adjusting entry at the end of each period. Expenditures made in the current period for assets not yet used would be recorded as assets and included in the current period's balance sheet, not recorded as expenses in the current period. As the assets are used, the related costs would be matched against revenues for that period by making an adjusting entry at the end of that period. If a company fails to make these adjustments at the proper time, the net income and assets of the company could be dramatically overstated.

As businesses have gotten more complex because of globalization, creative sales, and customer financing techniques, the proper period in which to recognize revenue has become less clear. Because, under the matching concept, the recognition of revenue triggers the recognition of the related expenses, this can have serious effects on a company's financial statements.

As a result, in recent years, there has been a dramatic increase in the number of companies restating prior years' earnings. In most instances, this has been prompted by the discovery that the original timing of the recognition of revenues and, therefore, the related expenses (the matching concept!) had been in error.

RECTIFICATION OF ERRORS

Financial accounting deals with recording and maintaining every monetary transaction of an organization. However, sometimes, a few entries might be either incorrect or used at the wrong place. In financial accounting, the process of correcting such mistakes is known as Rectification of Errors.

Once an error is located, it should be properly corrected. The correction of accounting errors in a systematic manner is called the rectification of errors. In other words, the process of systematically correcting the accounting errors is known as rectification of errors. The presence of accounting errors affects accuracy of the profit and loss and the financial position of the business shown by the final accounts, therefore, no error should be left uncorrected.

Methods of Rectification of Accounting Errors

The following method should be followed to rectify the accounting errors:

1. Rectification of errors located before preparation of trial balance.
2. Rectification of errors after preparation of trial balance.

Rectification of Errors Located before Preparation of Trial Balance

Errors may be detected in the process of closing books and accounts for preparation of trial balance. The errors detected in the process may be either one-sided errors or two-sided errors. However, once such errors are located they must be rectified immediately.

Rectification of One-sided Errors Located before Preparation of Trial Balance

One-sided errors are those errors which affect only one side of an account. Wrong totaling of subsidiary books, posting a wrong amount, posting on the wrong side are some of the examples of one-sided errors. Since two accounts are not involved in these errors, journal entry can not be passed for rectifying such errors. The one-sided error is rectified by making an additional posting on the affected side of the ledger account.

Rectification of Two-sided Errors Located before Preparation of Trial Balance

The errors that affect two or more accounts are called two-sided errors. Correction of such two-sided errors needs to make rectification journal entries since such errors involve two or more accounts. Therefore, one account is debited and another account is credited to rectify two-sided errors. The rules of debit and credit are applied to rectify these errors.

The following three steps are taken to rectify the two-sided errors.

1. Identify correct entry.
2. Rewrite wrong entry.
3. Find rectifying entry by making adjustment of correct entry and wrong entry.

Rectification of Errors after Preparation of Trial Balance

Sometimes, errors may be detected after an accounting year is over. Those are the errors detected after preparation of trial balance. The errors detected after the completion of accounting year may be one-sided and two-sided errors. Rectification of the errors seen after preparation of trial balance can be made by preparing rectifying journal entries in the subsequent year only.

Double entry system is followed to rectify the errors detected after preparation of trial balance. Two accounts are affected by the two-sided errors. Therefore, one account is debited and another affecting account is credited for such errors. But one-sided errors are rectified by opening 'Suspense Account'.

CLOSING ENTRY

A closing entry is a journal entry that is made at the end of the accounting period to transfer balances from a temporary account to a permanent account.

Companies use closing entries to reset the balances of temporary accounts – accounts that show balances over a single accounting period – to zero. By doing so, the company moves these balances into permanent accounts on the balance sheet. These permanent accounts show a company's long-standing financials.

Temporary Accounts

Temporary accounts are accounts in the general ledger that are used to accumulate transactions over a single accounting period. The balances of these accounts are eventually used to construct the income statement at the end of the fiscal year.

The income statement is a financial statement that is used to portray a company's financial performance and activities over a single fiscal year. It is for this reason that the date line in the annual income statement is written as "Year ended."

Below is an example of Amazon's 2017 annual income statement. You can see that for the date, it is written as 'Years ended December 31, YYYY'.

CONSOLIDATED STATEMENTS OF OPERATIONS (in millions, except per share data)			
	Year Ended December 31,		
	2015	2016	2017
Net product sales	$ 79,268	$94,665	$118,573
Net service sales	27,738	41,322	59,293
Total net Sales	107,006	135,987	177,866
Operating Expenses:			
Cost of Sales	71,651	88,265	111,934
Fulfilment	13,410	17,619	25,249
Marketing	5,254	7,233	10,069

Technology and Content	12,540	16,085	22,620
General and administrative	1,747	2,432	3,674
Other operating expense, net	171	167	214
Total operating Expenses	104,773	131,801	173,760
Operating income	2,233	4,186	4,106
Interest income	50	100	202
Interest expense	(459)	(484)	(848)
Other income (expense), net	(256)	90	346
Total non-operating income (expense)	(665)	(294)	(300)
Income before income taxes	1,568	3,892	3,806
Provision for income taxes	(950)	(1,425)	(769)
Equity- method investment activity , net of tax	(22)	(96)	(4)
Net income	$ 596	$ 2,371	$ 3,033
Basic earnings per Share	$ 1.28	$ 5.01	$ 6.32
Diluted earnings Per Share	$ 1.25	$ 4.90	$ 6.15
Weighted –average shares used in computation of earnings per share:	467	474	480
Basic	467	474	480
Diluted	477	484	493

As mentioned, temporary accounts in the general ledger consist of income statement accounts such as sales or expense accounts. After the income statement has been published at the end of the year, the balances of these accounts are transferred to the income summary, which is also a temporary account.

The income summary is used to transfer the balances of temporary accounts to retained earnings, which is a permanent account on the balance sheet.

Income Summary

The income summary is a temporary account used to make closing entries.

All temporary accounts must be reset to zero at the end of the accounting period. To do this, their balances are emptied into the income summary account. The income summary account then transfers the net balance of all the temporary accounts to retained earnings, which is a permanent account on the balance sheet.

Permanent Accounts

Permanent accounts are accounts that show the long-standing financial position of a company. Balance sheet accounts are permanent accounts. These accounts carry forward their balances throughout multiple accounting periods.

To understand this better, we can look at an account such as inventory. Below is an excerpt from

Amazon's 2017 annual balance sheet.

CONSOLIDATED BALANCE SHEETS (in millions, except per share data)		
ASSETS	December 31,	
	2016	2017
Current assets:		
Cash and cash equivalents	$ 19,334	$ 20,522
Marketable securities	6,647	10,464
Inventories	11,461	16,047
Accounts receivable, net and other	8,339	13,164
Total current assets	45,781	60,197
Property and equipment, net	29,114	48,886
Goodwill	3,784	13,350
Other assets	4,723	8,897
Total assets	$ 83,402	$ 131,310

The balance sheet captures a snapshot of a company at a given point in time. By looking at this balance sheet we can observe the following:

On December 31, 2016, Amazon reported $11,461 million of inventory. This amount was carried forward into the beginning of 2017.

On December 31, 2017, Amazon posted $16,047 million of inventory.

Amazon increased its inventories by $4,586 million in 2017 to come to the balance it reported on December 31, 2017.

By looking at it this way, we can see how Inventory is a permanent account that carries forward balances through multiple accounting periods.

Example of a Closing Entry

Below are examples of closing entries that 'zero' the temporary accounts in the income statement and transfer the balances to the permanent retained earnings account. This is done using the income summary account.

Close Revenue Accounts

Clear the balance of the revenue account by debiting revenue and crediting income summary.

Date	Accounts	Debit	Credit
2017 Dec. 31	Revenue	$100,000	
	Income Summary		$ 100,000

Close Expense Accounts

Clear the balance of the expense accounts by debiting income summary and crediting the corresponding expenses.

Date	Accounts	Debit	Credit
2017 Dec. 31	Income Summary	$92,000	
	Cost of goods sold		$ 55,000
	Depreciation expense		5,000
	Rent expense		15,000
	Wages expense		15,000
	Interest expense		2,000

Close Income Summary

Close the income summary account by debiting income summary and crediting retained earnings.

Date	Accounts	Debit	Credit
2017 Dec. 31	Income Summary	$ 8,000	
	Retained earnings		$ 8,000

Close Dividends

Close the dividends account by crediting retained earnings and crediting dividends.

Date	Accounts	Debit	Credit
2017 Dec. 31	Retained earnings	$4,000	
	Dividends		$ 4,000

STOCK EXCHANGE TRANSACTIONS

Stock exchange is an organized market where sale and purchase of listed securities of all description i.e. shares, stocks, debentures, government securities, etc. are done. It is a government approved market place where buyer and seller of securities of all kind find each other to buy and sell securities on the market price.

Meaning of Stock Exchange

"An association, organization or body of individuals, whether incorporated or not, established for the purpose of assisting, regulating and controlling business in buying, selling and dealing in securities."

A stock exchange is a common and authorized point of exchange, which offers the services for stock brokers and traders to buy or sell stocks, bonds, and other securities of such kind. Further, it also provides facilities for issue and redemption of securities, other financial instruments, and capital events. For example, payment of income and dividends.

Features and Characteristics of Stock Exchange

Following are the main features and characteristics of a stock exchange:

- Stock exchange is the market place where trading of listed securities can be done.
- Trading of un-listed securities is not allowed.
- There are certain rules and regulations that need to be followed while trading.
- Stock exchange is an association of persons, whether incorporated or not.
- Anyone can buy or sell securities whether he is investor or speculator.
- For doing business transaction i.e. sale & purchase of securities, membership is compulsory. Non-members are not allowed to do business transactions. Membership can be applied only when there is a vacancy in any stock exchange and after paying the prescribed fees of respective stock exchange, membership can be acquired. Members of stock exchange are called as brokers and commission charged by them for the transaction done is called as brokerage.
- Only a broker (member) can buy or sell securities, therefore, investors or speculators can do transaction through members only.

Functions and Services of Stock Exchange

Followings functions are performed by Stock Exchange:

- Anyone can sell and buy any industrial, financial, and Government securities. Stock Exchange is an organized ready market to do all this.
- Liquidity is provided by the stock exchange. Investors and speculators can buy and sell their securities at any time.
- Stock exchange provides collateral value to the securities that is helpful in borrowing from the bank on easy terms.
- Capital for the industrial growth is provided by the stock exchange that is helpful for the investor to participate in the industrial development.
- Price list and reports are prepared and published in the newspapers and broadcasted through the TV channels by stock exchange. It is helpful in knowing the true value of the investments. With the help of this, an investor or speculator can get to know the fair market value of his securities as per the latest market trend.
- Listing of securities is encouraged by the stock exchange. Listing of securities means — "a permission to trade" that is given by the stock exchange only after fulfillment of the prescribed standards.
- Listed companies have to provide the financial statements, reports, and other statements

time to time to stock exchange — necessary for the maintaining the record and deciding the value of securities.

Thus, stock exchange works as the center of providing business information at one platform.

Procedures for Dealing at Stock Exchange

Following procedures are normally followed for dealing at stock exchange:

- No one can directly deal in stock exchange, therefore, any person who wants to sell or buy securities, requires a broker through whom selling or buying of securities can be done.
- After finalization of a member or a broker, intending buyer or seller of the securities, places an order according to his choice, mentioning tentative quantity, and price. Thereupon, broker opens a new account for each client and start trading in the best possible way.
- After getting an order, broker tries to finalize the deal between seller and buyer. After finalization of deal, seller and buyer of securities send a selling and buying note respectively mentioning the detail of traded securities.
- Finally, settlement of account may be done in the following three manners:
    - When the settlement of account is done as per the fixed and agreed date, it is called as "liquidation in full."
    - When only difference of agreed price and ruling price is settled on the fixed date, it is called as "liquidation by payment of difference."
    - When a settlement is carried forward to the next settlement period, it is known as "carried over to next settlement period".

In case, when purchase is delayed and charge debited by the broker to purchaser is known as "contango" (Contango charge is also known as "Badla" Charge) and in case, where sale is delayed by the seller and charge debited by the broker is known as "backwardation."

Operators at Stock Exchange

The following figure shows the three operators at the Stock Exchange:

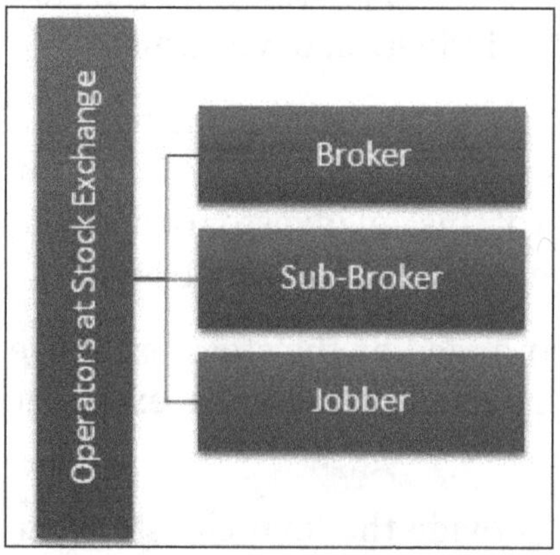

Broker

As studied earlier, no one can deal directly in stock exchange and every intended seller or buyer, who wants to sell or buy securities has to deal through members known as brokers. Membership of the stock exchange is restricted to prescribed numbers of members, to financially sound persons who have sufficient experience in dealing in securities.

A broker cannot buy or sell securities on his personal capacity. He charges commission from the parties, sellers, and buyers and deals on the behalf of his non-member clients.

Sub-broker

Sub-brokers are non-members of the stock exchange and deal only on behalf of the members or registered brokers. Commission is received by sub-brokers on the business procured by them out of total commission received by the brokers. Sub brokers are known as “half commission men” and “remisiers” too.

Jobbers

Jobbers are the independent dealers, who deal in securities at their own. A jobber cannot sell or buy securities on the behalf of others, but he deals in securities for his own profit through fluctuation of the prices. Difference between sale price and purchase price of securities is the profit of a jobber.

Important Terms used in Stock Exchange

Following are the significant terms more commonly used in stock exchange:

- Bull – Bulls are those brokers who strongly expect price hike of securities and with this hope, they buy shares to sell them at later stage (when price gets increased). Thus bull market means when buying of the securities are on much higher side instead of selling of the securities. Bulls first buy securities and sell when the price of securities is high.
- Bear – Bear is pessimist, who expect fall in the price of certain securities. A Bear first sells his securities and purchases at later stage when the price of securities are low and the difference of both is his profit.
- Stag – A cautious investor or speculator is known as a stag. Stag doesn’t sell or buy shares in his hand, but he tries to buy shares of new company with a hope that price of those shares will increase in the future.
- Blue Chips – Shares of well-recognized, well-renowned, financially strong, and well-established companies.
- Cash Shares – Settlement of some of the transactions are completed in cash are known as cash shares. These transactions are done by real and genuine investors who want to buy or sell shares for the actual investment purpose.
- Cleared Shares – Speculators are normally deals in such type of shares. In these types of

shares, settlement of the payments are done by the differential amounts only; however, actual delivery of the securities may not be done.

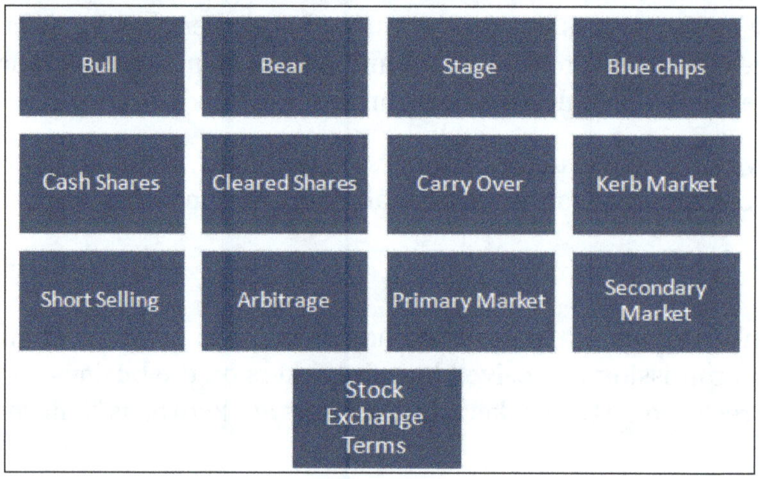

- Carry Over or Badla System – Speculator earns money by foreseeing the future. If their expectations come true, they earn profit and if not, they lose money. Speculator mostly does transactions on forward basis, when any speculator forwards his transactions from one settlement date to another, he has to pay charges called "Badla charge." Transaction of these natures is called as Badla System.

- Kerb Market – Transactions that done before and after the official hours are known as kerb market.

- Short Selling – Short selling means where the large volumes of securities are sold by the bear speculator without actually possessing.

- Arbitrage – Securities are traded at the different stock exchanges and there is normally a little difference in prices (among different stock exchanges). Therefore, arbitrage is practiced to take advantage of different rates.

- Primary Market – Primary market is the market where new securities are issued for the capital formation in the form of a new issue or in the form of a right issue to the existing shareholders.

- Secondary Market – Secondary market is the market where subsequent trading (sale and purchase) of securities are done called as secondary market and the transactions are known as secondary transactions.

- Group A Shares – Actively traded shares of the reputed companies are called a Group A shares.

- Group B Shares – Not actively traded shares or the shares of different stock exchanges are called as Group B shares.

References

- Chang, Hsihui; Kao, Yi-Ching; Mashruwala, Raj; Sorensen, Susan M. (10 April 2017). "Technical Inefficiency, Allocative Inefficiency, and Audit Pricing". Journal of Accounting, Auditing & Finance. 33 (4): 580–600. Doi:10.1177/0148558x17696760
- Money-measurement, concepts-and-principles, financial: accounting- simplified.com, Retrieved 12 June 2019
- Auditing and Assurance Vol.1. The Institute of Chartered Accountants of India. 2011. P. 3.4. ISBN 978-81-8441-135-5. Retrieved 27 August 2012
- Office, Australian National Audit (12 May 2016). "Auditor-General and the Office". Www.anao.gov.au. Retrieved 17 May 2016
- Closing-entry, accounting, knowledge, resources: corporatefinanceinstitute.com, Retrieved 16 January 2019
- Financial-accounting-stock-exchange-transactions, financial-accounting: tutorialspoint.com, Retrieved 29 March 2019
- Joseph Swanson and Peter Marshall, Houlihan Lokey and Lyndon Norley, Kirkland & Ellis International LLP (2008). A Practitioner's Guide to Restructuring, Andrew Miller's Valuation of a Distressed Company p. 24. ISBN 978-1-905121-31-1
- Explanation, financial-accounting: accountingcoach.com, Retrieved 12 July 2019
- "Consolidated Statements (Interco eliminations)". Findmybestcpa.com. Archived from the original on 2011-03-08. Retrieved 2011-04-15
- What-is-realization-concept-of-accounting: cashstock.in, Retrieved 30 April 2019
- "Accrual Accounting". Investopedia.com. Archived from the original on 5 January 2010. Retrieved 6 January 2010.
- Matching-Concept, Man-Mix, encyclopedia: referenceforbusiness.com, Retrieved 2 June 2019
- Rectification-of-accounting-errors-and: blogspot.com, Retrieved 29 March 2019

3

Financial Mathematics and Ratios

The application of mathematical methods to financial problems is known as financial mathematics. The relative magnitude of two selected numerical values that are taken from the financial statements of an enterprise is termed as financial ratio. This chapter discusses in detail the concepts and application related to financial mathematics and ratios such as accounting liquidity and bias ratio.

Financial Mathematics is the application of mathematical methods to financial problems. (Equivalent names sometimes used are quantitative finance, financial engineering, mathematical finance, and computational finance.) It draws on tools from probability, statistics, stochastic processes, and economic theory. Traditionally, investment banks, commercial banks, hedge funds, insurance companies, corporate treasuries, and regulatory agencies apply the methods of financial mathematics to such problems as derivative securities valuation, portfolio structuring, risk management, and scenario simulation. Industries that rely on commodities (e.g. energy, manufacturing) also use financial mathematics. Quantitative analysis has brought efficiency and rigor to financial markets and to the investment process and is becoming increasingly important in regulatory concerns.

Quantitative Finance as a sub-field of economics concerns itself with the valuation of assets and financial instruments as well as the allocation of resources. Centuries of experience have produced fundamental theories about the way economies function and the way we value assets. Models describe relationships between fundamental variables such as asset prices, market movements and interest rates. These mathematical tools allow us to draw conclusions that can be otherwise difficult to find or not immediately obvious from intuition. An example of the application of models is stress-testing of banks. Especially with the aid of modern computational techniques, we can store vast quantities of data and model many variables simultaneously, leading to the ability to model quite large and complicated systems. Thus the techniques of scientific computing, such as numerical analysis, Monte Carlo simulation and optimization are an important part of financial mathematics.

A large part of any science is the ability to create testable hypotheses based on a fundamental understanding of the objects of study and prove or contradict the hypotheses through repeatable studies. In this light, mathematics is the language for representing theories and provides tools for testing their validity. For example, in the theory of option pricing due to Black, Scholes and Merton, a model for the movement of stock prices is presented, and in conjunction with theory which states that a riskless investment will receive the risk-free rate of return, the researchers reasoned that a value can be assigned to an option.

This theory, for which Scholes and Merton were awarded the Nobel prize, is an excellent illustration of the interaction between math and financial theory, which ultimately led to a surprising insight into the nature of option prices. The mathematical contribution was the basic stochastic model (Geometric Brownian motion) for stock price movements and the partial differential equation and its solution providing the relationship between the option's value and other market variables. Their analysis also provided a completely specified strategy for managing option investment which permits practical testing of the model's consequences.

QUANTITIES OF MATHEMATICAL FINANCE

Greeks

In mathematical finance, the Greeks are the quantities representing the sensitivity of the price of derivatives such as options to a change in underlying parameters on which the value of an instrument or portfolio of financial instruments is dependent. The name is used because the most common of these sensitivities are denoted by Greek letters (as are some other finance measures). Collectively these have also been called the risk sensitivities, risk measures or hedge parameters.

Use of the Greeks

	Spot price (S)	Volatility (Δ)	Time to expiry (τ)
Value (V)	Δ Delta	$\mathcal{V}$ Vega	Θ Theta
Delta (Δ)	Gamma	Vanna	Charm
Vega ($\mathcal{V}$)	Vanna	Vomma	Veta
Theta (Θ)	Charm	Veta	
Gamma (Γ)	Speed	Zomma	Color
Vomma		Ultima	

Definition of Greeks as the sensitivity of an option's price and risk (in the first row) to the underlying parameter (in the first column). First-order Greeks are in blue, second-order Greeks are in green, and third-order Greeks are in yellow. Note that vanna, charm and veta appear twice, since partial cross derivatives are equal by Schwarz's theorem. Rho, lambda, epsilon, and vera are left out as they are not as important as the rest. Three places in the table are not occupied, because the respective quantities have not yet been defined in the financial literature.

The Greeks are vital tools in risk management. Each Greek measures the sensitivity of the value of a portfolio to a small change in a given underlying parameter, so that component risks may be treated in isolation, and the portfolio rebalanced accordingly to achieve a desired exposure.

The Greeks in the Black–Scholes model are relatively easy to calculate, a desirable property of financial models, and are very useful for derivatives traders, especially those who seek to hedge their portfolios from adverse changes in market conditions. For this reason, those Greeks which are particularly useful for hedging—such as delta, theta, and vega—are well-defined for measuring changes in Price, Time and Volatility. Although rho is a primary input into the Black–Scholes model, the overall impact on the value of an option corresponding to changes in the risk-free interest rate is generally insignificant and therefore higher-order derivatives involving the risk-free interest rate are not common.

The most common of the Greeks are the first order derivatives: delta, vega, theta and rho as well as gamma, a second-order derivative of the value function. The remaining sensitivities in this list are common enough that they have common names, but this list is by no means exhaustive.

First-order Greeks

Delta

Delta, Δ, measures the rate of change of the theoretical option value with respect to changes in the underlying asset's price. Delta is the first derivative of the value V of the option $\Delta = \frac{\partial V}{\partial S}$ with respect to the underlying instrument's price S.

Practical Use

For a vanilla option, delta will be a number between 0.0 and 1.0 for a long call (or a short put) and 0.0 and −1.0 for a long put (or a short call); depending on price, a call option behaves as if one owns 1 share of the underlying stock (if deep in the money), or owns nothing (if far out of the money), or something in between, and conversely for a put option. The difference between the delta of a call and the delta of a put at the same strike is close to but not in general equal to one, but instead is equal to the inverse of the discount factor. By put–call parity, long a call and short a put is equivalent to a forward *F*, which is linear in the spot *S*, with factor the inverse of the discount factor, so the derivative dF/dS is this factor.

These numbers are commonly presented as a percentage of the total number of shares represented by the option contract(s). This is convenient because the option will (instantaneously) behave like the number of shares indicated by the delta. For example, if a portfolio of 100 American call options on XYZ each have a delta of 0.25 (=25%), it will gain or lose value just like 2,500 shares of XYZ as the price changes for small price movements (100 option contracts covers 10,000 shares). The sign and percentage are often dropped – the sign is implicit in the option type (negative for put, positive for call) and the percentage is understood. The most commonly quoted are 25 delta put, 50 delta put/50 delta call, and 25 delta call. 50 Delta put and 50 Delta call are not quite identical, due to spot and forward differing by the discount factor, but they are often conflated.

Delta is always positive for long calls and negative for long puts (unless they are zero). The total delta of a complex portfolio of positions on the same underlying asset can be calculated by simply taking the sum of the deltas for each individual position – delta of a portfolio is linear in the constituents. Since the delta of underlying asset is always 1.0, the trader could delta-hedge his entire position in the underlying by buying or shorting the number of shares indicated by the total delta. For example, if the delta of a portfolio of options in XYZ (expressed as shares of the underlying) is +2.75, the trader would be able to delta-hedge the portfolio by selling short 2.75 shares of the underlying. This portfolio will then retain its total value regardless of which direction the price of XYZ moves. (Albeit for only small movements of the underlying, a short amount of time and not-withstanding changes in other market conditions such as volatility and the rate of return for a risk-free investment).

As a Proxy for Probability

The (absolute value of) Delta is close to, but not identical with, the percent moneyness of an option, i.e., the *implied* probability that the option will expire in-the-money (if the market moves under Brownian motion in the risk-neutral measure). For this reason some option traders use the absolute value of delta as an approximation for percent moneyness. For example, if an out-of-the-money call option has a delta of 0.15, the trader might estimate that the option has approximately a 15% chance of expiring in-the-money. Similarly, if a put contract has a delta of −0.25, the trader might expect the option to have a 25% probability of expiring in-the-money. At-the-money calls and puts have a delta of approximately 0.5 and −0.5 respectively with a slight bias towards higher deltas for ATM calls. The actual probability of an option finishing in the money is its dual delta, which is the first derivative of option price with respect to strike.

Relationship between Call and Put Delta

Given a European call and put option for the same underlying, strike price and time to maturity, and with no dividend yield, the sum of the absolute values of the delta of each option will be 1 – more precisely, the delta of the call (positive) minus the delta of the put (negative) equals 1. This is due to put–call parity: a long call plus a short put (a call minus a put) replicates a forward, which has delta equal to 1.

If the value of delta for an option is known, one can calculate the value of the delta of the option of the same strike price, underlying and maturity but opposite right by subtracting 1 from a known call delta or adding 1 to a known put delta.

$$\Delta(call) - \Delta(put) = 1, \text{ therefore: } \Delta(call) = \Delta(put) + 1 \text{ and } \Delta(put) = \Delta(call) - 1.$$

For example, if the delta of a call is 0.42 then one can compute the delta of the corresponding put at the same strike price by 0.42 − 1 = −0.58. To derive the delta of a call from a put, one can similarly take −0.58 and add 1 to get 0.42.

Vega

Vega measures sensitivity to volatility. Vega is the derivative of the option value with respect to the volatility of the underlying asset.

Vega is not the name of any Greek letter. The glyph used is a non-standard majuscule version of the Greek letter nu, ν, written as $\mathcal{V}$. Presumably the name *vega* was adopted because $\mathcal{V} = \frac{\partial V}{\partial \sigma}$ the Greek letter *nu* looked like a Latin *vee*, and *vega* was derived from *vee* by analogy.

The symbol kappa, κ, is sometimes used (by academics) instead of vega (as is tau (τ) or capital lambda (Λ), though these are rare).

Vega is typically expressed as the amount of money per underlying share that the option's value will gain or lose as volatility rises or falls by 1%. All options (both calls and puts) will gain value with rising volatility.

Vega can be an important Greek to monitor for an option trader, especially in volatile markets, since the value of some option strategies can be particularly sensitive to changes in volatility. The value of an option straddle, for example, is extremely dependent on changes to volatility.

Theta

Theta, Θ, measures the sensitivity of the value of the derivative to the passage of time the "time decay."

The mathematical result of the formula for theta is expressed in value per year. By convention, it is usual to divide the result by the number of days in a year, to arrive at the $\Theta = -\frac{\partial V}{\partial \tau}$ amount an option's price will drop, in relation to the underlying stock's price. Theta is almost always negative for long calls and puts, and positive for short (or written) calls and puts. An exception is a deep in-the-money European put. The total theta for a portfolio of options can be determined by summing the thetas for each individual position.

The value of an option can be analysed into two parts: the intrinsic value and the time value. The intrinsic value is the amount of money you would gain if you exercised the option immediately, so a call with strike $50 on a stock with price $60 would have intrinsic value of $10, whereas the corresponding put would have zero intrinsic value. The time value is the value of having the option of waiting longer before deciding to exercise. Even a deeply out of the money put will be worth something, as there is some chance the stock price will fall below the strike before the expiry date. However, as time approaches maturity, there is less chance of this happening, so the time value of an option is decreasing with time. Thus if you are long an option you are short theta: your portfolio will lose value with the passage of time (all other factors held constant).

Rho

Rho, ρ, measures sensitivity to the interest rate: it is the derivative of the option value with respect to the risk free interest rate (for the relevant outstanding term).

Except under extreme circumstances, the value of an option is less sensitive to changes in the risk free interest rate than to changes in other parameters. For this reason, rho is the least $\rho = \frac{\partial V}{\partial r}$ used of the first-order Greeks.

Rho is typically expressed as the amount of money, per share of the underlying, that the value of the option will gain or lose as the risk free interest rate rises or falls by 1.0% per annum (100 basis points).

Lambda

Lambda, λ, omega, Ω, or elasticity is the percentage change in option value per percentage change in the underlying price, a measure of leverage, sometimes called $\lambda = \Omega = \frac{\partial V}{\partial S} \times \frac{S}{V}$ gearing.

Epsilon

Epsilon, ϵ (also known as psi, ψ), is the percentage change in option value per percentage change in the underlying dividend yield, a measure of the dividend risk. The dividend $\epsilon = \psi = \frac{\partial V}{\partial q}$ yield impact is in practice determined using a 10% increase in those yields. Obviously, this sensitivity can only be applied to derivative instruments of equity products.

Second-order Greeks

Gamma

Gamma, Γ, measures the rate of change in the delta with respect to changes in the $\Gamma = \frac{\partial \Delta}{\partial S} = \frac{\partial^2 V}{\partial S^2}$ underlying price. Gamma is the second derivative of the value function with respect to the underlying price. Most long options have positive gamma and most short options have negative gamma. Long options have a positive relationship with gamma because as price increases, Gamma increases as well, causing Delta to approach 1 from 0 (long call option) and 0 from -1 (long put option). The inverse is true for short options.

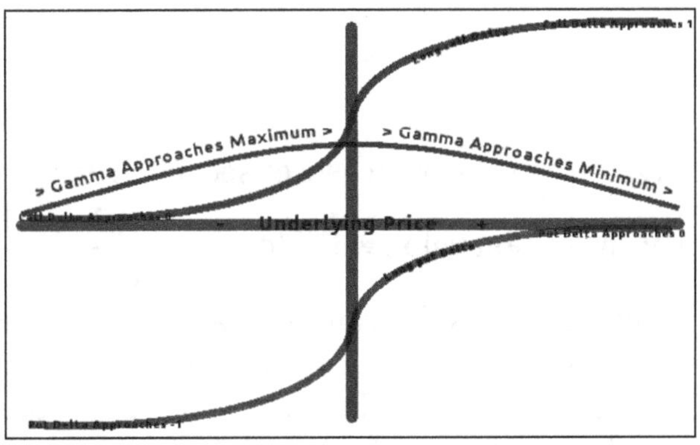

Long option delta, underlying price, and gamma.

Gamma is greatest approximately at-the-money (ATM) and diminishes the further out you go either in-the-money (ITM) or out-of-the-money (OTM). Gamma is important because it corrects for the convexity of value.

When a trader seeks to establish an effective delta-hedge for a portfolio, the trader may also seek to neutralize the portfolio's gamma, as this will ensure that the hedge will be effective over a wider range of underlying price movements.

Vanna

Vanna, also referred to as DvegaDspot and DdeltaDvol, is a second order derivative of the option value, once to the underlying spot price and once to volatility. It is mathematically equivalent to DdeltaDvol, the sensitivity of the option delta with respect to change in volatility; or alternatively, the partial of vega with respect to the underlying instrument's price. Vanna can be a useful sensitivity to monitor when maintaining a delta- or vega-hedged portfolio as vanna will help the trader to anticipate changes to the effectiveness of a delta-hedge as volatility changes or the effectiveness of a vega-hedge against change in the underlying spot price.

If the underlying value has continuous second partial derivatives, then

$$\text{Vanna} = \frac{\partial \Delta}{\partial \sigma} = \frac{\partial \mathcal{V}}{\partial S} = \frac{\partial^2 V}{\partial S \partial \sigma},$$

Charm

Charm or delta decay measures the instantaneous rate of change of delta over the passage of time. Charm has also been called DdeltaDtime. Charm $= -\frac{\partial \Delta}{\partial \tau} = -\frac{\partial \Theta}{\partial S} = -\frac{\partial^2 V}{\partial \tau \partial S}$ Charm can be an important Greek to measure/monitor when delta-hedging a position over a weekend. Charm is a second-order derivative of the option value, once to price and once to the passage of time. It is also then the derivative of theta with respect to the underlying's price.

The mathematical result of the formula for charm is expressed in delta/year. It is often useful to divide this by the number of days per year to arrive at the delta decay per day. This use is fairly accurate when the number of days remaining until option expiration is large. When an option nears expiration, charm itself may change quickly, rendering full day estimates of delta decay inaccurate.

Vomma

Vomma, volga, vega convexity, or DvegaDvol measures second order sensitivity to volatility. Vomma is the second derivative of the option value with Vomma $= \frac{\partial \mathcal{V}}{\partial \sigma} = \frac{\partial^2 V}{\partial \sigma^2}$ respect to the volatility, or, stated another way, vomma measures the rate of change to vega as volatility changes. With positive vomma, a position will become long vega as implied volatility increases and short vega as it decreases, which can be scalped in a way analogous to long gamma. And an initially vega-neutral, long-vomma position can be constructed from ratios of options at different strikes. Vomma is positive for options away from the money, and initially increases with distance from the money (but drops off as vega drops off). (Specifically, vomma is positive where the usual d1 and d2 terms are of the same sign, which is true when $d1 < 0$ or $d2 > 0$).

Veta

Veta or DvegaDtime measures the rate of change in the vega with respect to the passage of time. Veta is the second derivative of the value function; once Veta $= \frac{\partial \mathcal{V}}{\partial \tau} = \frac{\partial^2 V}{\partial \sigma \partial \tau}$ to volatility and once to time.

It is common practice to divide the mathematical result of veta by 100 times the number of days per year to reduce the value to the percentage change in vega per one day.

Vera

Vera (sometimes rhova) measures the rate of change in rho with respect to volatility. Vera is the second derivative of the value function; once to volatility and once Vera $= \frac{\partial \rho}{\partial \sigma} = \frac{\partial^2 V}{\partial \sigma \partial r}$ to interest rate. The word 'Vera' was coined by Dr. R. Naryshkin in early 2012 when this sensitivity needed to be used in practice to assess the impact of volatility changes on rho-hedging, but no name yet existed in the available literature. 'Vera' was picked to sound similar to a combination of Vega and

Rho, its respective first-order Greeks. This name is now in a wider use, including, for example, the Maple computer algebra software (which has 'BlackScholesVera' function in its Finance package).

Third-order Greeks

Speed

$$\text{Speed} = \frac{\partial \Gamma}{\partial S} = \frac{\partial^3 V}{\partial S^3}$$

Speed measures the rate of change in Gamma with respect to changes in the underlying price. This is also sometimes referred to as the gamma of the gamma or DgammaDspot. Speed is the third derivative of the value function with respect to the underlying spot price. Speed can be important to monitor when delta-hedging or gamma-hedging a portfolio.

Zomma

$$\text{Zomma} = \frac{\partial \Gamma}{\partial \sigma} = \frac{\partial \text{vanna}}{\partial S} = \frac{\partial^3 V}{\partial S^2 \partial \sigma}$$

Zomma measures the rate of change of gamma with respect to changes in volatility. Zomma has also been referred to as DgammaDvol. Zomma is the third derivative of the option value, twice to underlying asset price and once to volatility. Zomma can be a useful sensitivity to monitor when maintaining a gamma-hedged portfolio as zomma will help the trader to anticipate changes to the effectiveness of the hedge as volatility changes.

Color

$$\text{Color} = \frac{\partial \Gamma}{\partial \tau} = \frac{\partial^3 V}{\partial S^2 \partial \tau}$$

Color, gamma decay or DgammaDtime measures the rate of change of gamma over the passage of time. Color is a third-order derivative of the option value, twice to underlying asset price and once to time. Color can be an important sensitivity to monitor when maintaining a gamma-hedged portfolio as it can help the trader to anticipate the effectiveness of the hedge as time passes.

The mathematical result of the formula for color is expressed in gamma/year. It is often useful to divide this by the number of days per year to arrive at the change in gamma per day. This use is fairly accurate when the number of days remaining until option expiration is large. When an option nears expiration, color itself may change quickly, rendering full day estimates of gamma change inaccurate.

Ultima

$$\text{Ultima} = \frac{\partial \text{vomma}}{\partial \sigma} = \frac{\partial^3 V}{\partial \sigma^3}$$

Ultima measures the sensitivity of the option vomma with respect to change in volatility. Ultima has also been referred to as DvommaDvol. Ultima is a third-order derivative of the option value to volatility.

Greeks for Multi-asset Options

If the value of a derivative is dependent on two or more underlyings, its Greeks are extended to include the cross-effects between the underlyings.

Correlation delta measures the sensitivity of the derivative's value to a change in the correlation between the underlyings. It is also commonly known as cega.

Cross gamma measures the rate of change of delta in one underlying to a change in the level of another underlying.

Cross vanna measures the rate of change of vega in one underlying due to a change in the level of another underlying. Equivalently, it measures the rate of change of delta in the second underlying due to a change in the volatility of the first underlying.

Cross volga measures the rate of change of vega in one underlying to a change in the volatility of another underlying.

Formulas for European Option Greeks

Greeks for Multi-asset Options

If the value of a derivative is dependent on two or more underlyings, its Greeks are extended to include the cross-effects between the underlyings.

Correlation delta measures the sensitivity of the derivative's value to a change in the correlation between the underlyings. It is also commonly known as cega.

Cross gamma measures the rate of change of delta in one underlying to a change in the level of another underlying.

Cross vanna measures the rate of change of vega in one underlying due to a change in the level of another underlying. Equivalently, it measures the rate of change of delta in the second underlying due to a change in the volatility of the first underlying.

Cross volga measures the rate of change of vega in one underlying to a change in the volatility of another underlying.

Related Measures

Some related risk measures of financial derivatives are listed below.

Bond Duration and Convexity

In trading of fixed income securities (bonds), various measures of bond duration are used analogously to the delta of an option. The closest analogue to the delta is DV01, which is the reduction in price (in currency units) for an increase of one basis point (i.e. 0.01% per annum) in the yield (the yield is the underlying variable).

Analogous to the lambda is the modified duration, which is the *percentage* change in the market price of the bond(s) for a *unit* change in the yield (i.e. it is equivalent to DV01 divided by the market price). Unlike the lambda, which is an elasticity (a percentage change in output for a percentage change in input), the modified duration is instead a *semi*-elasticity—a percentage change in output for a *unit* change in input.

Bond convexity is a measure of the sensitivity of the duration to changes in interest rates, the second derivative of the price of the bond with respect to interest rates (duration is the first derivative). In general, the higher the convexity, the more sensitive the bond price is to the change in interest rates. Bond convexity is one of the most basic and widely used forms of convexity in finance.

For a bond with an embedded option, the standard yield to maturity based calculations here do not consider how changes in interest rates will alter the cash flows due to option exercise. To address this, effective duration and effective convexity are introduced. These values are typically calculated using a tree-based model, built for the entire yield curve (as opposed to a single yield to maturity), and therefore capturing exercise behavior at each point in the option's life as a function of both time and interest rates.

Beta

The beta (β) of a stock or portfolio is a number describing the volatility of an asset in relation to the volatility of the benchmark that said asset is being compared to. This benchmark is generally the overall financial market and is often estimated via the use of representative indices, such as the S&P 500.

An asset has a Beta of zero if its returns change independently of changes in the market's returns. A positive beta means that the asset's returns generally follow the market's returns, in the sense that they both tend to be above their respective averages together, or both tend to be below their respective averages together. A negative beta means that the asset's returns generally move opposite the market's returns: one will tend to be above its average when the other is below its average.

Fugit

The fugit is the expected time to exercise an American or Bermudan option. It is useful to compute it for hedging purposes—for example, one can represent flows of an American swaption like the flows of a swap starting at the fugit multiplied by delta, then use these to compute sensitivities.

Alpha

Alpha is a measure of the active return on an investment, the performance of that investment compared with a suitable market index. An alpha of 1% means the investment's return on investment over a selected period of time was 1% better than the market during that same period; a negative alpha means the investment underperformed the market. Alpha, along with beta, is one of two key coefficients in the capital asset pricing model used in modern portfolio theory and is closely related to other important quantities such as standard deviation, R-squared and the Sharpe ratio.

In modern financial markets, where index funds are widely available for purchase, alpha is commonly used to judge the performance of mutual funds and similar investments. As these funds include various fees normally expressed in percent terms, the fund has to maintain an alpha greater than its fees in order to provide positive gains compared with an index fund. Historically, the vast majority of traditional funds have had negative alphas, which has led to a flight of capital to index funds and non-traditional hedge funds.

It is also possible to analyze a portfolio of investments and calculate a theoretical performance, most commonly using the capital asset pricing model (CAPM). Returns on that portfolio can be compared with the theoretical returns, in which case the measure is known as Jensen's alpha. This is useful for non-traditional or highly focused funds, where a single stock index might not be representative of the investment's holdings.

The alpha coefficient (α_i) is a parameter in the single-index model (SIM). It is the intercept of the security characteristic line (SCL), that is, the coefficient of the constant in a market model regression.

$$\text{SCL}: R_{i,t} - R_f = \alpha_i + \beta_i (R_{M,t} - R_f) + \epsilon_{i,t}$$

where the following inputs are:

- R_i : the realized return (on the portfolio),
- R_M : the market return,
- R_f : the risk-free rate of return, and
- β_{iM} : the beta of the portfolio.

It can be shown that in an efficient market, the expected value of the alpha coefficient is zero. Therefore, the alpha coefficient indicates how an investment has performed after accounting for the risk it involved:

- $\alpha_i < 0$: the investment has earned too little for its risk (or, was too risky for the return).
- $\alpha_i = 0$: the investment has earned a return adequate for the risk taken.
- $\alpha_i > 0$: the investment has a return in excess of the reward for the assumed risk.

For instance, although a return of 20% may appear good, the investment can still have a negative alpha if it's involved in an excessively risky position.

In this context, because returns are being compared with the theoretical return of CAPM and not to a market index, it would be more accurate to use the term of Jensen's alpha.

A belief in efficient markets spawned the creation of market capitalization weighted index funds that seek to replicate the performance of investing in an entire market in the weights that each of the equity securities comprises in the overall market. The best examples for the US are the S&P 500 and the Wilshire 5000 which approximately represent the 500 most widely held equities and the largest 5000 securities respectively, accounting for approximately 80%+ and 99%+ of the total market capitalization of the US market as a whole.

In fact, to many investors, this phenomenon created a new standard of performance that must be matched: an investment manager should not only avoid losing money for the client and should make a certain amount of money, but in fact should make more money than the passive strategy of investing in everything equally (since this strategy appeared to be statistically more likely to be successful than the strategy of any one investment manager). The name for the additional return above the expected return of the beta adjusted return of the market is called "Alpha".

Relation to Beta

Besides an investment manager simply making more money than a passive strategy, there is another issue: although the strategy of investing in every stock appeared to perform better than 75 percent of investment managers, the price of the stock market as a whole fluctuates up and down, and could be on a downward decline for many years before returning to its previous price.

The passive strategy appeared to generate the market-beating return over periods of 10 years or more. This strategy may be risky for those who feel they might need to withdraw their money before a 10-year holding period, for example. Thus investment managers who employ a strategy which is less likely to lose money in a particular year are often chosen by those investors who feel that they might need to withdraw their money sooner.

Investors can use both alpha and beta to judge a manager's performance. If the manager has had a high alpha, but also a high beta, investors might not find that acceptable, because of the chance they might have to withdraw their money when the investment is doing poorly.

These concepts not only apply to investment managers, but to any kind of investment.

Beta

In finance, the beta (β or beta coefficient) of an investment is a measure of the risk arising from exposure to general market movements as opposed to idiosyncratic factors.

The market portfolio of all investable assets has a beta of exactly 1. A beta below 1 can indicate either an investment with lower volatility than the market, or a volatile investment whose price movements are not highly correlated with the market. An example of the first is a treasury bill: the price does not go up or down a lot, so it has a low beta. An example of the second is gold. The price of gold does go up and down a lot, but not in the same direction or at the same time as the market.

A beta greater than 1 generally means that the asset both is volatile and tends to move up and down with the market. An example is a stock in a big technology company. Negative betas are possible for investments that tend to go down when the market goes up, and vice versa. There are few fundamental investments with consistent and significant negative betas, but some derivatives like put options can have large negative betas.

Importance

Beta is important because it measures the risk of an investment that cannot be reduced by diversification. It does not measure the risk of an investment held on a stand-alone basis, but the amount of risk the investment adds to an already-diversified portfolio. In the capital asset pricing model

(CAPM), beta risk is the only kind of risk for which investors should receive an expected return higher than the risk-free rate of interest.

The definition above covers only theoretical beta. The term is used in many related ways in finance. For example, the betas commonly quoted in mutual fund analyses generally measure the risk of the fund arising from exposure to a benchmark for the fund, rather than from exposure to the entire market portfolio. Thus they measure the amount of risk the fund adds to a diversified portfolio of funds of the same type, rather than to a portfolio diversified among all fund types.

Beta decay refers to the tendency for a company with a high beta coefficient ($\beta > 1$) to have its beta coefficient decline to the market beta. It is an example of regression toward the mean.

Statistical Estimation

A statistical estimate of beta is calculated by a regression method. For a given asset and a benchmark, the goal is to find an approximate formula:

$$r_a \approx \alpha + \beta r_b$$

where, r_a is the return of the asset, alpha (α) is the active return, and r_b is return of the benchmark.

Since practical data are typically available as a discrete time series of samples, the statistical model is

$$r_{a,t} = \alpha + \beta r_{b,t} + \varepsilon_t,$$

where ε_t is an error term (the unexplained return). The best (in the sense of least squared error) estimates for α and β are those such that $\Sigma\varepsilon_t^2$ is as small as possible.

A common expression for beta is

$$\beta = \frac{\mathrm{Cov}(r_a, r_b)}{\mathrm{Var}(r_b)},$$

where Cov and Var are the covariance and variance operators.

By using the relationships between standard deviation, variance and correlation:

$$\sigma_a = \sqrt{\mathrm{Var}(r_a)}, \sigma_b = \sqrt{\mathrm{Var}(r_b)}, \rho_{a,b} = \mathrm{Cov}(r_a, r_b) / \sqrt{\mathrm{Var}(r_a)\mathrm{Var}(r_b)},$$

the above expression can also be written as:

$$\beta = \rho_{a,b}\frac{\sigma_a}{\sigma_b},$$

where $\rho_{a,b}$ is the correlation of the two returns, and σ_a and σ_b are the respective volatilities. If *a* refers to the investment and *b* refers to the market, it now becomes clear that the interpretation of beta as 'the volatility of an investment relative to the market volatility' is inconsistent with how beta is calculated; this is due to the presence of the correlation in the above formula.

Beta can be computed for prices in the past, where the data is known, which is historical beta. However, what most people are interested in is *future beta*, which relates to risks going forward. Estimating future beta is a difficult problem. One guess is that future beta equals historical beta.

From this, we find that beta can be explained as "correlated relative volatility". This has three components:

- Correlated,
- Relative,
- Volatility.

Beta is also referred to as financial elasticity or correlated relative volatility, and can be referred to as a measure of the sensitivity of the asset's returns to market returns, its non-diversifiable risk, its systematic risk, or market risk. On an individual asset level, measuring beta can give clues to volatility and liquidity in the marketplace. In fund management, measuring beta is thought to separate a manager's skill from his or her willingness to take risk.

The portfolio of interest in the CAPM formulation is the market portfolio that contains all risky assets, and so the r_b terms in the formula are replaced by r_m, the rate of return of the market. The regression line is then called the security characteristic line (SCL).

$$\mathrm{SCL}: r_{a,t} = \alpha_a + \beta_a r_{m,t} + \varepsilon_{a,t}$$

α_a is called the asset's alpha and β_a is called the asset's beta coefficient. Both coefficients have an important role in modern portfolio theory.

For example, in a year where the broad market or benchmark index returns 25% above the risk free rate, suppose two managers gain 50% above the risk free rate. Because this higher return is theoretically possible merely by taking a leveraged position in the broad market to double the beta so it is exactly 2.0, we would expect a skilled portfolio manager to have built the outperforming portfolio with a beta somewhat less than 2, such that the excess return not explained by the beta is positive. If one of the managers' portfolios has an average beta of 3.0, and the other's has a beta of only 1.5, then the CAPM simply states that the extra return of the first manager is not sufficient to compensate us for that manager's risk, whereas the second manager has done more than expected given the risk. Whether investors can expect the second manager to duplicate that performance in future periods is of course a different question.

Security Market Line

The SML graphs the results from the capital asset pricing model (CAPM) formula. The x-axis represents the risk (beta), and the y-axis represents the expected return. The market risk premium is determined from the slope of the SML.

The relationship between β and required return is plotted on the *security market line* (SML) which shows expected return as a function of β. The intercept is the nominal risk-free rate R_f available for the market, while the slope is $E(R_m) - R_f$ (for market return R_m). The security market line can be regarded as representing a single-factor model of the asset price, where beta is exposure to changes in value of the market. The equation of the SML, giving the expected value of the return on asset *i*, is thus:

$$\text{SML}: E(R_i) - R_f = \beta_i(E(R_M) - R_f).$$

It is a useful tool in determining if an asset being considered for a portfolio offers a reasonable expected return for risk. Individual securities are plotted on the SML graph. If the security's risk versus expected return is plotted above the SML, it is undervalued because the investor can expect a greater return for the inherent risk. A security plotted below the SML is overvalued because the investor would be accepting a lower return for the amount of risk assumed.

Choice of Benchmark

In the U.S., published betas typically use a stock market index such as the S&P 500 as a benchmark. The S&P 500 is a popular index of U.S. large-cap stocks. Other choices may be an international index such as the MSCI EAFE. The benchmark is often chosen to be similar to the assets chosen by the investor. For example, for a person who owns S&P 500 index funds and gold bars, the index would combine the S&P 500 and the price of gold. In practice a standard index is used.

The choice of the index need not reflect the portfolio under question; e.g., beta for gold bars compared to the S&P 500 may be low or negative carrying the information that gold does not track stocks and may provide a mechanism for reducing risk. The restriction to stocks as a benchmark is somewhat arbitrary. A model portfolio may be stocks plus bonds. Sometimes the market is defined as "all investable assets"; unfortunately, this includes lots of things for which returns may be hard to measure.

Investing

By definition, the market itself has a beta of 1, and individual stocks are ranked according to how much they deviate from the macro market (for simplicity purposes, the S&P 500 Index is sometimes used as a proxy for the market as a whole). A stock whose returns vary more than the market's returns over time can have a beta whose absolute value is greater than 1.0 (whether it is, in fact, greater than 1.0 will depend on the correlation of the stock's returns and the market's returns). A stock whose returns vary less than the market's returns has a beta with an absolute value less than 1.0.

A stock with a beta of 2 has returns that change, on average, by twice the magnitude of the overall market; when the market's return falls or rises by 3%, the stock's return will fall or rise (respectively) by 6% on average. (However, because beta also depends on the correlation of returns, there can be considerable variance about that average; the higher the correlation, the less variance; the lower the correlation, the higher the variance.) Beta can also be negative, meaning the stock's returns tend to move in the opposite direction of the market's returns. A stock with a beta of −3 would see its return decline 9% (on average) when the market's return goes up 3%, and would see its return climb 9% (on average) if the market's return falls by 3%.

Higher-beta stocks tend to be more volatile and therefore riskier, but provide the potential for higher returns. Lower-beta stocks pose less risk but generally offer lower returns. Some have challenged this idea, claiming that the data show little relation between beta and potential reward, or even that lower-beta stocks are both less risky and more profitable (contradicting CAPM). In the same way a stock's beta shows its relation to market shifts, it is also an indicator for required returns on investment (ROI). Given a risk-free rate of 2%, for example, if the market (with a beta of 1) has an expected return of 8%, a stock with a beta of 1.5 should return 11% (= 2% + 1.5(8% – 2%)) in accordance with the financial CAPM model.

Adding to a Portfolio

Suppose an investor has all his money in an asset class X and wishes to move a small amount to an asset class Y. For example, X could be U.S. stocks, while Y could be stocks of a different country, or bonds. Then the new portfolio, Z, can be expressed symbolically:

$$Z = (1-\delta)X + \delta Y.$$

The variance can be computed as:

$$\mathrm{Var}(Z) = (1-\delta)^2\,\mathrm{Var}(X) + 2\delta(1-\delta)\,\mathrm{Cov}(X,Y) + \delta^2\,\mathrm{Var}(Y)$$

which can be simplified by ignoring δ^2 terms:

$$\mathrm{Var}(Z) \approx (1-2\delta)\,\mathrm{Var}(X) + 2\delta\,\mathrm{Cov}(X,Y).$$

The first formula is exact, while the second one is only valid for small δ. Using the formula for β of Y relative to X,

$$\beta = \mathrm{Cov}(X,Y)\,/\,\mathrm{Var}(X),$$

we can compute:

$$Var(Z)\,/\,Var(X) \approx 1 + 2\delta(\beta - 1).$$

This suggests that an asset with β greater than 1 will increase variance, while an asset with β less than 1 will decrease variance, if added in the right amount. This assumes that variance is an accurate measure of risk, which is usually good. However, the beta does need to be computed with respect to what the investor currently owns.

Academic Theory

Academic theory claims that higher-risk investments should have higher returns over the long-term. Wall Street has a saying that "higher return requires higher risk", not that a risky investment will automatically do better. Some things may just be poor investments (e.g., playing roulette). Further, highly rational investors should consider correlated volatility (beta) instead of simple volatility (sigma). Theoretically, a negative beta equity is possible; for example, an inverse ETF should have negative beta to the relevant index. Also, a short position should have opposite beta.

This expected return on equity, or equivalently, a firm's cost of equity, can be estimated using the capital asset pricing model (CAPM). According to the model, the expected return on equity is a function of a firm's equity beta (βE) which, in turn, is a function of both leverage and asset risk (βA):

$$K_E = R_F + \beta_E(R_M - R_F)$$

where,

K_E = firm's cost of equity,

R_F = risk-free rate (the rate of return on a "risk free investment"; e.g., U.S. Treasury Bonds),

R_M = return on the market portfolio.

$$\beta_E = \beta = \left[\beta_A - \beta_D\left(\frac{D}{V}\right)\right]\frac{V}{E}$$

because,

$$\beta_A = \beta_D\left(\frac{D}{V}\right) + \beta_E\left(\frac{E}{V}\right)$$

and

Firm value (V) + cash and risk-free securities = debt value (D) + equity value (E).

An indication of the systematic riskiness attaching to the returns on ordinary shares. It equates to the asset Beta for an ungeared firm, or is adjusted upwards to reflect the extra riskiness of shares in a geared firm., i.e. the Geared Beta.

Multiple Beta Model

The arbitrage pricing theory (APT) has multiple betas in its model. In contrast to the CAPM that has only one risk factor, namely the overall market, APT has multiple risk factors. Each risk factor has a corresponding beta indicating the responsiveness of the asset being priced to that risk factor.

Multiple-factor models contradict CAPM by claiming that some other factors can influence return, therefore one may find two stocks (or funds) with equal beta, but one may be a better investment.

Estimation

To estimate beta, one needs a list of returns for the asset and returns for the index; these returns can be daily, weekly or any period. Then one uses standard formulas from linear regression. The slope of the fitted line from the linear least-squares calculation is the estimated Beta. The y-intercept is the alpha.

Myron Scholes and Joseph Williams provided a model for estimating betas from nonsynchronous data.

Beta specifically gives the volatility ratio multiplied by the correlation of the plotted data. To take an extreme example, something may have a beta of zero even though it is highly volatile, provided it is uncorrelated with the market. Tofallis provides a discussion of this, together with a real example involving AT&T Inc. The graph showing monthly returns from AT&T is visibly more volatile than the index and yet the standard estimate of beta for this is less than one.

The relative volatility ratio described above is actually known as Total Beta (at least by appraisers who practice business valuation). Total beta is equal to the identity: beta/R or the standard deviation of the stock divided by the standard deviation of the market. Total beta captures the security's risk as a stand-alone asset (because the correlation coefficient, R, has been removed from beta), rather than part of a well-diversified portfolio. Because appraisers frequently value closely held companies as stand-alone assets, total beta is gaining acceptance in the business valuation industry. Appraisers can now use total beta in the following equation: total cost of equity (TCOE) = risk-free rate + total beta·equity risk premium. Once appraisers have a number of TCOE benchmarks, they can compare/contrast the risk factors present in these publicly traded benchmarks and the risks in their closely held company to better defend/support their valuations.

Interpretations

Some interpretations of beta are explained in the following table:

Value of Beta	Interpretation	Example
$\beta < -1$	Asset moves in the opposite direction, and in a greater amount than the negative of the benchmark.	An inverse fund, such as the Direxion 3X Bear ETF, which seeks 300% the inverse of the S&P 500 Index.
$-1 < \beta < 0$	Asset movement is in the opposite direction of the benchmark.	An inverse exchange-traded fund or a short position.
$\beta = 0$	Asset movement is uncorrelated to the benchmark.	Fixed-yield asset, whose growth is unrelated to the movement of the stock market.
$0 < \beta < 1$	Asset moves in the same direction, but in a lesser amount than the benchmark.	Stable, "staple" stock such as a company that makes soap. Moves in the same direction as the market at large, but less susceptible to day-to-day fluctuation.
$\beta = 1$	Asset moves in the same direction and in the same amount as the benchmark.	A representative stock, or a stock that is a strong contributor to the index itself.
$\beta > 1$	Asset moves in the same direction, but in a greater amount than the benchmark.	Stocks which are very strongly influenced by day-to-day market news, or by the general health of the economy.

It measures the part of the asset's statistical variance that cannot be removed by the diversification provided by the portfolio of many risky assets, because of the correlation of its returns with the returns of the other assets that are in the portfolio. Beta can be estimated for individual companies using regression analysis against a stock market index. An alternative to standard beta is downside beta.

Beta is always measured in respect to some benchmark. Therefore, an asset may have different betas depending on which benchmark is used. Just a number is useless if the benchmark is not known.

Extreme and Interesting Cases

- Beta has no upper or lower bound, and betas as large as 3 or 4 will occur with highly volatile stocks.

- Beta can be zero. Some zero-beta assets are risk-free, such as treasury bonds and cash. However, simply because a beta is zero does *not* mean that it is risk-free. A beta can be zero simply because the correlation between that item's returns and the market's returns is zero. An example would be betting on horse racing. The correlation with the market will be zero, but it is certainly not a risk-free endeavor.
- On the other hand, if a stock has a moderately low but positive correlation with the market, but a high volatility, then its beta may still be high.
- A negative beta simply means that the stock is inversely correlated with the market.
- A negative beta might occur even when both the benchmark index and the stock under consideration have positive returns. It is possible that lower positive returns of the index coincide with higher positive returns of the stock, or vice versa. The slope of the regression line in such a case will be negative.
- Using beta as a measure of relative risk has its own limitations. Most analyses consider only the magnitude of beta. Beta is a statistical variable and should be considered with its statistical significance (R square value of the regression line). Closer to 1 R square value implies higher correlation and a stronger relationship between returns of the asset and benchmark index.
- If beta is a result of regression of one stock against the market where it is quoted, betas from different countries are not comparable.
- Utility stocks commonly show up as examples of low beta. These have some similarity to bonds, in that they tend to pay consistent dividends, and their prospects are not strongly dependent on economic cycles. They are still stocks, so the market price will be affected by overall stock market trends, even if this does not make sense.
- Staple stocks are thought to be less affected by cycles and usually have lower beta. Procter & Gamble, which makes soap, is a classic example. Other similar ones are Philip Morris (tobacco) and Johnson & Johnson (Health & Consumer Goods).
- 'Tech' stocks are commonly equated with higher beta. This is based on experience of the dot-com bubble around year 2000. Although tech did very well in the late 1990s, it also fell sharply in the early 2000s, much worse than the decline of the overall market. More recently, this is not a good example.
- During the 2008 market fall, finance stocks did very poorly, much worse than the overall market. Then in the following years they gained the most, although not to make up for their losses.
- Foreign stocks may provide some diversification. World benchmarks such as S&P Global 100 have slightly lower betas than comparable US-only benchmarks such as S&P 100. However, this effect is not as good as it used to be; the various markets are now fairly correlated, especially the US and Western Europe.
- Derivatives and other non-linear assets. Beta relies on a linear model. An out of the money option may have a distinctly non-linear payoff. The change in price of an option relative to

the change in the price of the underlying asset (for example a stock) is not constant. For example, if one purchased a put option on the S&P 500, the beta would vary as the price of the underlying index (and indeed as volatility, time to expiration and other factors) changed.

Criticism

Seth Klarman wrote in Margin of Safety: "I find it preposterous that a single number reflecting past price fluctuations could be thought to completely describe the risk in a security. Beta views risk solely from the perspective of market prices, failing to take into consideration specific business fundamentals or economic developments. The price level is also ignored, as if IBM selling at 50 dollars per share would not be a lower-risk investment than the same IBM at 100 dollars per share. Beta fails to allow for the influence that investors themselves can exert on the riskiness of their holdings through such efforts as proxy contests, shareholder resolutions, communications with management, or the ultimate purchase of sufficient stock to gain corporate control and with it direct access to underlying value. Beta also assumes that the upside potential and downside risk of any investment are essentially equal, being simply a function of that investment's volatility compared with that of the market as a whole. This too is inconsistent with the world as we know it. The reality is that past security price volatility does not reliably predict future investment performance (or even future volatility) and therefore is a poor measure of risk."

At the industry level, beta tends to underestimate downside beta two-thirds of the time (resulting in value overestimation) and overestimate upside beta one-third of the time resulting in value underestimation.

Another weakness of beta can be illustrated through an easy example by considering two hypothetical stocks, A and B. The returns on A, B and the market follow the probability distribution below:

Probability	Market	Stock A	Stock B
0.25	−30%	−15%	−60%
0.25	−15%	−7.5%	−30%
0.25	15%	30%	7.5%
0.25	30%	60%	15%

The table shows that stock A goes down half as much as the market when the market goes down and up twice as much as the market when the market goes up. Stock B, on the other hand, goes down twice as much as the market when the market goes down and up half as much as the market when the market goes up. Most investors would label stock B as more risky. In fact, stock A has better return in every possible case. However, according to the capital asset pricing model, stock A and B would have the same beta, meaning that theoretically, investors would require the same rate of return for both stocks. Of course it is entirely expected that this example could break the CAPM as the CAPM relies on certain assumptions one of the most central being the nonexistence of arbitrage, However, in this example buying stock A and selling stock B is an example of an arbitrage as stock A is worth more in every scenario. This is an illustration of how using standard beta might mislead investors. The dual-beta model, in contrast, takes into account this issue and differentiates downside beta from upside beta, or downside risk from upside risk, and thus allows investors to make better informed investing decisions.

FINANCIAL RATIO

Financial ratios are one of the most common tools of managerial decision making. A ratio is a comparison of one number to another—mathematically, a simple division problem. Financial ratios involve the comparison of various figures from the financial statements in order to gain information about a company's performance. It is the interpretation, rather than the calculation, that makes financial ratios a useful tool for business managers. Ratios may serve as indicators, clues, or red flags regarding noteworthy relationships between variables used to measure the firm's performance in terms of profitability, asset utilization, liquidity, leverage, or market valuation.

Use and Users of Ratio Analysis

There are basically two uses of financial ratio analysis: to track individual firm performance over time, and to make comparative judgments regarding firm performance. Firm performance is evaluated using trend analysis—calculating individual ratios on a per-period basis, and tracking their values over time. This analysis can be used to spot trends that may be cause for concern, such as an increasing average collection period for outstanding receivables or a decline in the firm's liquidity status. In this role, ratios serve as red flags for troublesome issues, or as benchmarks for performance measurement.

Another common usage of ratios is to make relative performance comparisons. For example, comparing a firm's profitability to that of a major competitor or observing how the firm stacks up versus industry averages enables the user to form judgments concerning key areas such as profitability or management effectiveness. Users of financial ratios include parties both internal and external to the firm. External users include security analysts, current and potential investors, creditors, competitors, and other industry observers. Internally, managers use ratio analysis to monitor performance and pinpoint strengths and weaknesses from which specific goals, objectives, and policy initiatives may be formed.

Profitability Ratios

Perhaps the type of ratios most often used and considered by those outside a firm are the profitability ratios. Profitability ratios provide measures of profit performance that serve to evaluate the periodic financial success of a firm. One of the most widely-used financial ratios is net profit margin, also known as return on sales.

Return on sales provides a measure of bottom-line profitability. For example, a net profit margin of 6 percent means that for every dollar in sales, the firm generated six cents in net income.

Two other margin measures are gross profit margin and operating margin.

Gross margin measures the direct production costs of the firm. A gross profit margin of 30 percent would indicate that for each dollar in sales, the firm spent seventy cents in direct costs to produce the good or service that the firm sold.

Operating margin goes one step further, incorporating nonproduction costs such as selling, general, and administrative expenses of the firm. Operating profit is also commonly referred to as earnings before interest and taxes, or EBIT. An operating margin of 15 percent would indicate that the firm spent an additional fifteen cents out of every dollar in sales on nonproduction expenses, such as sales commissions paid to the firm's sales force or administrative labor expenses.

Two very important measures of the firm's profitability are return on assets and return on equity.

Return on assets (ROA) measures how effectively the firm's assets are used to generate profits net of expenses. An ROA of 7 percent would mean that for each dollar in assets, the firm generated seven cents in profits. This is an extremely useful measure of comparison among firms's competitive performance, for it is the job of managers to utilize the assets of the firm to produce profits.

Return on equity (ROE) measures the net return per dollar invested in the firm by the owners, the common shareholders. An ROE of 11 percent means the firm is generating an 11-cent return per dollar of net worth.

One should note that in each of the profitability ratios mentioned above, the numerator in the ratio comes from the firm's income statement. Hence, these are measures of periodic performance, covering the specific period reported in the firm's income statement. Therefore, the proper interpretation for a profitability ratio such as an ROA of 11 percent would be that, over the specific period (such as fiscal year 2004), the firm returned eleven cents on each dollar of asset investment.

- Gross profit margin,
- Operating margin,
- Net profit margin,
- Return on assets,
- Return on equity.

Asset Utilization Ratios

Asset utilization ratios provide measures of management effectiveness. These ratios serve as a guide to critical factors concerning the use of the firm's assets, inventory, and accounts receivable collections in day-to-day operations. Asset utilization ratios are especially important for internal monitoring concerning performance over multiple periods, serving as warning signals or benchmarks from which meaningful conclusions may be reached on operational issues. An example is the total asset turnover (TAT) ratio.

This ratio offers managers a measure of how well the firm is utilizing its assets in order to generate sales revenue. An increasing TAT would be an indication that the firm is using its assets more productively. For example, if the TAT for 2003 was 2.2×, and for 2004 was 3×, the interpretation would follow that in 2004, the firm generated $3 in sales for each dollar of assets, an additional 80 cents in sales per dollar of asset investment over the previous year. Such change may be an indication of increased managerial effectiveness.

A similar measure is the fixed asset turnover (FAT) ratio. Fixed assets (such as plant and equipment) are often more closely associated with direct production than are current assets (such as cash and accounts receivable), so many analysts prefer this measure of effectiveness. A FAT of 1.6× would be interpreted as the firm generated $1.60 in sales for every $1 it had in fixed assets.

Two other asset utilization ratios concern the effectiveness of management of the firm's current assets. Inventory is an important economic variable for management to monitor since dollars invested in inventory have not yet resulted in any return to the firm. Inventory is an investment, and it is important for the firm to strive to maximize its inventory turnover. The inventory turnover ratio is used to measure this aspect of performance.

Cost of goods sold (COGS) derives from the income statement and indicates the expense dollars attributed to the actual production of goods sold during a specified period. Inventory is a current asset on the balance sheet. Because the balance sheet represents the firm's assets and liabilities at one point in time, an average figure is often used from two successive balance sheets. Managers attempt to increase this ratio, since a higher turnover ratio indicates that the firm is going through its inventory more often due to higher sales. A turnover ratio of 4.75×, or 475 percent, means the firm sold and replaced its inventory stock more than four and one-half times during the period measured on the income statement.

One of the most critical ratios that management must monitor is days sales outstanding (DSO), also known as average collection period.

This represents a prime example of the use of a ratio as an internal monitoring tool. Managers strive to minimize the firm's average collection period, since dollars received from customers become immediately available for reinvestment. Periodic measurement of the DSO will "red flag" a lengthening of the firm's time to collect outstanding accounts before customers get used to taking longer to pay. A DSO of thirty-six means that, on average, it takes thirty-six days to collect on the firm's outstanding accounts. This is an especially critical measure for firms in industries where extensive trade credit is offered, but any company that extends credit on sales should be aware of the DSO on a regular basis.

- Total asset turnover,
- Inventory turnover,
- Days sales outstanding,
- Fixed asset turnover.

Leverage Ratios

Leverage ratios, also known as capitalization ratios, provide measures of the firm's use of debt financing. These are extremely important for potential creditors, who are concerned with the firm's ability to generate the cash flow necessary to make interest payments on outstanding debt. Thus, these ratios are used extensively by analysts outside the firm to make decisions concerning the provision of new credit or the extension of existing credit arrangements. It is also important for management to monitor the firm's use of debt financing. The commitment to service outstanding debt is a fixed cost to a firm, resulting in decreased flexibility and higher break-even production rates. Therefore, the use of debt financing increases the risk associated with the firm. Managers and creditors must constantly monitor the trade-off between the additional risk that comes with borrowing money and the increased opportunities that the new capital provides. Leverage ratios provide a means of such monitoring.

Perhaps the most straightforward measure of a firm's use of debt financing is the total-debt ratio.

It is important to recall that there are only two ways to finance the acquisition of any asset: debt (using borrowed funds) and equity (using funds from internal operations or selling stock in the company). The total debt ratio captures this idea. A debt ratio of 35 percent means that, for every dollar of assets the firm has, 35 cents was financed with borrowed money. The natural corollary is that the other 65 cents came from equity financing. This is known as the firm's capital structure—35 percent debt and 65 percent equity. Greater debt means greater leverage, and more leverage means more risk. How much debt is too much is a highly subjective question, and one that managers constantly attempt to answer. The answer depends, to a large extent, on the nature of the business or industry. Large manufacturers, who require heavy investment in fixed plant and equipment, will require higher levels of debt financing than will service firms such as insurance or advertising agencies.

The total debt of a firm consists of both long- and short-term liabilities. Short-term (or current) liabilities are often a necessary part of daily operations and may fluctuate regularly depending on factors such as seasonal sales. Many creditors prefer to focus their attention on the firm's use of long-term debt. Thus, a common variation on the total debt ratio is the long-term debt ratio, which does not incorporate current liabilities in the numerator.

In a similar vein, many analysts prefer a direct comparison of the firm's capital structure. Such a measure is provided by the debt-to-equity ratio.

This is perhaps one of the most misunderstood financial ratios, as many confuse it with the total debt ratio. A debt-to-equity ratio of 45 percent would mean that for each dollar of equity financing, the firm has 45 cents in debt financing. This does not mean that the firm has 45 percent of its total financing as debt; debt and equity percentages, together, must sum to one (100 percent of the firm's total financing). A little algebra will illustrate this point. Let x = the percent of equity financing (in decimal form), so $0.45\,x$ is the percent of debt financing. Then $x + 0.45\,x = 1$, and $x = 0.69$. So, a debt to equity ratio of 45 percent indicates that each dollar of the firm's assets are financed with 69 cents of equity and 31 cents with debt. The point here is to caution against confusing the interpretation of the debt-to-equity ratio with that of the total debt ratio.

Two other leverage ratios that are particularly important to the firm's creditors are the times-interest-earned and the fixed-charge coverage ratios. These measure the firm's ability to meet its on-going commitment to service debt previously borrowed. The times-interest-earned (TIE) ratio, also known as the EBIT coverage ratio, provides a measure of the firm's ability to meet its interest expenses with operating profits.

For example, a TIE of 3.6× indicates that the firm's operating profits from a recent period exceeded the total interest expenses it was required to pay by 360 percent. The higher this ratio, the more financially stable the firm and the greater the safety margin in the case of fluctuations in sales and operating expenses. This ratio is particularly important for lenders of short-term debt to the firm, since short-term debt is usually paid out of current operating revenue.

Similarly, the fixed charge coverage ratio, also known as the debt service coverage ratio, takes into account all regular periodic obligations of the firm.

The adjustment to the principal repayment reflects the fact that this portion of the debt repayment is not tax deductible. By including the payment of both principal and interest, the fixed charge coverage ratio provides a more conservative measure of the firm's ability to meet fixed obligations.

- Total debt ratio,
- Times interest earned,
- Long-term debt ratio,
- Fixed charge coverage,
- Debt-to-equity ratio.

Liquidity Ratios

Managers and creditors must closely monitor the firm's ability to meet short-term obligations. The liquidity ratios are measures that indicate a firm's ability to repay short-term debt. Current liabilities represent obligations that are typically due in one year or less. The current and quick ratios are used to gauge a firm's liquidity.

A current ratio of 1.5× indicates that for every dollar in current liabilities, the firm has $1.50 in current assets. Such assets could, theoretically, be sold and the proceeds used to satisfy the liabilities if the firm ran short of cash. However, some current assets are more liquid than others. Obviously, the most liquid current asset is cash. Accounts receivable are usually collected within one to three months, but this varies by firm and industry. The least liquid of current assets is often inventory. Depending on the type of industry or product, some inventory has no ready market. Since the economic definition of liquidity is the ability to turn an asset into cash at or near fair market value, inventory that is not easily sold will not be helpful in meeting short-term obligations. The quick (or acid test) ratio incorporates this concern.

By excluding inventories, the quick ratio is a more strident liquidity measure than the current ratio. It is a more appropriate measure for industries that involve long product production cycles, such as in manufacturing.

- Current ratio,
- Quick ratio.

Market Value Ratios

Managers and investors are interested in market ratios, which are used in valuing the firm's stock. The price-earnings ratio and the market-to-book value ratio are often used in valuation analysis. The price/earnings ratio, universally known as the PE ratio, is one of the most heavily-quoted statistics concerning a firm's common stock. It is reported in the financial pages of newspapers, along with the current value of the firm's stock price.

A note of caution is warranted concerning the calculation of PE ratios. Analysts use two different components in the denominator: trailing earnings and forecast earnings. Trailing earnings refer to the firm's reported earnings, per share, over the last twelve months of operation. Forecast earnings are based on security analyst forecasts of what they expect the firm to earn in the coming twelve-month period. Neither definition is more correct than the other; one should simply pay attention to which measure is used when consulting published PE ratios. A PE ratio of sixteen can be interpreted as investors are willing to pay $16 for $1 worth of earnings. PE ratios are used extensively, on a comparative basis, to analyze investment alternatives. In investment lingo, the PE ratio is often referred to as the firm's "multiple." A high PE is often indicative of investors's belief that the firm has very promising growth prospects, while firms in more mature industries often trade at lower multiples.

A related measure used for valuation purposes is the market-to-book value ratio. The book value of a firm is defined as:

> Technically, the book value represents the value of the firm if all the assets were sold off, and the proceeds used to retire all outstanding debt. The remainder would represent the equity that would be divided, proportionally, among the firm's shareholders. Many investors like to compare the current price of the firm's common stock with its book, or break-up, value.

This is also known as the price/book ratio. If the ratio is greater than one, which is often the case, then the firm is trading at a premium to book value. Many investors regard a market-to-book ratio of less than one an indication of an undervalued firm. While the interpretation one draws from market ratios is highly subjective (do high PE or low PE firms make better investments?), these measures provide information that is valued both by managers and investors regarding the market price of a firm's stock.

- Price/earnings ratio,
- Market-to-book ratio.

Cautions on the use and Interpretation of Financial Ratios

Financial ratios represent tools for insight into the performance, efficiency, and profitability of a firm. Two noteworthy issues on this subject involve ratio calculation and interpretation. For example, if someone refers to a firm's "profit margin" of 18 percent, are they referring to gross profit margin, operating margin, or net profit margin? Similarly, is a quotation of a "debt ratio" a reference to the total debt ratio, the long-term debt ratio, or the debt-to-equity ratio? These types of confusions can make the use of ratio analysis a frustrating experience.

Interpreting financial ratios should also be undertaken with care. A net profit margin of 12 percent may be outstanding for one type of industry and mediocre to poor for another. This highlights the fact that individual ratios should not be interpreted in isolation. Trend analyses should include a series of identical calculations, such as following the current ratio on a quarterly basis for two consecutive years. Ratios used for performance evaluation should always be compared to some benchmark, either an industry average or perhaps the identical ratio for the industry leader.

Another factor in ratio interpretation is for users to identify whether individual components, such as net income or current assets, originate from the firm's income statement or balance sheet. The income statement reports performance over a specified period of time, while the balance sheet gives static measurement at a single point in time. These issues should be recognized when one attempts to interpret the results of ratio calculations.

Despite these issues, financial ratios remain useful tools for both internal and external evaluations of key aspects of a firm's performance. A working knowledge and ability to use and interpret ratios remains a fundamental aspect of effective financial management. The value of financial ratios to investors became even more apparent during the stock market decline of 2000, when the bottom dropped out of the soaring "dot.com" economy. Throughout the long run-up, some financial analysts warned that the stock prices of many technology companies—particularly Internet start-up businesses—were overvalued based on the traditional rules of ratio analysis. Yet investors largely ignored such warnings and continued to flock to these companies in hopes of making a quick return. In the end, however, it became clear that the old rules still applied, and that financial ratios remained an important means of measuring, comparing, and predicting firm performance.

ACCOUNTING LIQUIDITY

In accounting, liquidity (or accounting liquidity) is a measure of the ability of a debtor to pay their debts as and when they fall due. It is usually expressed as a ratio or a percentage of current liabilities. Liquidity is the ability to pay short-term obligations.

Calculating Liquidity

For a corporation with a published balance sheet there are various ratios used to calculate a measure of liquidity. These include the following:

- The current ratio is the simplest measure and calculated by dividing the total current assets by the total current liabilities. A value of over 100% is normal in a non-banking corporation. However, some current assets are more difficult to sell at full value in a hurry.
- The quick ratio is calculated by deducting inventories and prepayments from current assets and then dividing by current liabilities, giving a measure of the ability to meet current liabilities from assets that can be readily sold. A better way for a trading corporation to meet liabilities is from cash flows, rather than through asset sales.
- The operating cash flow ratio can be calculated by dividing the operating cash flow by current liabilities. This indicates the ability to service current debt from current income, rather than through asset sales.

Understanding the Ratios

For different industries and differing legal systems the use of differing ratios and results would be appropriate. For instance, in a country with a legal system that gives a slow or uncertain result a higher level of liquidity would be appropriate to cover the uncertainty related to the valuation of assets. A manufacturer with stable cash flows may find a lower quick ratio more appropriate than an Internet-based start-up corporation.

Liquidity in Banking

Liquidity is a prime concern in a banking environment and a shortage of liquidity has often been a trigger for bank failures. Holding assets in a highly liquid form tends to reduce the income from that asset (cash, for example, is the most liquid asset of all but pays no interest) so banks will try to reduce liquid assets as far as possible. However, a bank without sufficient liquidity to meet the demands of their depositors risks experiencing a bank run. The result is that most banks now try to forecast their liquidity requirements and maintain emergency standby credit lines at other banks. Banking regulators also view liquidity as a major concern.

ACCOUNTING RATE OF RETURN

Accounting rate of return, also known as the Average rate of return, or ARR is a financial ratio used in capital budgeting. The ratio does not take into account the concept of time value of money. ARR calculates the return, generated from net income of the proposed capital investment. The ARR is a percentage return. Say, if ARR = 7%, then it means that the project is expected to earn seven cents out of each dollar invested (yearly). If the ARR is equal to or greater than the required rate of return, the project is acceptable. If it is less than the desired rate, it should be rejected. When comparing investments, the higher the ARR, the more attractive the investment. More than half of large firms calculate ARR when appraising projects.

The key advantage of ARR is that it is easy to compute and understand. The main disadvantage of ARR is that it disregards the time factor in terms of time value of money or risks for long term investments. The ARR is built on evaluation of profits and it can be easily manipulated with changes in depreciation methods. The ARR can give misleading information when evaluating investments of different size.

Basic Formulas

$$\text{ARR} = \frac{\text{Average return during period}}{\text{Average investment}}$$

where,

$$\text{Average investment} = \frac{\text{Book value at beginning of year 1} + \text{Book value at end of useful life}}{2}$$

Average return during period

$$= \frac{\text{Incremental revenue} - \text{Incremental expenses (including depreciation)}}{\text{Initial investment}}$$

$$\text{Average profit} = \frac{\text{Profit after tax}}{\text{Life of investment}}$$

Pitfalls

- This technique is based on profits rather than cash flow. It ignores cash flow from investment. Therefore, it can be affected by non-cash items such as bad debts and depreciation when calculating profits. The change of methods for depreciation can be manipulated and lead to higher profits.
- This technique does not adjust for the risk to long term forecasts.
- ARR doesn't take into account the time value of money.

BIAS RATIO

The bias ratio is an indicator used in finance to analyze the returns of investment portfolios, and in performing due diligence.

The bias ratio is a concrete metric that detects valuation bias or deliberate price manipulation of portfolio assets by a manager of a hedge fund, mutual fund or similar investment vehicle, without requiring disclosure (transparency) of the actual holdings. This metric measures abnormalities in the distribution of returns that indicate the presence of bias in subjective pricing. The formulation of the Bias Ratio stems from an insight into the behavior of asset managers as they address the expectations of investors with the valuation of assets that determine their performance.

The bias ratio measures how far the returns from an investment portfolio – e.g. one managed by a hedge fund – are from an unbiased distribution. Thus the bias ratio of a pure equity index will usually be close to 1. However, if a fund smooths its returns using subjective pricing of illiquid assets the bias ratio will be higher. As such, it can help identify the presence of illiquid securities where they are not expected.

The bias ratio was first defined by Adil Abdulali, a risk manager at the investment firm Protégé Partners. The concepts behind the bias ratio were formulated between 2001 and 2003 and privately used to screen money managers. The first public discussions on the subject took place in 2004 at New York University's Courant Institute and in 2006 at Columbia University.

The bias ratio has since been used by a number of Risk Management professionals to spot suspicious funds that subsequently turned out to be frauds. The most spectacular example of this was reported in the *Financial Times* on 22 January 2009 titled "Bias ratio seen to unmask Madoff".

Imagine that you are a hedge fund manager who invests in securities that are hard to value, such as mortgage-backed securities. Your peer group consists of funds with similar mandates, and all have track records with high Sharpe ratios, very few down months, and investor demand from the "[one per cent per month]" crowd. You are keenly aware that your potential investors look carefully at the characteristics of returns, including such calculations as the percentage of months with negative and positive returns.

Furthermore, assume that no pricing service can reliably price your portfolio, and the assets are often sui generis with no quoted market. In order to price the portfolio for return calculations, you poll dealers for prices on each security monthly and get results that vary widely on each asset. The following real-world example illustrates this theoretical construct.

When pricing this portfolio, standard market practice allows a manager to discard outliers and average the remaining prices. But what constitutes an outlier? Market participants contend that outliers are difficult to characterize methodically and thus use the heuristic rule "you know it when you see it." Visible outliers consider the particular security's characteristics and liquidity as well as the market environment in which quotes are solicited. After discarding outliers, a manager sums up the relevant figures and determines the net asset value ("NAV"). Now let's consider what happens when this NAV calculation results in a small monthly loss, such as -0.01%. Lo and behold, just before the CFO publishes the return, an aspiring junior analyst notices that the pricing process included a dealer quote 50% below all the other prices for that security. Throwing out that one quote would raise the monthly return to +0.01%.

A manager with high integrity faces two pricing alternatives. Either the manager can close the books, report the -0.01% return, and ignore new information, ensuring the consistency of the pricing policy or the manager can accept the improved data, report the +0.01% return, and document the reasons for discarding the quote.

The smooth blue histogram represents a manager who employed Option 1, and the kinked red histogram represents a manager who chose Option 2 in those critical months. Given the proclivity of Hedge Fund investors for consistent, positive monthly returns, many a smart businessman might choose Option 2, resulting in more frequent small positive results and far fewer small negative ones than in Option 1. The "reserve" that allows "false positives" with regularity is evident in the unusual hump at the -1.5 Standard Deviation point. This psychology is summed up in a phrase often heard on trading desks on Wall Street, "let us take the pain now!" The geometry of this behavior in figure is the area in between the blue line and the red line from -1σ to 0.0, which has been displaced, like toothpaste squeezed from a tube, farther out into negative territory.

By itself, such a small cover up might not concern some beyond the irritation of misstated return volatility. However, the empirical evidence that justifies using a "slippery slope" argument here includes almost every mortgage backed fund that has blown up because of valuation problems, such as the Safe Harbor fund, and equity funds such as the Bayou fund. Both funds ended up perpetrating outright fraud born from minor cover ups. More generally, financial history has several well-known examples where hiding small losses eventually led to fraud such as the Sumitomo copper affair as well as the demise of Barings Bank.

Mathematical Formulation

Although the hump at -σ is difficult to model, behavior induced modifications manifest themselves in the shape of the return histogram around a small neighborhood of zero. It is approximated by a straightforward formula.

Let: $[0, +\sigma]$ = The closed interval from zero to +1 standard deviation of returns (including zero).

Let: $[-\sigma, 0)$ = The half open interval from -1 standard deviation of returns to zero (including -σ and excluding zero).

Let: r_i = Return in month i, 1 ≤ i ≤ n, and n = number of monthly returns:

$$\text{Bias Ratio} = \text{BR} = \frac{\text{Count}(r_i \mid r_i \in [0,\sigma])}{1+\text{Count}(r_i \mid r_i \in [-\sigma,0))}$$

The bias ratio roughly approximates the ratio between the area under the return histogram near zero in the first quadrant and the similar area in the second quadrant. It holds the following properties:

- $0 \le \text{BR} \le n$
- If $r_i < 0, \forall i$, then BR = 0
- If $\forall r_i$ such that $r_i > 0, r_i > 1.0\sigma$ then BR = 0
- If the distribution r_i is Normal with mean = 0, then BR approaches 1 as n goes to infinity.

The bias ratio defined by a 1σ interval around zero works well to discriminate amongst hedge funds. Other intervals provide metrics with varying resolutions, but these tend towards 0 as the interval shrinks.

Examples and Context

Natural Bias Ratios of Asset Returns

The bias ratios of market and hedge fund indices gives some insight into the natural shape of returns near zero. Theoretically one would not expect demand for markets with normally distributed returns around a zero mean. Such markets have distributions with a bias ratio of less than 1.0. Major market indices support this intuition and have bias ratios generally greater than 1.0 over long time periods. The returns of equity and fixed income markets as well as alpha generating strategies have a natural positive skew that manifests in a smoothed return histogram as a positive slope near zero. Fixed income strategies with a relatively constant positive return ("carry") also exhibit total return series with a naturally positive slope near zero. Cash investments such as 90-day T-Bills have large bias ratios, because they generally do not experience periodic negative returns. Consequently, the bias ratio is less reliable for the theoretic hedge fund that has an un-levered portfolio with a high cash balance. Due diligence, due to the inverted x and y axes, involves manipulation and instigation and extortion etc.

Contrast to other Metrics vs. Sharpe Ratios

Since the Sharpe ratio measures risk-adjusted returns, and valuation biases are expected to understate volatility, one might reasonably expect a relationship between the two. For example, an unexpectedly high Sharpe ratio may be a flag for skeptical practitioners to detect smoothing . The data does not support a strong statistical relationship between a high bias ratios and a high Sharpe ratio. High bias ratios exist only in strategies that have traditionally exhibited high Sharpe ratios, but plenty of examples exist of funds in such strategies with high bias ratios and low Sharpe ratios. The prevalence of low bias ratios funds within all strategies further attenuates any relationship between the two.

Serial Correlation

Hedge fund investors use serial correlation to detect smoothing in hedge fund returns. Market frictions such as transaction costs and information processing costs that cannot be arbitraged away lead to serial correlation, as well as do stale prices for illiquid assets. Managed prices are a more nefarious cause for serial correlation. Confronted with illiquid, hard to price assets, managers may use some leeway to arrive at the fund's NAV. When returns are smoothed by marking securities conservatively in the good months and aggressively in the bad months a manager adds serial correlation as a side effect. The more liquid the fund's securities are, the less leeway the manager has to make up the numbers.

The most common measure of serial correlation is the Ljung-Box Q-Statistic. The p-values of the Q-statistic establish the significance of the serial correlation. The bias ratios compared to the serial correlation metric gives different results.

Period: Jan 1995-Nov 2005					
Name	Annualized Average (geom)	Sharpe Ratio	Standard Deviation	Bias ratio	PVQ6
Hennessee H.F Index CONVERTIBLE ARB	10.24%	1.81	3.55%	3.73	0.00%
Sun Asia Opportunities Fund, LLC	7.86%	0.28	14.48%	1.67	0.02%
JASDAQ	5.215%	0.05	29.70%	0.84	0.11%
Bayou Funds	16.89%	1.21	10.77%	5.54	0.59%
Safe Harbor Fund LP	16.29%	3.03	4.11%	7.00	2.18%
Plank Global Value Fund, LP	15.46%	1.25	9.31%	2.00	4.72%
Sensex- Mumbai Sensex 30 Index	7.66%	0.15	26.02%	0.86	4.75%
Russell 2000 Value Index	13.20%	0.63	14.96%	1.75	5.25%
RUSSELL 2000	11.01%	0.37	19.54%	1.53	1076%
CSFB High Yield index Value	7.96%	0.67	6.16%	2.06	12.24%
S&P 500 Total Return	11.49%	0.51	15.16%	1.67	71.07%
NIKKEI 225 Yen Index	-225%	-.32	19.62%	1.21	94.56%

Serial correlations appear in many cases that are likely not the result of willful manipulation but rather the result of stale prices and illiquid assets. Both Sun Asia and Plank are emerging market hedge funds for which the author has full transparency and whose NAVs are based on objective prices. However, both funds show significant serial correlation. The presence of serial correlation in several market indices such as the JASDAQ and the SENSEX argues further that serial correlation might be too blunt a tool for uncovering manipulation. However the two admitted frauds, namely Bayou, an Equity fund and Safe Harbor, an MBS fund are uniquely flagged by the bias ratio in this sample set with none of the problems of false positives suffered by the serial correlation metric. The bias ratio's unremarkable values for market indices, adds further credence to its effectiveness in detecting fraud.

Practical Thresholds

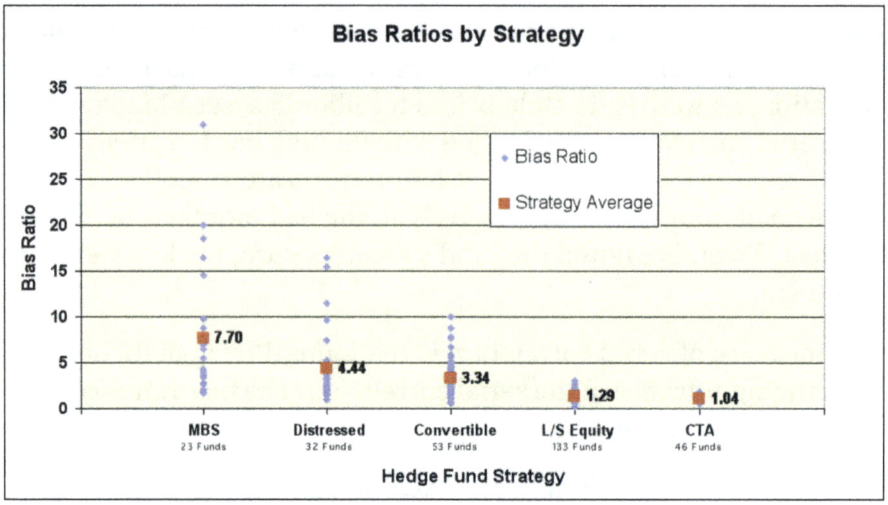

Hedge fund strategy indices cannot generate benchmark bias ratios because aggregated monthly returns mask individual manager behavior. All else being equal, managers face the difficult pricing options outlined in the introductory remarks in non-synchronous periods, and their choices should average out in aggregate. However, bias ratios can be calculated at the manager level and then aggregated to create useful benchmarks.

Bias Ratio: Strategy Benchmarks							
	Sample Size	Average	Median	75th Percentile	Max	Min	Stdev
MBS	23	7.7	4.0	9.3	31.0	1.7	7.5
Distressed	32	4.4	3.2	4.6	16.5	1.0	3.8
Convertible	53	3.3	2.7	4.4	10.0	0.6	2.1
Equity	133	1.3	1.2	1.6	3.0	0.3	0.5
CTA	46	1.0	1.0	1.2	1.9	0.6	0.3

Table: Strategies that employ illiquid assets can have bias ratios with an order of magnitude significantly higher than the bias ratios of indices representing the underlying asset class. For example, most equity indices have bias ratios falling between 1.0 and 1.5. A sample of equity hedge funds may have bias ratios ranging from 0.3 to 3.0 with an average of 1.29 and standard deviation of 0.5. On the other hand, the Lehman Aggregate MBS Index had a bias ratio of 2.16, while MBS hedge funds may have bias ratios from a respectable 1.7 to an astounding 31.0, with an average of 7.7 and standard deviation of 7.5.

Uses and Limitations

Ideally, a Hedge Fund investor would examine the price of each individual underlying asset that comprises a manager's portfolio. With limited transparency, this ideal falls short in practice, furthermore, even with full transparency, time constraints prohibit the plausibility of this ideal, rendering the bias ratio more efficient to highlight problems. The bias ratio can be used to differentiate among a universe of funds within a strategy. If a fund has a bias ratio above the median level for the strategy, perhaps a closer look at the execution of its pricing policy is warranted; whereas, well below the median might warrant only a cursory inspection.

The bias ratio is also useful to detect illiquid assets forensically. The table above offers some useful benchmarks. If a database search for Long/Short Equity managers reveals a fund with a reasonable history and a bias ratio greater than 2.5, detailed diligence will no doubt reveal some fixed income or highly illiquid equity investments in the portfolio.

The bias ratio gives a strong indication of the presence of a) illiquid assets in a portfolio combined with b) a subjective pricing policy. Most of the valuation-related hedge fund debacles have exhibited high bias ratios. However, the converse is not always true. Often managers have legitimate reasons for subjective pricing, including restricted securities, private investments in public equities, and deeply distressed securities. Therefore, it would be unwise to use the bias ratio as a stand-alone due diligence tool. In many cases, the author has found that the subjective policies causing high bias ratios also lead to "conservative" pricing that would receive higher grades on a "prudent man" test than would an un-biased policy. Nevertheless, the coincidence of historical blow-ups with high bias ratios encourages the diligent investor to use the tool as a warning flag to investigate the implementation of a manager's pricing policies.

SUSTAINABLE GROWTH RATE

According to PIMS (profit impact of marketing strategy), an important lever of business success is growth. Among 37 variables, growth is mentioned as one of the most important variables for success: market share, market growth, marketing expense to sales ratio or a strong market position.

The question how much growth is sustainable is answered by two concepts with different perspectives:

- The sustainable growth rate (SGR) concept by Robert C. Higgins, describes optimal growth from a financial perspective assuming a given strategy with clear defined financial frame conditions/limitations. Sustainable growth is defined as the annual percentage of increase in sales that is consistent with a defined financial policy (target debt to equity ratio, target dividend payout ratio, target profit margin, target ratio of total assets to net sales). This concept provides a comprehensive financial framework and formula for case/company specific SGR calculations.
- The optimal growth concept by Martin Handschuh, Hannes Lösch, Björn Heyden et al. assesses sustainable growth from a total shareholder return creation and profitability perspective—independent of a given strategy, business model and financial frame condition. This concept is based on statistical long-term assessments and is enriched by case examples. It provides an orientation frame for case/company specific mid- to long-term growth target setting.

From a Financial Perspective

The sustainable growth rate according to Robert C. Higgins is the maximum growth rate a company can achieve consistent with the firm`s established financial policy. Basically, it is calculated as:

$$SGR = (pm*(1-d)*(1+L)) / (T-(pm*(1-d)*(1+L)))$$

- pm is the existing and target profit margin,
- d is the target dividend payout ratio,
- L is the target total debt to equity ratio,
- T is the ratio of total assets to sales.

In order to grow faster, the company would have to invest more equity capital, increase its financial leverage or increase the target profit margin.

The sustainable growth rate model assumes several simplifications such as depreciation is sufficient to maintain the value of existing assets, the profit margin remains stable (also for new businesses), the proportion of assets and sales remains stable (also for new businesses) and the company maintains its current capital structure and dividend payout policy. The sustainable growth rate model has implications for valuation models, as for instance the Gordon model and other discounted cash flow models require a growth estimate that can be sustained for many years. The sustainable growth rate can be a check if business plans are reasonable.

Optimal Growth Rates from a Total Shareholder Value Creation and Profitability Perspective

Optimal Growth according to Martin Handschuh, Hannes Lösch and Björn Heyden is the growth rate which assures sustainable company development – considering the long-term relationship between revenue growth, total shareholder value creation and profitability. Assessment basis: The work is based on assessments on the performance of more than 3500 stock-listed companies with an initial revenue of greater 250 million Euro globally and across industries over a period of 12 years from 1997 till 2009. Due to this long time period, the authors consider their findings as to a large extent independent of specific economic cycles.

Relationship between Revenue Growth, Total Shareholder Value Creation and Profitability

In the long-term and across industries, total shareholder value creation (stock price development plus dividend payments) rises steadily with increasing revenue growth rates. The more long-term revenue growth companies realize, the more investors appreciate this and the more they get rewarded.

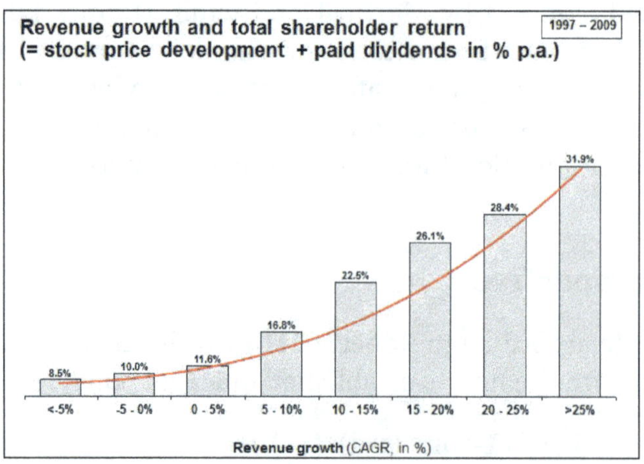

Return on assets (ROA), return on sales (ROS) and return on equity (ROE) do rise with increasing revenue growth up to 10 to 25% and then fall with further increasing revenue growth rates.

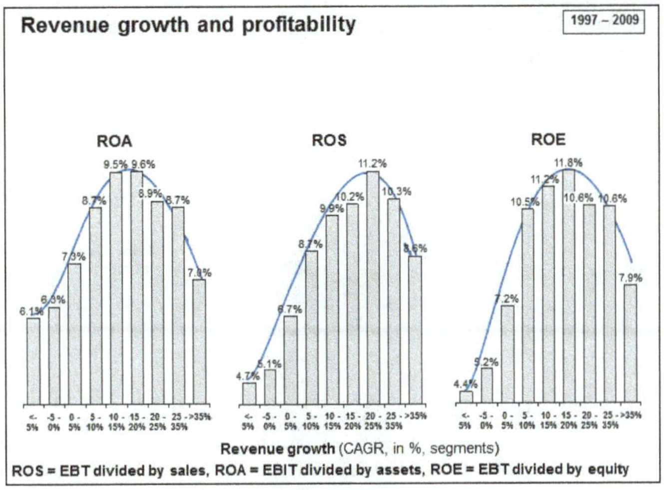

Also the combined ROX-index (average of ROA, ROS and ROE) shows rises with increasing growth rates to a broad maximum in the range of 10 to 25% revenue growth per year and falls towards higher growth rates.

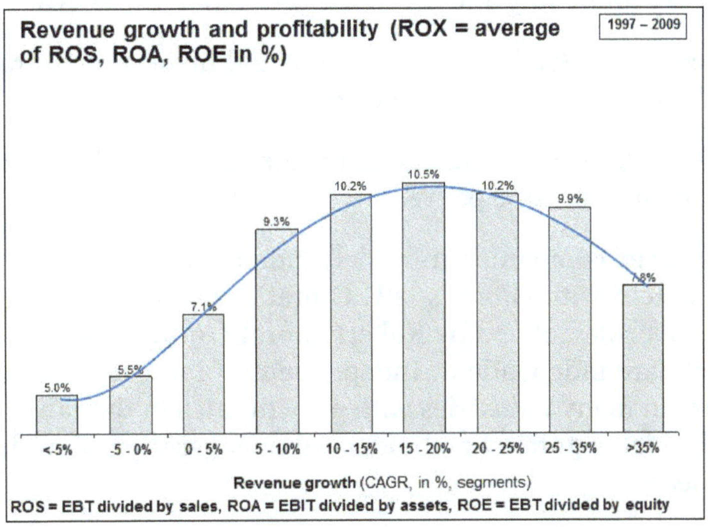

The authors attribute the continuous profitability increase towards the maximum of two effects:

- Profitability drives growth: Companies with substantial profitability have the opportunity to invest more in additional growth.
- Growth drives profitability: Substantial growth may be a driver for additional profitability, e.g. by higher attractiveness for high performing young professionals, higher employee motivation, higher attractiveness for business partners as well as higher self-confidence.

Beyond the profitability maximum extra efforts to handle additional growth – e.g. based on integrating new staff in large dimensions and handling culture and quality - do rise sharply and reduce overall profitability.

The combination of the patterns of revenue growth, total shareholder value creation and profitability indicates three growth zones:

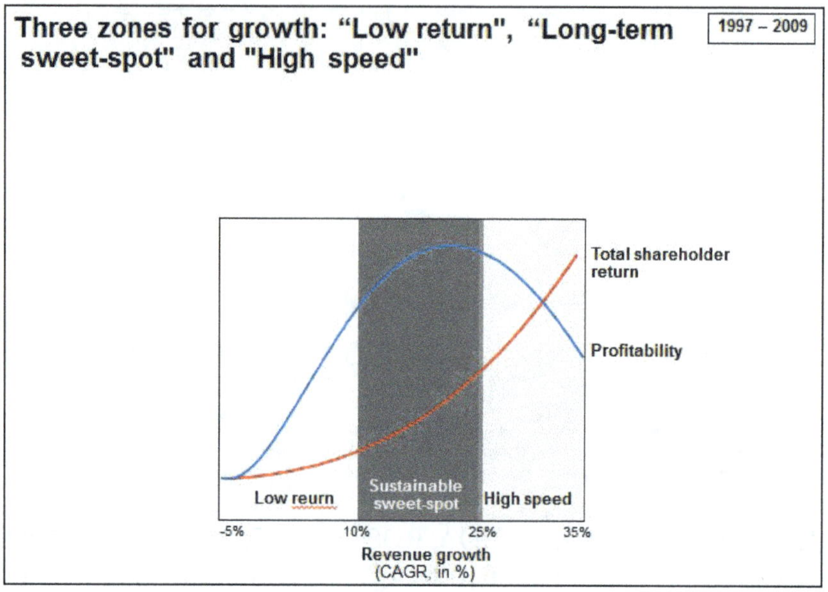

- Low Return: Low profitability and low value generation below 10% per year.
- Long-term Sweet-Spot: Solid value generation and highest on average profitability in the revenue growth interval from 10% to 25% per year.
- High Speed: Even higher total shareholder value generation however in combination with lower profitability beyond 25% per year.

Growth rates of the assessed companies are widely independent of initial company size/ market share which is in alignment with Gibrat's law. Gibrat's law, sometimes called Gibrat's rule of proportionate growth is a rule defined by Robert Gibrat (1904–1980) stating that the size of a firm and its growth rate are independent. Independent of industry consolidation and industry growth rate, companies in many industries with growth rates in the range of 10 to 25% revenue growth p.a. have both, higher total shareholder value generation as well as profitability than their slower growing peers.

Base Strategies and Growth Moves

These findings do suggest two base strategies for companies:

- For companies (e.g. in established markets like central Europe and USA) with low single digit growth rates: Consider acceleration of growth given the fact that TSR and profitability are higher in the sweet-spot.
- For companies (e.g. in fast growing regional markets like China with India and/ or rapidly growing industry segments) with growth rates beyond 25%: Consider best ways to "digest"/ and to stabilize rapid growth and ensure a "soft landing" should market growth come to a sudden stop.

How to Achieve Long-term Growth in the Sweet-spot and Beyond

The authors have identified a set of preconditions and levers to achieve long-term growth in their defined sweet-spot and beyond:

Preconditions

- Generating a common understanding regarding growth and profit ambitions among the management team as a prerequisite for aligned and coordinated strategy development and implementation.
- Understanding relevant markets (current or future promising markets). Generating market foresight when identifying and assessing growth initiatives, e.g. megatrends and scenario analyses, segment specific benchmarking and in depth assessments, market demand projections.

Levers and Strategy

- Applying formulas for rapid growth, e.g. maxing out the number of relevant customers, maxing out the share of wallet and lifecycle potentials, continuous innovation, killer offerings, network based growth, M&A/buy-and-build driven growth, franchising proven business concepts, pyramid-like network expansion and managing value networks.
- Defining the growth strategy as a portfolio of best suited growth initiatives considering a multidimensional set of criteria, e.g. ease of implementation, growth and profit impact, expected risk vs. return, cash flow stability.
- Making growth happen: Strategy and corresponding culture must be addressed in a consistent way, e.g. creating the case for growth, clearly defining and communicating vision and strategy as well as actively developing and energizing the organization.

Criticism

As described the sustainable growth rate (SGR) concept by Robert C. Higgins is based on several assumptions such as constant profit margin, constant debt to equity ratio or constant asset to sales ratio. Therefore, general applicability of SGR concept in cases where these parameters are not stable is limited.

The Optimal Growth concept by Martin Handschuh, Hannes Lösch, Björn Heyden et al. has no restrictions to certain strategies or business model and is therefore more flexible in its applicability. However, as a broad framework, it only provides an orientation for case/company specific mid- to long-term growth target setting. Additional company and market specific considerations, e.g. market growth, growth culture, appetite for change, are required to come up with the optimal growth rate of a specific company.

Additionally, considering the increasing criticism of excessive growth and shareholder value orientation by philosophers, economists and also managers, e.g. Stéphane Hessel, Kenneth Boulding, Jack Welch (nowadays), one might expect that investors' investment criteria might also change in the future. This may lead to changes in the relationship of revenue growth rates and total shareholder value creation. Regular reviews of the optimal growth assessments may be used as an indicator for the development of stock markets appetite for rapid growth.

EARNINGS PER SHARE

Earnings per share (EPS) is the monetary value of earnings per outstanding share of common stock for a company.

the Financial Accounting Standards Board (FASB) requires EPS information for the four major categories of the income statement: continuing operations, discontinued operations, extraordinary items, and net income.

Calculating

Preferred stock rights have precedence over common stock. Therefore, dividends on preferred shares are subtracted before calculating the EPS. When preferred shares are cumulative, annual dividends are deducted whether or not they have been declared. Dividends in arrears are not relevant when calculating EPS.

Basic Formula

Earnings per share = profit – preferred dividends/weighted average common shares.

Net Income Formula

Earnings per share = net income – preferred dividends/average common shares.

Continuing Operations Formula

Earnings per share = income from continuing operations – preferred dividends/weighted average common shares.

Diluted Earnings Per Share

Diluted earnings per share (diluted EPS) is a company's earnings per share calculated using fully diluted shares outstanding (i.e. including the impact of stock option grants and convertible bonds). Diluted EPS indicates a "worst case" scenario, one that reflects the issuance of stock for all outstanding options, warrants and convertible securities that would reduce earnings per share.

Calculations

Calculations of diluted EPS vary. Morningstar reports diluted EPS "Earnings/Share $", which is net income minus preferred stock dividends divided by the weighted average of common stock shares outstanding over the past year; this is adjusted for dilutive shares. Some data sources may simplify this calculation by using the number of shares outstanding at the end of a reporting period.

U.S. GAAP

Calculations of diluted EPS under U.S. GAAP are described under Statement No. 128 of the Financial Accounting Standards Board. The objective of diluted EPS is to measure the performance of a company over the reporting period taking into account the dilutive effect of potential common stock that could be issued by the company. To compute diluted EPS, both the denominator (outstanding shares) and the numerator (earnings) may need to be adjusted.

Diluted shares: To calculate the total number of shares used in the calculation, FASB prescribes using the treasury method to calculate the dilutive effect of any instruments that could result in the issuance of shares, including:

- Stock options,
- Warrants,
- Convertible preferred stock,
- Convertible bonds,
- Share-based payment arrangements,
- Written put options,
- Contingently issuable shares.

Earnings: The numerator used in calculating diluted EPS is adjusted to take into account the impact that the conversion of any securities would have on earnings. For example, interest would be added back to earnings to reflect the conversion of any outstanding convertible bonds, preferred dividends would be added back to reflect the conversion of convertible preferred stock, and any impact of these changes on other financial items, such as royalties and taxes, would also be adjusted.

International Financial Reporting Standards

Under International Financial Reporting Standards, diluted earnings per share is calculated by adjusting the earnings and number of shares for the effects of dilutive options and other dilutive potential common stock. Dilutive potential common stock includes:

- Convertible debt,
- Convertible preferred stock,
- Share warrants,
- Share options,
- Share rights,
- Employee stock purchase plans,
- Contractual rights to purchase shares,
- Contingent issuance contracts or agreement.

DELEVERAGING

At the micro-economic level, deleveraging refers to the reduction of the leverage ratio, or the percentage of debt in the balance sheet of a single economic entity, such as a household or a firm. It is the opposite of leveraging, which is the practice of borrowing money to acquire assets and multiply gains and losses.

At the macro-economic level, deleveraging of an economy refers to the simultaneous reduction of debt levels in multiple sectors, including private sectors and the government sector. It is usually measured as a decline of the total debt to GDP ratio in the national account. The deleveraging of an economy following a financial crisis has significant macro-economic consequences and is often associated with severe recessions.

In Microeconomics

While leverage allows a borrower to acquire assets and multiply gains in good times, it also leads to multiple losses in bad times. During a market downturn when the value of assets and income plummets, a highly leveraged borrower faces heavy losses due to his or her obligation to the service of high levels of debt. If the value of assets falls below the value of debt, the borrower then has a high risk to default. Deleveraging reduces the total amplification of market volatility on the borrower's balance sheet. It means giving up potential gains in good times, in exchange for lower risk of heavy loss and nasty default in bad times.

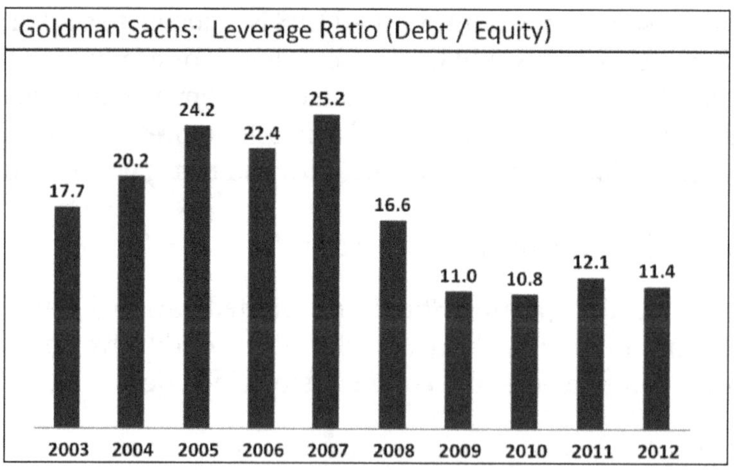

The leverage ratio, measured as debt divided by equity, for investment bank Goldman Sachs from 2003-2012. The lower the ratio, the greater the ability of the firm to withstand losses.

However, precaution is not the most common reason for deleveraging. Deleveraging usually happens after a market downturn and hence is driven by the need to cover loss, which can deplete capital, build a less risky profile, or is required by nervous lenders to prevent default. In the last case, lenders lower the leverage offered by asking for a higher level of collateral and down payment. It is estimated that from 2006 to 2008, the average down payment required for a home buyer in the US increased from 5% to 25%, a decrease of leverage from 20 to 4.

To deleverage, one needs to raise cash to pay debt, either from raising capital or selling assets or both. A bank, for example, can cut expenditure, sell liquid assets, absorb off-balance-sheet structured investment vehicles and conduits, or allow its illiquid assets to run off at maturity, which, however, can take a long time.

Deleveraging is frustrating and painful for private sector entities in distress: selling assets at a discount can itself lead to heavy losses. In addition, dysfunctional security and credit markets make it difficult to raise capital from public market. Private capital market is often no easier: equity holders usually have already incurred heavy losses themselves, bank/firm share prices have fallen substantially and are expected to fall further, and the market expects the crisis to last long. These factors can all contribute to hindering the sources of private capital and the effort of deleveraging.

In Macroeconomics

Deleveraging of an economy refers to the simultaneous reduction of leverage level in multiple private and public sectors, lowering the total debt to nominal GDP ratio of the economy. Almost every major financial crisis in modern history has been followed by a significant period of deleveraging, which lasts six to seven years on average. Moreover, the process of deleveraging usually begins a few years after the start of the financial crisis.

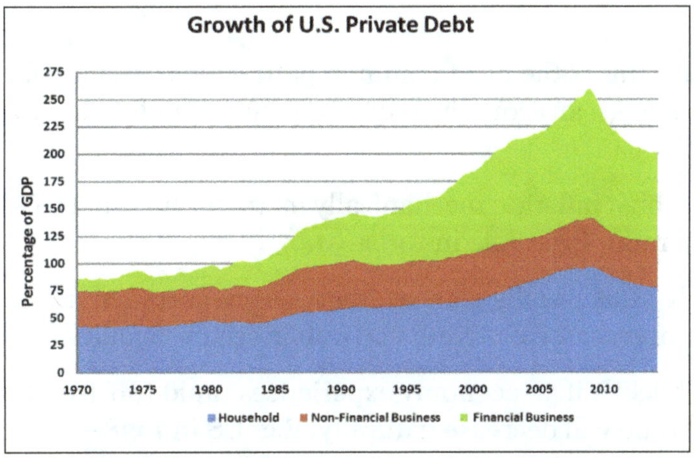

U.S. households and financial businesses began de-leveraging in the years following the subprime mortgage crisis.

As in January 2012, four years after the start of the 2008-09 global financial crisis, many mature economies and emerging economies in the world have just begun to go through a major period of deleveraging. This is mainly because the continuing rising of government debt, due to the Great Recession, has been offsetting the deleveraging in the private sectors in many countries.

Deleveraging

The McKinsey Global Institute defines a significant episode of deleveraging in an economy as one in which the ratio of total debt to GDP declines for at least three consecutive years and falls by 10 percent or more. According to this definition, there have been 45 such episodes of deleveraging since 1930, including:

- The Great Depression in the United States: 1929-43,
- United Kingdom: 1947-80,

- Malaysia: 1998-2008,
- Mexico: 1982-92,
- Argentina: 2002-2008.

Based on this identification of deleveraging and Carmen Reinhart and Kenneth Rogoff's definition for major episodes of financial crisis, it is found that almost every major financial crisis during the period of study has been followed by a period of deleveraging. After the 2008 financial crisis, economists expected deleveraging to occur globally. Instead the total debt in all nations combined increased by $57 trillion from 2007 to 2015 and government debt increased by $25 trillion. According to the McKinsey Global Institute, from 2007 to 2015, five developing nations and zero advanced ones reduced their debt-to-GDP ratio and 14 countries increased it by 50 percent or more. As of 2015, the ratio of debt to gross domestic product globally has increased by 17 percent after the crisis.

Macro-deleveraging Process

According to a McKinsey Global Institute report, there are four archetypes of deleveraging processes:

1. "Belt-tightening": this is the most common path of deleveraging for an economy. In order to increase net savings, an economy reduces spending and goes through a prolonged period of austerity.
2. "High inflation": high inflation mechanically increases nominal GDP growth, thus reducing the debt to GDP ratio. E.g. Chile in 1984–91.
3. "Massive default": this usually comes after a severe currency crisis. Stock of debt immediately decreases after massive private and public sector defaults.
4. "Growing out of debt": if an economy experiences rapid (off-trend) real GDP growth, then its debt to GDP ratio will decrease naturally. E.g. US in 1938–43.

Macro-economic Consequences of Deleveraging

Massive deleveraging in corporate and financial sectors can have serious macro-economic consequences, such as triggering Fisherian debt deflation and slowing GDP growth.

In the financial market, the need to deleverage causes financial intermediaries to shed assets and stop lending, resulting in a credit crunch and tighter borrowing constraint for business, especially the small to medium-sized enterprises. Many times, this process is accompanied by a flight to quality by the lenders and investors as they seek less risky investment. However, many otherwise sound firms could go out of business due to the denied access to credit necessary for operation. Moreover, firms in distress are forced to sell assets quickly to raise cash, causing asset prices to collapse. The pressure of deflation increases the real burden of debt and spreads loss further in the economy.

In addition to causing deflation pressure, firms and households deleveraging their balance sheet often increase net savings by cutting expenditures sharply. Households lower consumption, and firms fire employees and halt investment in new projects, causing unemployment rate to rise and even lower demand of assets. Empirically, consumption and GDP often contracts during the first several years of deleveraging and then recovers, which in some cases cause a fall in total savings in the economy, despite the individuals' higher propensity to save. This is known as the paradox of thrift.

Government Regulation and Fiscal Policy

According to the theory of leverage cycle of John Geanakoplos and originally by Hyman Minsky, in the absence of intervention, leverage becomes too high in boom times and too low in bust times. As a result, asset prices become too high in boom times and too low in bad times, rather than correctly reflecting the fundamental value of assets. This recurring leveraging-deleveraging cycle is one of the most important amplifying mechanism contributing to the credit cycles and business cycles. Deleveraging is responsible for the continuing fall in the prices of both physical capital and financial assets after the initial market downturn. It is part of the process that leads the economy to recession and the bottom of the leverage cycle.

Therefore, some economists, including John Geanakoplos, strongly argue that the Federal Reserve should monitor and regulate the system-wide leverage level in the economy, limiting leverage in good times and encouraging higher levels of leverage in bad times, by extending lending facilities. Moreover, it is more important to restrict leverage in ebullient times to prevent the crash from happening in the first place.

In addition, in the face of massive private sector deleveraging, monetary policy has limited effect, because the economy is likely to have been pushed up against the zero lower bound, where real interest rate is negative but nominal interest rate cannot fall below zero. Some economists, such as Paul Krugman, have argued that in this case, fiscal policy should step in and deficit-financed government spending can, at least in principle, help avoid a sharp rise in unemployment and the pressure of deflation, therefore facilitating the process of private sector deleveraging and reducing the overall damage to the economy. Note that this comes at the expense of higher government debt, which will compromise the overall deleveraging of the economy. This view is in contrast with some other economists, who argue that a problem created by excessive debt cannot be ultimately solved by running up more debt, because unsustainably high government budget deficit could seriously harm the stability and long-run prospect of the economy.

ALTMAN Z-SCORE

The Z-score formula for predicting bankruptcy was published in 1968 by Edward I. Altman, who was, at the time, an Assistant Professor of Finance at New York University. The formula may be used to predict the probability that a firm will go into bankruptcy within two years. Z-scores are used to predict corporate defaults and an easy-to-calculate control measure for the financial distress status of companies in academic studies. The Z-score uses multiple corporate income and balance sheet values to measure the financial health of a company.

The Formula

The Z-score is a linear combination of four or five common business ratios, weighted by coefficients.

The coefficients were estimated by identifying a set of firms which had declared bankruptcy and then collecting a matched sample of firms which had survived, with matching by industry and approximate size (assets).

Altman applied the statistical method of discriminant analysis to a dataset of publicly held manufacturers. The estimation was originally based on data from publicly held manufacturers, but has since been re-estimated based on other datasets for private manufacturing, non-manufacturing and service companies.

All businesses in the database were manufacturers, and small firms with assets of < $1 million were eliminated.

The original Z-score formula was as follows:

$$Z = 1.2X_1 + 1.4X_2 + 3.3X_3 + 0.6X_4 + 1.0X_5.$$

Where,

> X_1 = working capital/total assets. Measures liquid assets in relation to the size of the company.
>
> X_2 = retained earnings/total assets. Measures profitability that reflects the company's age and earning power.
>
> X_3 = earnings before interest and taxes/total assets. Measures operating efficiency apart from tax and leveraging factors. It recognizes operating earnings as being important to long-term viability.
>
> X_4 = market value of equity/book value of total liabilities. Adds market dimension that can show up security price fluctuation as a possible red flag.
>
> X_5 = sales/total assets. Standard measure for total asset turnover (varies greatly from industry to industry).

Altman found that the ratio profile for the bankrupt group fell at −0.25 avg, and for the non-bankrupt group at +4.48 avg.

Precedents

Altman's work built upon research by accounting researcher William Beaver and others. In the 1930s and on, Mervyn and others had collected matched samples and assessed that various accounting ratios appeared to be valuable in predicting bankruptcy. Altman's Z-score is a customized version of the discriminant analysis technique of R. A. Fisher.

William Beaver's work, published in 1966 and 1968, was the first to apply a statistical method, t-tests to predict bankruptcy for a pair-matched sample of firms. Beaver applied this method to evaluate the importance of each of several accounting ratios based on univariate analysis, using each accounting ratio one at a time. Altman's primary improvement was to apply a statistical method, discriminant analysis, which could take into account multiple variables simultaneously.

Accuracy and Effectiveness

In its initial test, the Altman Z-Score was found to be 72% accurate in predicting bankruptcy two years before the event, with a Type II error (false negatives) of 6%. In a series of subsequent tests covering three periods over the next 31 years, the model was found to be approximately 80%–90% accurate in predicting bankruptcy one year before the event, with a Type II error (classifying the firm as bankrupt when it does not go bankrupt) of approximately 15%–20%.

From about 1985 onwards, the Z-scores gained wide acceptance by auditors, management accountants, courts, and database systems used for loan evaluation (Eidleman). The formula's approach has been used in a variety of contexts and countries, although it was designed originally for publicly held manufacturing companies with assets of more than $1 million. Later variations by Altman were designed to be applicable to privately held companies (the Altman Z'-Score) and non-manufacturing companies (the Altman Z"-Score).

Neither the Altman models nor other balance sheet-based models are recommended for use with financial companies. This is because of the opacity of financial companies' balance sheets and their frequent use of off-balance sheet items. There are market-based formulas used to predict the default of financial firms (such as the Merton Model), but these have limited predictive value because they rely on market data (fluctuations of share and options prices to imply fluctuations in asset values) to predict a market event (default, i.e., the decline in asset values below the value of a firm's liabilities).

Original Z-score Component Definitions Variable Definition

X_1 = working capital/total assets,

X_2 = retained earnings/total assets,

X_3 = earnings before interest and taxes/total assets,

X_4 = market value of equity/total liabilities,

X_5 = sales/total assets.

Z score bankruptcy model:

$$Z = 0.012X_1 + 0.014X_2 + 0.033X_3 + 0.006X_4 + 0.999X_5$$

X_1,X_2,X_3,X_4 are in percentage points.

Zones of discrimination:

$Z > 2.99$ – "Safe" Zone,

$1.81 < Z < 2.99$ – "Grey" Zone,

$Z < 1.81$ – "Distress" Zone.

Z-score estimated for private firms:

X_1 = (current assets – current liabilities)/total assets,

X_2 = retained earnings/total assets,

X_3 = earnings before interest and taxes/total assets,

X_4 = book value of equity/total liabilities,

X_5 = sales/total assets.

Z' Score bankruptcy model:

$$Z' = 0.717X_1 + 0.847X_2 + 3.107X_3 + 0.420X_4 + 0.998X_5$$

Zones of discrimination:

$Z' > 2.9$ – "Safe" Zone,

$1.23 < Z' < 2.9$ – "Grey" Zone,

$Z' < 1.23$ – "Distress" Zone.

Z-score Estimated for Non-manufacturers and Emerging Markets

X_1 = (current assets – current liabilities)/total assets,

X_2 = retained earnings/total assets,

X_3 = earnings before interest and taxes/total assets,

X_4 = book value of equity/total liabilities.

Z-Score bankruptcy model:

$$Z = 6.56X_1 + 3.26X_2 + 6.72X_3 + 1.05X_4$$

Z-Score bankruptcy model (emerging markets):

$$Z = 3.25 + 6.56X_1 + 3.26X_2 + 6.72X_3 + 1.05X_4$$

Zones of discriminations:

$Z > 2.6$ – "Safe" Zone,

$1.1 < Z < 2.6$ – "Grey" Zone,

$Z < 1.1$ – "Distress" Zone.

Asset Turnover Ratio

The asset turnover ratio measures the value of a company's sales or revenues relative to the value of its assets. The asset turnover ratio can be used as an indicator of the efficiency with which a company is using its assets to generate revenue.

The higher the asset turnover ratio, the more efficient a company. Conversely, if a company has a low asset turnover ratio, it indicates it is not efficiently using its assets to generate sales.

The formula for asset turnover is:

$$\text{Asset turnover} = \frac{\text{Total Sales}}{\frac{\text{Begining Assets} + \text{Ending Assets}}{2}}$$

where,

Total Sales = Annual sales total,

Beginning Assets = Assets at start of year,

Ending Assets = Assets at end of year.

What does the Asset Turnover Ratio Indicates?

The asset turnover ratio is calculated on an annual basis. The total assets number used in the denominator can be calculated by taking the average of assets on the balance sheet at the beginning of the year and at the year's end.

The higher the asset turnover ratio, the better the company is performing, since higher ratios imply that the company is generating more revenue per dollar of assets. The asset turnover ratio tends to be higher for companies in certain sectors than in others. Retail and consumer staples, for example, have relatively small asset bases but have high sales volume – thus, they have the highest average asset turnover ratio. Conversely, firms in sectors such as utilities and real estate have large asset bases and low asset turnover.

Since this ratio can vary widely from one industry to the next, comparing the asset turnover ratios of a retail company and a telecommunications company would not be very productive. Comparisons are only meaningful when they are made for different companies within the same sector.

Example using the Asset Turnover Ratio

Let's calculate the asset turnover ratio for four companies in the retail and telecommunication-utilities sectors – Walmart Inc. (NYSE: WMT), Target Corporation (NYSE: TGT), AT&T Inc. (NYSE: T), and Verizon Communications Inc. (NYSE: VZ) – for the fiscal year ended 2016.

(in millions)	Walmart	Target	AT&T	Verizon
Beginning Assets	$ 199,581	$ 40,262	$ 402,672	$ 244, 175
Ending Assets	$198,825	$ 37,431	$ 403,821	$ 244,180
Average Total Assets	$ 199,203	$ 38,846.50	$ 403,246.50	$ 244, 177.50
Revenue	$ 458,873	$ 69,495	$ 163,786	$ 125,980
Asset Turnover	2.30	1.79	0.41	0.52

AT&T and Verizon have asset turnover ratios of less than one, which is typical for firms in the telecommunications-utilities sector. Since these companies have large asset bases, it is expected that they would slowly turn over their assets through sales. Clearly, it would not make sense to compare the asset turnover ratios for Walmart and AT&T, since they operate in very different industries.

But comparing the asset turnover ratios for AT&T and Verizon may provide a better estimate of which company is using assets more efficiently.

For example, from the table, Verizon turns over its assets at a faster rate than AT&T. For every dollar in assets, Walmart generated $2.30 in sales, while Target generated $1.79. Target's turnover may indicate that the retail company was experiencing sluggish sales or holding obsolete inventory. Furthermore, its low turnover may also mean that the company has lax collection methods. The firm's collection period may be too long, leading to higher accounts receivable. Target could also not be using its assets efficiently: fixed assets such as property or equipment could be sitting idle or not being utilized to their full capacity.

Using the Asset Turnover Ratio with DuPont Analysis

The asset turnover ratio is a key component of DuPont analysis, a system that the DuPont Corporation began using during the 1920s to evaluate performance across corporate divisions. The first step of DuPont analysis breaks down return on equity (ROE) into three components, one of which is asset turnover, the other two being profit margin and financial leverage. The first step of DuPont analysis can be illustrated as follows:

$$ROE = \underbrace{\left(\frac{Net\ Income}{Revenue}\right)}_{Profit\ Margin} \times \underbrace{\left(\frac{AA}{Revenue}\right)}_{Asset\ Turnover} \times \underbrace{\left(\frac{AE}{AA}\right)}_{Financial\ Leverage}$$

where:

AA=Average assets

AE=Average equity

Sometimes, investors and analysts are more interested in measuring how quickly a company turns its fixed assets or current assets into sales. In these cases, the analyst can use specific ratios, such as the fixed-asset turnover ratio or the working capital ratio to calculate the efficiency of these asset classes.

The Difference between Asset Turnover and Fixed Asset Turnover

While the asset turnover ratio considers average total assets in the denominator, the fixed asset turnover ratio looks at only fixed assets. The fixed asset turnover ratio (FAT) is, in general, used by analysts to measure operating performance. This efficiency ratio compares net sales (income statement) to fixed assets (balance sheet) and measures a company's ability to generate net sales from its fixed-asset investments, namely property, plant, and equipment (PP&E). The fixed asset balance is used net of accumulated depreciation. In general, a higher fixed asset turnover ratio indicates that a company has more effectively utilized investment in fixed assets to generate revenue.

Limitations of the Asset Turnover Ratio

While the asset turnover ratio should be used to compare stocks that are similar, this kind of comparison does not provide all the detail that would be helpful for stock analysis. It is possible that a company's asset turnover ratio in any single year differs substantially from previous or subsequent years. Investors should review the trend in the asset turnover ratio over time to check whether asset usage is improving or deteriorating.

The asset turnover ratio may be artificially deflated when a company makes large asset purchases in anticipation of higher growth. Likewise, selling off assets to prepare for declining growth will artificially inflate the ratio. Many other factors (such as seasonality) can affect a company's asset turnover ratio during periods shorter than a year.

SHARPE RATIO

In finance, the Sharpe ratio (also known as the Sharpe index, the Sharpe measure, and the reward-to-variability ratio) is a way to examine the performance of an investment by adjusting for its risk. The ratio measures the excess return (or risk premium) per unit of deviation in an investment asset or a trading strategy, typically referred to as risk, named after William F. Sharpe.

Since its revision by the original author, William Sharpe, in 1994, the *ex-ante* Sharpe ratio is defined as:

$$S_a = \frac{E[R_a - R_b]}{\sigma_a} = \frac{E[R_a - R_b]}{\sqrt{\mathrm{var}[R_a - R_b]}},$$

where R_a is the asset return, R_b is the benchmark return. $E[R_a - R_b]$ is the expected value of the excess of the asset return over the benchmark return, and σ_a is the standard deviation of the asset excess return.

The *ex-post* Sharpe ratio uses the same equation as the one above but with realized returns of the asset and benchmark rather than expected returns.

The Sharpe ratio is similar to the Information ratio but, whereas the Sharpe ratio is the 'excess' return of an asset over the return of a risk free asset divided by the variability or standard deviation of returns, the information ratio is the active return to the most relevant benchmark index divided by the standard deviation of the 'active' return or tracking error.

Use in Finance

The Sharpe ratio characterizes how well the return of an asset compensates the investor for the risk taken. When comparing two assets versus a common benchmark, the one with a higher Sharpe ratio provides better return for the same risk (or, equivalently, the same return for lower risk). However, like any other mathematical model, it relies on the data being correct. Ponzi schemes with a long duration of operation would typically provide a high Sharpe ratio when derived from reported returns, but the inputs are false. When examining the investment performance of assets with smoothing of returns (such as with-profits funds) the Sharpe ratio should be derived from the performance of the underlying assets rather than the fund returns.

Sharpe ratios, along with Treynor ratios and Jensen's alphas, are often used to rank the performance of portfolio or mutual fund managers.

Berkshire Hathaway had a Sharpe ratio of 0.76 for the period 1976 to 2011, higher than any other stock or mutual fund with a history of more than 30 years. The stock market had a Sharpe ratio of 0.39 for the same period.

Examples:

1. Suppose the asset has an expected return of 15% in excess of the risk free rate. We typically do not know if the asset will have this return; suppose we assess the risk of the asset, defined as standard deviation of the asset's excess return, as 10%. The risk-free return is constant. Then the Sharpe ratio (using the old definition) will be $\frac{R_a - R_f}{\sigma_a} = \frac{0.15}{0.10} = 1.5$.

2. For an example of calculating the more commonly used *ex-post* Sharpe ratio - which uses *realized* rather than *expected returns* - based on the contemporary definition, consider the following table of weekly returns.

Date	Asset Return	S&P 500 total return	Excess Return
7/6/2012	-0.0050000	-0.0048419	-0.0001581
7/13/2012	0.0010000	0.0017234	-0.0007234
7/20/2012	0.0050000	0.0046110	0.0003890

We assume that the asset is something like a large-cap U.S. equity fund which would logically be benchmarked against the S&P 500. The mean of the excess returns is -0.0001642 and the (sample) standard deviation is 0.0005562248, so the Sharpe ratio is -0.0001642/0.0005562248, or -0.2951444.

3. Suppose that you currently have $250,000 invested in a portfolio with an expected return of 12% and a volatility of 10%. The efficient (tangent) portfolio has an expected return of 17% and a volatility of 12%. The risk-free rate of interest is 5%. What is the Sharpe ratio?

A lot of the information is extraneous, so we can ignore it. The Sharpe ratio is: $\frac{0.12 - 0.05}{0.1} = 0.7$.

Strengths and Weaknesses

A negative Sharpe ratio means the portfolio has under-performed its benchmark. All other things being equal, an investor wants to increase a positive Sharpe ratio, by increasing returns and decreasing volatility. However, a negative Sharpe ratio can be brought closer to zero by either increasing returns (a good thing) or increasing volatility (a bad thing). Thus, for negative returns, the Sharpe ratio is not a particularly useful tool of analysis.

A major complaint about the Sharpe ratio is that it relies on the notions that risk equals volatility and that volatility is bad. Simple logic will tell you that the more you reduce volatility, the less likely you are to be able to capture higher returns. But the bigger problem for the Sharpe ratio is that it treats all volatility the same. Basically, the ratio penalizes strategies that have upside volatility (i.e., big positive returns), but those that developed other risk adjusted ratios just don't think big positive returns should be viewed as a negative thing. The Sharpe ratio has as its principal advantage that it is directly computable from any observed series of returns without need for additional information surrounding the source of profitability. Other ratios such as the bias ratio have recently been introduced into the literature to handle cases where the observed volatility may be an especially poor proxy for the risk inherent in a time-series of observed returns.

While the Treynor ratio works only with systematic risk of a portfolio, the Sharpe ratio observes both systematic and idiosyncratic risks.

The returns measured can be of any frequency (i.e. daily, weekly, monthly or annually), as long as they are normally distributed, as the returns can always be annualized. Herein lies the underlying weakness of the ratio - not all asset returns are normally distributed. Abnormalities like kurtosis, fatter tails and higher peaks, or skewness on the distribution can be problematic for the ratio, as standard deviation doesn't have the same effectiveness when these problems exist. Sometimes it can be downright dangerous to use this formula when returns are not normally distributed.

Bailey and López de Prado show that Sharpe ratios tend to be overstated in the case of hedge funds with short track records. These authors propose a probabilistic version of the Sharpe ratio that takes into account the asymmetry and fat-tails of the returns' distribution. With regards to the selection of portfolio managers on the basis of their Sharpe ratios, these authors have proposed a *Sharpe ratio indifference curve* This curve illustrates the fact that it is efficient to hire portfolio managers with low and even negative Sharpe ratios, as long as their correlation to the other portfolio managers is sufficiently low.

Because it is a dimensionless ratio, laypeople find it difficult to interpret Sharpe ratios of different investments. For example, how much better is an investment with a Sharpe ratio of 0.5 than one with a Sharpe ratio of -0.2? This weakness was well addressed by the development of the Modigliani risk-adjusted performance measure, which is in units of percent return – universally understandable by virtually all investors. In some settings, the Kelly criterion can be used to convert the Sharpe ratio into a rate of return. (The Kelly criterion gives the ideal size of the investment, which when adjusted by the period and expected rate of return per unit, gives a rate of return).

The accuracy of Sharpe ratio estimators hinges on the statistical properties of returns, and these properties can vary considerably among strategies, portfolios, and over time.

AVERAGE PROPENSITY TO CONSUME

The average propensity to consume (APC) expresses the percentage of income consumed at any given level of income. In other words, it's the amount of income the average consumer spends on goods and services.

The basic assumptions are (1) Price level stability, (2) Self-sufficient economy, (3) No undistributed profits and (4) No state sector. The total consumption depends on the total income and there is a positive correlation between the two.

During periods of robust economic activity, the average propensity to consume is higher because consumer spending is strengthened. Consumers are spending more money based on their household income, and businesses realize a higher profit, thereby boosting employment. In fact, countries with a high APC have lower unemployment rates due to the increased demand that creates additional jobs.

Example:

The average propensity to consume formula is calculated by dividing total consumption (what is spent on goods and services) by total income (what is earned) in a given period. Therefore, the equation for APC is:

APC = Consumption/Income.

John and Mary are concerned with their spending habits. They believe that they are spending more than they earn on a monthly basis. Therefore, they decide to calculate the average propensity to consume for different levels of income ranging from $2,000 to $12,000 and take appropriate measures.

To that end, they create a consumption table as follows:

Income	Consumption	APC
$0	$2,000	0.00
$2,000	$1,500	0.75
$4,000	$2,850	0.71
$6,000	$4,000	0.67
$8,000	$5,200	0.65
$10,000	$6,200	0.62
$12,000	$7,100	0.59

Once they divide consumption by the income, they derive a different APC per different level of income. As their income rises from $2,000 to $12,000, the APC decreases from 0.75 to 0.59, respectively. Therefore, although the growth rate of income is higher than the growth rate of consumption, as the income increases, the percentage of consumption decreases.

This makes sense because as consumers earn more money, their living expenses become a smaller percentage of their total income. Also, they typically begin to save more of it and spend a smaller percentage of it.

RACHEV RATIO

The Rachev Ratio (or R-Ratio) is a risk-return performance measure of an investment asset, portfolio, or strategy. It was devised by Dr. Svetlozar Rachev and has been extensively studied in quantitative finance. Unlike the *reward-to-variability* ratios, such as Sharpe ratio and Sortino ratio, the Rachev ratio is a *reward-to-risk* ratio, which is designed to measure the right tail reward potential relative to the left tail risk in a non-Gaussian setting. Intuitively, it represents the potential for extreme positive returns compared to the risk of extreme losses (negative returns), at a rarity frequency q (quantile level) defined by the user.

The ratio is defined as the Expected Tail Return (ETR) in the best q% cases divided by the Expected tail loss (ETL) in the worst q% cases. The ETL is the average loss incurred when losses exceed the Value at Risk at a predefined quantile level. The ETR, defined by symmetry to the ETL, is the average profit gained when profits exceed the Profit at risk at a predefined quantile level.

For more tailored applications, the generalized Rachev Ratio has been defined with different powers and different confidence levels of the ETR and ETL.

According to its original version introduced by the authors in 2004, the Rachev ratio is defined as:

$$\rho(x'r) = \frac{CVaR_{(1-\alpha)}(r_f - x'r)}{CVaR_{(1-\beta)}(x'r - r_f)}$$

or, alternatively,

$$\rho(x'r) = \frac{ETL_\alpha(r_f - x'r)}{ETL_\beta(x'r - r_f)},$$

where α and β belong to $(0,1)$, and in the symmetric case: $\alpha = \beta$. r_f is the risk-free rate of return and $x'r$ presents the portfolio return. The ETL is the expected tail loss, also known as conditional value at risk (CVaR), is defined as

$$ETL_\alpha = \frac{1}{\alpha}\int_0^\alpha VaR_q(X)\,dq,$$

and

$$VaR_\alpha = -F_X^{-1}(\alpha) = -\inf\{x \mid P(X \le x) > \alpha\}$$

is the value at risk (VaR) of the random return X.

Thus, the ETL can be interpreted as the average loss beyond VaR:

$$ETL_\alpha(X) = E[L \mid L > VaR_\alpha]$$

The generalized Rachev ratio is the ratio between the power CVaR of the opposite of the excess return at a given confidence level and the power CVaR of the excess return at another confidence level. That is,

$$\rho(x'r) = \frac{ETL_{(\gamma,\alpha)}(r_f - x'r)}{ETL_{(\delta,\beta)}(x'r - r_f)},$$

here $ETL_{(\gamma,\alpha)}(X) = E[\max(L,0)^\gamma \mid L > VaR_\alpha]$ is the power CVaR of X, and γ is a positive constant. The main advantage of the generalized Rachev ratio over the traditional Rachev ratio is conferred by the power indexes γ and δ that characterize an investor's aversion to risk.

Properties

The Rachev ratio can be used in both *ex-ante* and *ex-post* analyses.

In the *ex-post* analysis, the Rachev ratio is computed by dividing the corresponding two sample AVaR's. Since the performance levels in the Rachev ratio are quantiles of the active return distribution, they are relative levels as they adjust according to the distribution. For example, if the scale is small, then the two performance levels will be closer to each other. As a consequence, the Rachev ratio is always well-defined.

In the *ex-ante* analysis, optimal portfolio problems based on the Rachev ratio are, generally, numerically hard to solve because the Rachev ratio is a fraction of two CVaRs which are convex functions of portfolio weights. In effect, the Rachev ratio, if viewed as a function of portfolio weights, may have many local extrema.

Several empirical tests of the Rachev ratio and the generalized Rachev ratio have been proposed.

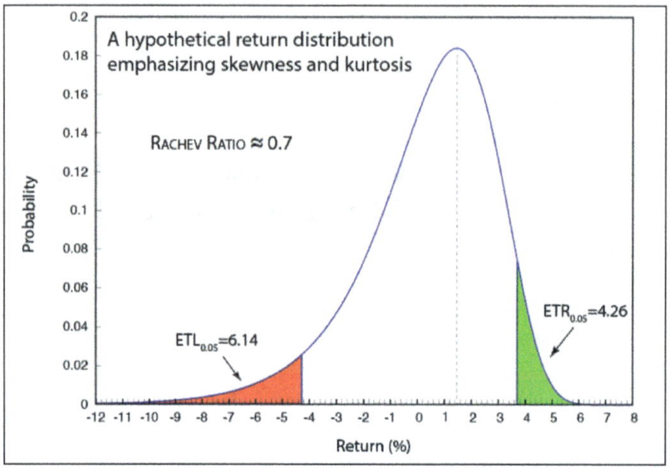

The 5% ETL and 5% ETR of a non-Gaussian return distribution. Although the most probable return is positive, the Rachev ratio is 0.7 < 1, which means that the excess loss is not balanced by the excess profit in the investment.

Example: In quantitative finance, non-Gaussian return distributions are common. The Rachev ratio, as a risk-adjusted performance measurement, characterizes the skewness and kurtosis of the return distribution.

RATE OF RETURN

A rate of return (RoR) is the net gain or loss on an investment over a specified time period, expressed as a percentage of the investment's initial cost. Gains on investments are defined as income received plus any capital gains realized on the sale of the investment.

Formula for RoR

$$Rate\,of\;return = [\frac{(Current\,value - Initial\,value)}{Initial\,value}] \times 100$$

This simple rate of return is sometimes called the basic growth rate, or alternatively, return on investment, or ROI. If you also consider the effect of the time value of money and inflation, the real rate of return can also be defined as the net amount of discounted cash flows received on an investment after adjusting for inflation.

What does the RoR Tell you?

A rate of return can be applied to any investment vehicle, from real estate to bonds, stocks, and fine art.

RoR works with any asset provided the asset is purchased at one point in time and produces cash flow at some point in the future. Investments are assessed based, in part, on past rates of return, which can be compared against assets of the same type to determine which investments are the most attractive.

RoR vs. Stocks and Bonds

The rate of return calculations for stocks and bonds are slightly different. Assume an investor buys a stock for $60 a share, owns the stock for five years, and earns a total amount of $10 in dividends. If the investor sells the stock for $80, his per share gain is $80 - $60 = $20. In addition, he has earned $10 in dividend income for a total gain of $20 + $10 = $30. The rate of return for the stock is thus $30 gain per share, divided by the $60 cost per share, or 50%.

On the other hand, consider an investor that pays $1,000 for a $1,000 par value 5% coupon bond. The investment earns $50 in interest income per year. If the investor sells the bond for $1,100 premium value and earns $100 in total interest, the investor's rate of return is the $100 gain on the sale plus $100 interest income divided by the $1,000 initial cost or 20%.

Real vs. Nominal Rates of Return

The simple rate of return used in the first example above with buying a home is considered a nominal rate of return since it does not account for the effect of inflation over time. Inflation reduces the purchasing power of money, and so $335,000 six years from now is not the same as $335,000 today.

Likewise, $250,000 today is not worth the same as $250,000 six years from now. Discounting is one way to account for the time value of money. Once the effect of inflation is taken into account, we call that the real rate of return (or the inflation-adjusted rate of return).

RoR vs. CAGR

A closely related concept to the simple rate of return is the compound annual growth rate, or CAGR. The CAGR is the mean annual rate of return of an investment over a specified period of time longer than one year, which means the calculation must factor in growth over multiple periods.

To calculate compound annual growth rate, we divide the value of an investment at the end of the period in question by its value at the beginning of that period, raise the result to the power of one divided by the number of holding periods, such as years, and subtract one from the subsequent result.

Example of how to use the RoR

The rate of return can be calculated for any investment, dealing with any kind of asset. Let's take the example of purchasing a home as a basic example for understanding how to calculate the RoR. Say that you buy a house for $250,000 (for simplicity let's assume you pay 100% cash).

Six years later, you decide to sell the house—maybe your family is growing and you need to move into a larger place. You are able to sell the house for $335,000, after deducting any realtor's fees and taxes. The simple rate of return on the purchase and sale of the house is as follows:

$$\frac{(335,000-250,000)}{250,000}\times 100 = 34\%$$

Now, what if, instead, you sold the house for less than you paid for it—say, for $187,500? The same equation can be used to calculate your loss, or the negative rate of return, on the transaction:

$$\frac{(187,500-250,000)}{250,000}\times 100=-25\%.$$

Example of IRR and DCF

The next step in understanding RoR over time is to account for the time value of money (TVM), which the CAGR ignores. Discounted cash flows take the earnings on investment and discount each of the cash flows based on a discount rate. The discount rate represents a minimum rate of return acceptable to the investor, or an assumed rate of inflation. In addition to investors, businesses use discounted cash flows to assess the profitability of their investments.

Assume, for example, a company is considering the purchase of a new piece of equipment for $10,000, and the firm uses a discount rate of 5%. After a $10,000 cash outflow, the equipment is used in the operations of the business and increases cash inflows by $2,000 a year for five years. The business applies present value table factors to the $10,000 outflow and to the $2,000 inflow each year for five years.

The $2,000 inflow in year five would be discounted using the discount rate at 5% for five years. If the sum of all the adjusted cash inflows and outflows is greater than zero, the investment is profitable. A positive net cash inflow also means the rate of return is higher than the 5% discount rate.

The rate of return using discounted cash flows is also known as the internal rate of return, or IRR. The internal rate of return is a discount rate that makes the net present value (NPV) of all cash flows from a particular project or investment equal to zero. IRR calculations rely on the same formula as NPV does and utilize the time value of money (using interest rates). The formula for IRR is as follows:

$$IRR = NPV = \sum_{t=1}^{T}\frac{C_t}{(1+r)^t} - C_0 = 0$$

where,

T=total number of time periods,

t=time period,

C_t=net cash inflow-outflows during a single period t,

C_0=baseline cash inflow-outflows,

r=discount rate.

ASSET TURNOVER RATIO

Asset turnover ratio determines the ability of a company to generate revenue from its assets by comparing the net sales of the company with the total assets. It is calculated by dividing net sales by average total assets of a company. In other words, it aims to measure sales as a percentage of average assets to determine how much sales is generated by each rupee of assets.

There can be several variants of this ratio depending on the type of assets considered to calculate the ratio, viz.

With fixed assets, there is fixed asset turnover ratio, and similar for current assets and total assets.

How to Interpret Asset Turnover Ratio?

Asset turnover ratio shows the comparison between the net sales and the average assets of the company. An asset turnover ratio of 3 means, for every 1 USD worth of assets, 3 USD worth of sale is generated. So, a higher asset turnover ratio is preferred as it reflects more efficient asset utilization. However, as with other ratios, the asset turnover ratio needs to be analyzed while keeping in Improve Asset Turnover Ratiomind the industry standards.

Some industries are designed to use assets in a better way than others. A higher asset turnover ratio implies that the company is more efficient at using its assets. A low asset turnover ratio, on the other hand, reflects the bad management of assets by the company. It may also indicate production or management problems.

Why is it Necessary to Improve Asset Turnover Ratio?

Since asset turnover ratio measures the efficiency of a company in managing its resources to generate its sales, it is very obvious that higher turnover ratios are preferred to reflect a better state of affairs at the company. This ratio gives an insight to the creditors and investors into the internal management of the company. A low asset turnover ratio will surely signify excess production, bad inventory management or poor collection practices. Thus, it is very important to improve the asset turnover ratio of a company.

How to Improve Asset Turnover Ratio

If a company analyzes that its asset turnover ratio is declining over time, there are several ways in which the asset turnover ratio can be improved:

Asset turnover

$$\text{Asset turnover} = \frac{\text{Revenue (sales)}}{\text{Net assets}}$$

Example

Revenue = £21,450k
Net assets = £4,455k
Asset turnover = 4.8 times

Increase Revenue

The easiest way to improve asset turnover ratio is to focus on increasing revenue. The assets might be properly utilized, but the sales could be slow resulting in a low asset turnover ratio. The company needs to increase its sales by more promotions and by quick movements of the finished goods.

Liquidate Assets

Obsolete or unused assets should be liquidated quickly. Assets, that are not used frequently, should be analyzed to see whether there is a sense in retaining those. Basically, the company should sell those assets that do not add to the bottom line regularly.

Leasing

Another efficient way is to lease assets, instead of buying them. Any leased equipment is not counted as a fixed asset.

Improve Efficiency

The asset turnover ratio could be low because of inefficient use of assets. The company should analyze how the assets are used and ways to improve the productivity of each asset. The output should increase without any significant increase in any other expenses.

Accelerate Accounts Receivables

The Slow collection of accounts receivables will lower the sales in the period, hence reducing the asset turnover ratio. The company should focus on quick collection practices. This can include outsourcing the delinquent accounts to a collection agency, hiring an employee just for collecting pending invoices and reducing the amount of time given to customers to pay.

Better Inventory Management

The company needs to check its inventory management to figure out the time spent in the movement of the goods throughout the process. If the company's delivery system is slow, there will be delays in getting the product to the customer and collecting the payment on time. The company should invest in technology and automate the order, billing and inventory systems. This will improve the sales and increase the asset turnover ratio.

RETURN OF CAPITAL

Return of capital occurs when an investor receives a portion of his or her original investment, and these payments are not considered income or capital gains from the investment.

Note that a return of capital reduces an investor's adjusted cost basis. Once the stock's adjusted cost basis has been reduced to zero, any subsequent return will be taxable as a capital gain.

Return of capital should not be confused with return on capital, where the latter is the return earned on invested capital (and is taxable).

How Return of Capital Works

When you make an investment, you put principal to work in hopes of generating a return—an amount known as the cost basis. When the principal is returned to an investor, that is the return on capital. Since it does not include gains (or losses) it is not considered taxable—it's like getting your original money back.

Some types of investments allow investors to first receive their capital back before receiving gains (or losses) for tax purposes. Examples include qualified retirement accounts like 401(k) plans or IRAs as well as cash accumulated inside of permanent life insurance policies. These products are examples of first-in-first-out (FIFO) in that you get your first dollar back before touching gains.

Cost basis is defined as an investor's total cost paid for an investment, and cost basis for a stock is adjusted for stock dividends and stock splits, as well as for the cost of commissions to purchase the stock. It's important for investors and financial advisors to track the cost basis of each investment so that any return of capital payments can be identified.

When an investor buys an investment and sells it for a gain, the taxpayer must report the capital gain on a personal tax return, and the sale price less the investment's cost basis is the capital gain on the sale. If an investor receives an amount that is less than or equal to the cost basis, the payment is a return of capital and not a capital gain.

Example of Stock Splits and Return of Capital

Assume, for example, that an investor buys 100 shares of XYZ common stock at $20 per share and the stock has a 2-for-1 stock split so that the investor's adjusted holdings total 200 shares at $10 per share. If the investor sells the shares for $15, the first $10 is considered a return of capital and is not taxed. The additional $5 per share is a capital gain and is reported on the personal tax return.

Factoring in Partnership Return of Capital

A partnership is defined as a business in which two or more people contribute assets and operate an entity to share in the profits. The parties create a partnership using a partnership agreement, though calculating return of capital for a partnership can be difficult.

A partner's interest in a partnership is tracked in the partner's capital account, and the account is increased by any cash or assets contributed by the partner, along with the partner's share of profits. The partner's interest is reduced by any withdrawals or guaranteed payments, and by the partner's share of partnership losses. A withdrawal up to the partner's capital account balance is considered a return of capital and is not a taxable event.

Once the entire capital account balance is paid to the partner, however, any additional payments are considered income to the partner and are taxed on the partner's personal tax return.

References

- What-is-financial-math: math.ncsu.edu, Retrieved 22 May 2019
- Banks, Erik; Siegel, Paul (2006). The options applications handbook: hedging and speculating techniques for professional investors. Mcgraw-Hill Professional. P. 263. ISBN 9780071453158. ISBN 0-07-145315-6

- Financial-Ratios, Ex-Gov, management: referenceforbusiness.com, Retrieved 23 February 2019
- Ilmanen, Antti (2011). Expected Returns: An Investor's Guide to Harvesting Market Rewards. John Wiley & Sons. ISBN 978-1119990727
- "How to Calculate Accounting Rate of Return | Tiduko.com | Never Stop Learning". Tiduko.com. Retrieved 2017-04-25
- Chapter 4 in Robert C. Higgins (2018). Analysis for Financial Management (12th Edition). Mcgraw-Hill. ISBN 978-1259918964
- "Earnings/Share $ - Morningstar.com Glossary E-F". Morningstar. Archived from the original on 2008-03-17. Retrieved 2008-03-02
- How-to-analyze-and-improve-asset-turnover-ratio, financial-analysis: efinancemanagement.com, Retrieved 13 March 2019
- Haug, Espen Gaardner (2007). The Complete Guide to Option Pricing Formulas. Mcgraw-Hill Professional. ISBN 9780071389976. ISBN 0-07-138997-0
- "Debt and deleveraging: The global credit bubble and its economic consequences". Mckinsey Global Institute. January 2010. Retrieved January 14, 2016
- Average-propensity-to-consume, accounting-dictionary: myaccountingcourse.com, Retrieved 2 February 2019
- Rachev, Svetlozar T.; Stoyanov, Stoyan V.; Fabozzi, Frank J. (2008). Advanced Stochastic Models, Risk Assessment, and Portfolio Optimization (1st ed.). Wiley. ISBN 978-0-470-05316-4.

4

Financial Capital

The money which is used to acquire items and equipment that are needed to offer services and build products is termed as financial capital. Some of the key types of financial capital are capital expenditure, working capital, share capital, fixed capital, etc. The diverse applications of these types of financial capital have been thoroughly discussed in this chapter.

Financial capital is the money, credit, and other forms of funding that build wealth. Individuals use financial capital to invest, by making a down payment on a home or creating a portfolio for retirement.

Capital in Business

In business accounting, capital is how companies invest in their businesses. They use financial capital to buy more equipment, buildings, or materials. Managers can't use the money to give themselves raises, increase dividends, or lower prices. They must use it to produce greater future gains. A business uses this investment capital to transform itself into something more profitable.

Types of Business Capital

There are three types of financial capital in the business world. The first is debt. Companies receive capital now that they pay back with interest. At first, many entrepreneurs borrow from family members or their credit cards.

As these businesses continue to grow, they become large enough to issue individual bonds to investors. The advantage of debt is that owners don't have to share the profits. The disadvantage is that they must repay the loan even if the business fails.

The second type of capital is equity. The business receives cash now from investors for a share of the profits later. Most entrepreneurs use their own cash to get started. They put their own equity into the business in hopes of receiving 100 percent of the return later. If the company is profitable, they forgo spending some of the cash flow now and instead invest it in the business.

A larger firm gets equity from partners, venture capitalists, or angel investors. It must give up some control and ownership of the business in exchange for the cash.

Once a company becomes really large and successful, it can get additional capital from issuing stocks. This is called an initial public offering. It means any investor can purchase the company's stock.

The third type of capital is specialty capital. It's extra cash flow that comes from managing the company's operations better.

Vendor financing is when the company's suppliers are willing to accept delayed payment for their goods or services.

A popular form of specialty capital is supply chain financing. It's like a pay-day loan for businesses. Banks lend the company the amount of an invoice, minus a fee. They receive payment for the loan when the invoice is paid.

Company finance managers also create extra capital through investing wisely. In a bull market, some companies make more money from their investments than from their operations.

Capital Structure

How a company creates and manages its capital is known as its capital structure. Most public companies use a combination of debt, through bonds, and equity, through various types of stock.

Many analysts use a simple formula, the debt-to-equity ratio, to determine how solid a company is. Companies with a ratio of 50 percent or more have more debt than equity. Analysts consider them to be highly leveraged and therefore riskier.

Another component of the capital structure is working capital. It's the cash on hand needed to run the company's operations. The formula is current assets minus current liabilities.

The working capital ratio is current assets divided by current liabilities. A working capital ratio of 2:1 means the company has enough liquidity to meet its immediate needs. If the ratio is higher, it means the company is not putting its money to use to build future profits.

Capital Markets

Easy access to capital has been one of the most important drivers of U.S. economic success. America has the world's most sophisticated capital markets.

The transparency of the U.S. stock market allows investors to gain up-to-date information about every aspect of companies in which they might invest.

The U.S. bond market is serviced by the best investment banks in the world. They have the experience to walk the company through the bond process. They have the financial clout to underwrite the bonds and guarantee their success. And they have the contacts among investors to sell the bonds for the best price.

Financial Capital versus Capital in Economics

Financial capital should not be confused with the economics term capital. It's one of the four factors of production that drive supply. That includes capital goods, such as machinery, equipment, and tools.

The other three factors are:

1. Natural resources, which are the raw materials.

2. Entrepreneurship or the drive to profit from innovation.
3. Labor, which refers to the number of employees. Labor includes human capital, which is the skills and abilities of people. Social capital is the value of a network of people.

A market economy automatically provides these components of supply to meet demand from consumers.

Sometimes financial capital is called the fifth factor of production, although that's not exactly accurate. It facilitates production by providing income to the owners of production, but it is not itself a factor of production.

Capital Structure Substitution Theory

In finance, the capital structure substitution theory (CSS) describes the relationship between earnings, stock price and capital structure of public companies. The CSS theory hypothesizes that managements of public companies manipulate capital structure such that earnings per share (EPS) are maximized. Managements have an incentive to do so because shareholders and analysts value EPS growth. The theory is used to explain trends in capital structure, stock market valuation, dividend policy, the monetary transmission mechanism, and stock volatility, and provides an alternative to the Modigliani–Miller theorem that has limited descriptive validity in real markets. The CSS theory is only applicable in markets where share repurchases are allowed. Investors can use the CSS theory to identify undervalued stocks.

The Formula

The CSS theory assumes that company managements can freely change the capital structure of the company – substituting bonds for stock or vice versa – on a day-to-day basis and in small denominations without paying transaction costs. Companies can decide to buy back one single share for the current market price P and finance this by issuing one extra corporate bond with face value P or do the reverse. In mathematical terms these substitutions are defined as:

$$\left[\frac{\partial D}{\partial n}\right]_{\mathrm{x,t}} = -P_{\mathrm{x,t}}$$

where D is the corporate debt and n the number of shares of company x at time t. The negative sign indicates that a reduction of the number of shares n leads to a larger debt D and vice versa. The earnings-per-share change when one share with price P is repurchased and one bond with face value P is issued:

1. The earnings that were 'allocated' to the one share that was repurchased are redistributed over the remaining outstanding shares, causing an increase in earnings per share of: E/n.
2. The earnings are reduced by the additional interest payments on the extra bond. As interest payments are tax-deductible the real reduction in earnings is obtained by multiplying with the tax shield. The additional interest payments thus reduce the EPS by: $P \cdot R \cdot [1-T]/n$.

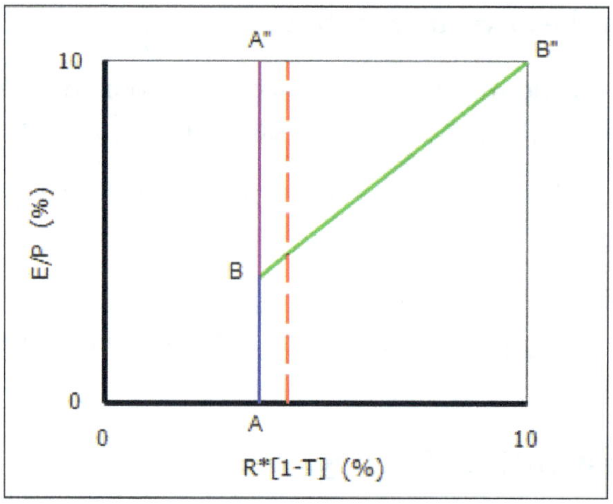

CSS equilibrium conditions: (1) companies fulfilling the equilibrium condition are found on B-B", (2) companies cannot issue debt with interest rates below 'Aaa' rated bonds on line A-A", (3) high valued companies with E/P<R*[1-T] are not expected to hold long term debt, pay no dividends and are found on line A-B.

Combining these two effects, the marginal change in EPS as function of the total number of outstanding shares becomes:

$$\left[\frac{\partial E}{\partial n}\right]_{x,t} = -\frac{E_{x,t}}{n} + \frac{P_{x,t}\, R_{x,t}\,[1-T]}{n}$$

where,

E is the earnings-per-share.

R is the nominal interest rate on corporate bonds.

T is the corporate tax rate.

EPS is maximized when substituting one more share for one bond or vice versa leads to no marginal change in EPS or:

$$\frac{\mathrm{E}_{x,t}}{P_{x,t}} = R_{x,t}\,[1-T]$$

This equilibrium condition is the central result of the CCS theory, linking stock prices to interest rates on corporate bonds.

Capital Structure

The two main capital structure theories as taught in corporate finance textbooks are the Pecking order theory and the Trade-off theory. The two theories make some contradicting predictions and for example Fama and French conclude: "In sum, we identify one scar on the tradeoff model (the negative relation between leverage and profitability), one deep wound on the pecking order (the large equity issues of small low-leverage growth firms)". The capital structure substitution theory has the potential to close these gaps. It predicts a negative relation between leverage and valuation (=reverse of earnings yield) which in turn can be linked to profitability. But it also predicts that high valued small growth firms will avoid the use of debt as especially for these companies the cost of borrowing ($R_{x,t}$) is higher than for large companies, which in turn has a negative effect on their EPS. This is consistent with the finding that "firms with higher current stock prices (relative to their past stock prices, book values or earnings) are more likely to issue equity rather than debt and repurchase debt rather than equity".

Asset Pricing

The equilibrium condition can be easily rearranged to an asset pricing formula:

$$P_{x,t} = \frac{E_{x,t}}{R_{x,t}[1-T]}$$

The CSS theory suggests that company share prices are not set by shareholders but by bondholders. As a result of active repurchasing or issuing of shares by company managements, equilibrium pricing is no longer a result of balancing shareholder demand and supply. In a way the CSS theory turns asset pricing upside-down, with bondholders setting share prices and shareholders determining company leverage. The asset pricing formula only applies to debt-holding companies. Some companies are offering stock screeners based on the CSS theory.

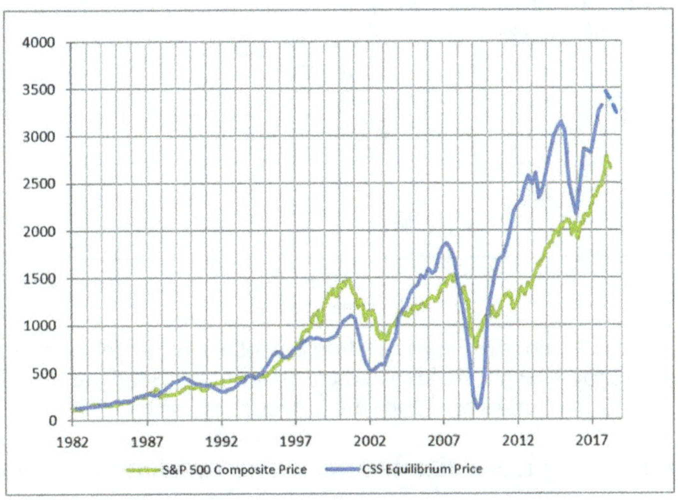

S&P 500 Composite Index compared to the CSS asset pricing formula - June 2018.

The asset pricing formula can be used on a market aggregate level as well. For the S&P 500 composite index, data from Shiller can be used for composite earnings level, and Federal Reserve Economic Data can be used for the interest rate on corporate bonds (BAA) and an estimate of corporate tax rate (by looking at the ratio of corporate profits and corporate profits after tax).

The resulting graph shows at what times the S&P 500 Composite was overpriced and at what times it was under-priced relative to the Capital Structure Substitution theory equilibrium. In times when the market is under-priced, corporate buyback programs will allow companies to drive up earnings-per-share, and generate extra demand in the stock market. In times when the index was under-priced relative to the model equilibrium, repurchase programs will be stopped and demand is reduced. Not surprisingly the index was overpriced in the period around the tech bubble. What may come more as a surprise that the market is currently (June 2018) not over-priced relative to the model as earnings are high and corporate interest rates are low. In order to reach equilibrium conditions the index would have to gain ~20% or about US$4.9 trillion in market capitalization.

Fed Model Equilibrium

In the US, a positive relationship between the average earnings yield of the S&P 500 index and government bond yields has been present over the last several decades. This relationship has become popular as the Fed model and states in its strongest form an equality between the one year forward looking E/P ratio or earnings yield and the 10-year government bond yield. The CSS equilibrium condition suggests that the Fed model is misspecified: the S&P 500 earnings yield is not in equilibrium with the government bond yield but with the average after-tax interest rate on corporate bonds. The CSS theory suggests that the Fed equilibrium was only observable after 1982, the year in which the United States Securities and Exchange Commission allowed open-market repurchases of shares.

Dividend Policy

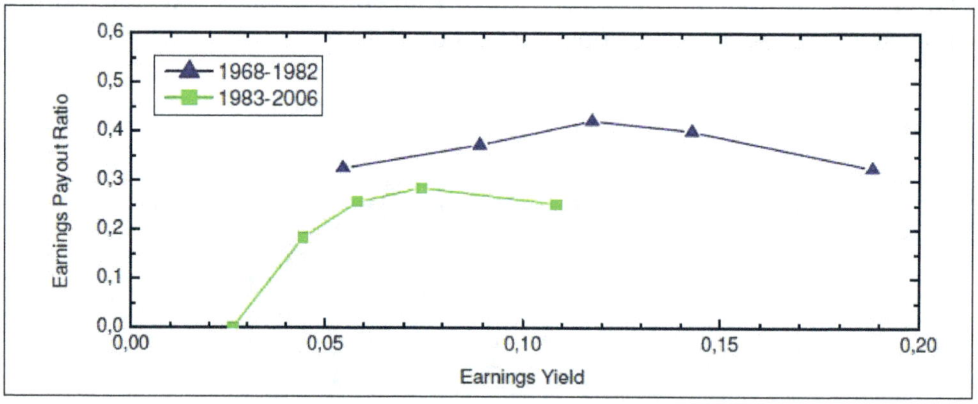

Earnings payout ratio (dividend) as a function of earnings yield for companies belonging to the S&P 500 index. Median values of dividend are used for the quintiles to reduce the influence of outliers.

It can be shown that repurchasing has a disadvantage over dividends for companies with a debt-equity ratio above,

$$\frac{D}{E_q} > \frac{1-T_C}{1-T_D} - 1$$

Under the assumptions described above, low valued, high leveraged companies with limited investment opportunities and a high profitability are expected to use dividends as the preferred means to distribute cash. From the earnings payout graph it can be seen that S&P 500 companies with a low earnings yield (=highly valued) on aggregate changed their dividend policy after 1982, when SEC rule 10b-18 was introduced which allowed public companies open-market repurchases of their own stock.

Monetary Policy

An unanticipated 25-basis-point cut in the federal funds rate target is associated with a 1% increase in broad stock indexes in the US. The CSS theory suggests that the monetary policy transmission mechanism is indirect but straightforward: a change in the federal funds rate affects the corporate bond market which in turn affects asset prices through the equilibrium condition.

Corporate Tax

One unexpected result of the CSS theory is possibly that a reduction in corporate tax rate would have a negative effect of share prices and valuation ratios. A reduction of the nominal corporate tax rate from 35% to 20% as proposed in the United States (Nov 2017) would lead to a -17% drop in share prices to reestablish equilibrium.

$$\frac{dP_{x,t}}{dT} = \frac{E_{x,t}}{R_{x,t}[T-1]^2}$$

Beta

The CSS equilibrium condition can be used to deduct a relationship for the beta of a company x at time t:

$$Beta_{x,t} = \overline{R_t} \cdot \left[\frac{P}{E}\right]_{x,t} \cdot [1-T]$$

where $\overline{R_t}$ is the market average interest rate on corporate bonds. The CSS theory predicts that companies with a low valuation and high leverage will have a *low* beta. This is counter-intuitive as traditional finance theory links leverage to risk, and risk to *high* beta.

Assumptions

- Managements of public companies manipulate capital structure such that earnings-per-share are maximized.
- Managements can freely change the capital structure of the company – substituting bonds for stock or vice versa – on a day-to-day basis and in small denominations.
- Shares can only be repurchased through open market buybacks. Information about share price is available on a daily basis.
- Companies pay a uniform corporate tax rate T.

CAPITAL EXPENDITURE

Capital expenditure or capital expense (capex or CAPEX) is the money a company spends to buy, maintain, or improve its fixed assets, such as buildings, vehicles, equipment, or land. It is considered a capital expenditure when the asset is newly purchased or when money is used towards extending the useful life of an existing asset, such as repairing the roof.

Capital expenditures contrast with operating expenses (opex), which are ongoing expenses that are inherent to the operation of the asset. Opex includes items like electricity or cleaning. The difference between opex and capex may not be immediately obvious for some expenses; for instance, repaving the parking lot may be thought of inherent to the operation of a shopping mall. The dividing line for items like these is that the expense is considered capex if the financial benefit of the expenditure extends beyond the current fiscal year.

Usage

Capital expenditures are the funds used to acquire or upgrade a company's fixed assets, such as expenditures towards property, plant, or equipment (PP&E). In the case when a capital expenditure constitutes a major financial decision for a company, the expenditure must be formalized at an annual shareholders meeting or a special meeting of the Board of Directors. In accounting, a capital expenditure is added to an asset account, thus increasing the asset's basis (the cost or value of an asset adjusted for tax purposes). capex is commonly found on the cash flow statement under "Investment in Plant, Property, and Equipment" or something similar in the Investing subsection.

Accounting Rules

For tax purposes, capex is a cost that cannot be deducted in the year in which it is paid or incurred and must be capitalized. The general rule is that if the acquired property's useful life is longer than the taxable year, then the cost must be capitalized. The capital expenditure costs are then amortized or depreciated over the life of the asset in question. Further to the above, capex creates or adds basis to the asset or property, which once adjusted, will determine tax liability in the event of sale or transfer. In the US, Internal Revenue Code 263 and 263A deal extensively with capitalization requirements and exceptions.

Included in capital expenditures are amounts spent on:

1. Acquiring fixed, and in some cases, intangible assets,
2. Repairing an existing asset so as to improve its useful life,
3. Upgrading an existing asset if it results in a superior fixture,
4. Preparing an asset to be used in business,
5. Restoring property or adapting it to a new or different use,
6. Starting or acquiring a new business.

An ongoing question for the accounting of any company is whether certain costs incurred should be *capitalized* or *expensed*. Costs which are expensed in a particular month simply appear on the financial statement as a cost incurred that month. Costs that are capitalized, however, are amortized or depreciated over multiple years. Capitalized expenditures show up on the balance sheet. Most ordinary business costs are either expensable or capitalizable, but some costs could be treated either way, according to the preference of the company. Capitalized interest if applicable is also spread out over the life of the asset.

The counterpart of capital expenditure is operating expense or operational cost (opex).

WORKING CAPITAL

Working capital (abbreviated WC) is a financial metric which represents operating liquidity available to a business, organisation or other entity, including governmental entities. Along with fixed assets such as plant and equipment, working capital is considered a part of operating capital. Gross working capital is equal to current assets. Working capital is calculated as current assets minus current liabilities. If current assets are less than current liabilities, an entity has a working capital deficiency, also called a working capital deficit.

A company can be endowed with assets and profitability but may fall short of liquidity if its assets cannot be readily converted into cash. Positive working capital is required to ensure that a firm is able to continue its operations and that it has sufficient funds to satisfy both maturing short-term debt and upcoming operational expenses. The management of working capital involves managing inventories, accounts receivable and payable, and cash.

Calculation

Working capital is the difference between current assets and current liabilities. It is not to be confused with trade working capital (the latter excluding cash).

The basic calculation of working capital is based on the entity's gross current assets.

Working capital = current asset + current liability.

Inputs

Current assets and current liabilities include four accounts which are of special importance. These accounts represent the areas of the business where managers have the most direct impact:

- Cash and cash equivalents (current asset),
- Accounts receivable (current asset),
- Inventory (current asset),
- Accounts payable (current liability).

The current portion of debt (payable within 12 months) is critical because it represents a short-term claim to current assets and is often secured by long-term assets. Common types of short-term debt are bank loans and lines of credit.

An increase in net working capital indicates that the business has either increased current assets (that it has increased its receivables or other current assets) or has decreased current liabilities—for example has paid off some short-term creditors, or a combination of both.

Working Capital Cycle

Working capital is computed as the sum of: Inventories (+) Trade receivables (+) Cash (-) Trade payables. The working capital cycle (WCC), also known as the cash conversion cycle, is the amount of time it takes to turn the net current assets and current liabilities into cash. The longer this cycle, the longer a business is tying up capital in its working capital without earning a return on it. Companies strive to reduce their working capital cycle by collecting receivables quicker or sometimes stretching accounts payable. Under certain conditions, minimizing working capital might adversely affect the company's ability to realize profitability, e.g. when unforeseen hikes in demand exceed inventories, or when a shortfall in cash restricts the company's ability to acquire trade or production inputs.

A positive working capital cycle balances incoming and outgoing payments to minimize net working capital and maximize free cash flow. For example, a company that pays its suppliers in 30 days but takes 60 days to collect its receivables has a working capital cycle of 30 days. This 30-day cycle usually needs to be funded through a bank operating line, and the interest on this financing is a carrying cost that reduces the company's profitability. Growing businesses require cash, and being able to free up cash by shortening the working capital cycle is the most inexpensive way to grow. Sophisticated buyers review closely a target's working capital cycle because it provides them with an idea of the management's effectiveness at managing their balance sheet and generating free cash flows.

As an absolute rule of funders, each of them wants to see a positive working capital. Such situation gives them the possibility to think that your company has more than enough current assets to cover financial obligations. Though, the same can't be said about the negative working capital. A large number of funders believe that businesses can't be sustainable with a negative working capital, which is a wrong way of thinking. In order to run a sustainable business with a negative working capital, it's essential to understand some key components.

- Approach your suppliers and persuade them to let you purchase the inventory on 1-2 month credit terms, but keep in mind that you must sell the purchased goods, to consumers, for money.
- Effectively monitor your inventory management, make sure that it's often refilled and with the help of your supplier, back up your warehouse.

Plus, big companies like McDonald's, Amazon, Dell, General Electric and Wal-Mart are using negative working capital.

Working Capital Management

Corporate finance.

Decisions relating to working capital and short-term financing are referred to as *working capital management.* These involve managing the relationship between a firm's short-term assets and its short-term liabilities. The goal of working capital management is to ensure that the firm is able to continue its operations and that it has sufficient cash flow to satisfy both maturing short-term debt and upcoming operational expenses.

A managerial accounting strategy focusing on maintaining efficient levels of both components of working capital, current assets, and current liabilities, in respect to each other. Working capital management ensures a company has sufficient cash flow in order to meet its short-term debt obligations and operating expenses.

Decision Criteria

By definition, working capital management entails short-term decisions—generally, relating to the next one-year period—which are "reversible". These decisions are therefore not taken on the same basis as capital-investment decisions (NPV or related, as above); rather, they will be based on cash flows, or profitability, or both.

- One measure of cash flow is provided by the cash conversion cycle—the net number of days from the outlay of cash for raw material to receiving payment from the customer. As a management tool, this metric makes explicit the inter-relatedness of decisions relating to inventories, accounts receivable and payable, and cash. Because this number effectively corresponds to the time that the firm's cash is tied up in operations and unavailable for other activities, management generally aims at a low net count.
- In this context, the most useful measure of profitability is return on capital (ROC). The result is shown as a percentage, determined by dividing relevant income for the 12 months by capital employed; return on equity (ROE) shows this result for the firm's shareholders. Firm value is enhanced when, and if, the return on capital, which results from working-capital management, exceeds the cost of capital, which results from capital investment decisions as above. ROC measures are therefore useful as a management tool, in that they link short-term policy with long-term decision making.
- Credit policy of the firm: Another factor affecting working capital management is credit policy of the firm. It includes buying of raw material and selling of finished goods either in cash or on credit. This affects the cash conversion cycle.

Management of Working Capital

Guided by the above criteria, management will use a combination of policies and techniques for the management of working capital. The policies aim at managing the *current assets* (generally cash and cash equivalents, inventories and debtors) and the short-term financing, such that cash flows and returns are acceptable.

- Cash management: Identify the cash balance which allows for the business to meet day to day expenses, but reduces cash holding costs.
- Inventory management: Identify the level of inventory which allows for uninterrupted production but reduces the investment in raw materials—and minimizes reordering costs

and hence increases cash flow. Besides this, the lead times in production should be lowered to reduce Work in Process (WIP) and similarly, the Finished Goods should be kept on as low level as possible to avoid overproduction—Debtors management. Identify the appropriate credit policy, i.e. credit terms which will attract customers, such that any impact on cash flows and the cash conversion cycle will be offset by increased revenue and hence Return on Capital (or *vice versa*).

- Short-term financing: Identify the appropriate source of financing, given the cash conversion cycle: the inventory is ideally financed by credit granted by the supplier; however, it may be necessary to utilize a bank loan (or overdraft), or to "convert debtors to cash" through "factoring".

EQUITY

In accounting, equity (or owner's equity) is the difference between the value of the assets and the value of the liabilities of something owned. It is governed by the following equation:

$$\text{equity} = \text{assets value} - \text{liabilities}$$

For example, if someone owns a car worth $15,000 (an asset), but owes $5,000 on a loan against that car (a liability), the car represents $10,000 of equity. Equity can be negative if liabilities exceed assets.

Shareholders' equity (or *stockholders' equity, shareholders' funds, shareholders' capital* or similar terms) represents the equity of a company as divided among shareholders of common or preferred stock. Negative shareholders' equity is often referred to as a shareholders' deficit.

Alternatively, equity can also refer to a corporation's share capital (capital stock in American English). The value of the share capital depends on the corporation's future economic prospects. For a company in liquidation proceedings, the equity is that which remains after all liabilities have been paid.

Owner's Equity

When starting a business, the owners fund the business to finance various operations. Under the model of a private limited company, the business and its owners are separate entities, so the business is considered to owe these funds to its owners as a liability in the form of share capital. Throughout the business's existence, the equity of the business will be the difference between its assets and debt liabilities; this is the accounting equation.

When a business liquidates during bankruptcy, the proceeds from the assets are used to reimburse creditors. The creditors are ranked by priority, with secured creditors being paid first, other creditors being paid next, and owners being paid last. Owner's equity (also known as risk capital or liable capital) is this remaining or residual claim against assets, which is paid only after all other creditors are paid. In such cases where even creditors could not get enough money to pay their bills, the owner's equity is reduced to zero because nothing is left to reimburse it.

Accounting

In financial accounting, owner's equity consists of the net assets of an entity. Net assets is the difference between the total assets and total liabilities. Equity appears on the balance sheet (also known as the statement of financial position), one of the four primary financial statements.

The assets of an entity can be both tangible and intangible items. Intangible assets include items such as brand names, copyrights or goodwill. Tangible assets include land, equipment, and cash. The types of accounts and their description that comprise the owner's equity depend on the nature of the entity and may include:

- Share capital (common stock),
- Preferred stock,
- Capital surplus,
- Retained earnings,
- Treasury stock,
- Stock options,
- Reserve.

Book Value

The book value of equity will change in the case of the following events:

- Changes in assets relative to liabilities. For example, a profitable firm receives more cash for its products than the cost at which it produced these goods, and so in the act of making a profit, increases its retained earnings, therefore its shareholders' equity.
- Issue of new equity in which the firm obtains new capital increases the total shareholders' equity.
- Share repurchases, in which a firm returns money to investors, reducing on the asset side its financial assets, and on the liability side the shareholders' equity. For practical purposes (except for its tax consequences), share repurchasing is similar to a dividend payment. Rather than giving money to all shareholders immediately in the form of a dividend payment, a share repurchase reduces the number of shares outstanding.
- Dividends paid out to preferred stock owners are considered an expense to be subtracted from net income(from the point of view of the common share owners).
- Other reasons - Assets and liabilities can change without any effect being measured in the Income Statement under certain circumstances; for example, changes in accounting rules may be applied retroactively. Sometimes assets bought and held in other countries get translated back into the reporting currency at different exchange rates, resulting in a changed value.

Shareholders' Equity

When the owners are shareholders, the interest can be called shareholders' equity; the accounting remains the same, and it is ownership equity spread out among shareholders. If all shareholders are in one and the same class, they share equally in ownership equity from all perspectives. However, shareholders may allow different priority ranking among themselves by the use of share classes and options. This complicates analysis for both stock valuation and accounting.

Shareholders' equity is obtained by subtracting total liabilities from the total assets of the shareholders. These assets and liabilities can be:

- Equity (beginning of year).
- + net income.
- − dividends.
- +/− gain/loss from changes to the number of shares outstanding.
- = Equity (end of year) if one gets more money during the year or less or not anything.

Equity Stock

Equity Investments

An equity investment generally refers to the buying and holding of shares of stock on a stock market by individuals and firms in anticipation of income from dividends and capital gains. Typically, equity holders receive voting rights, meaning that they can vote on candidates for the board of directors (shown on a diversification of the fund(s) and to obtain the skill of the professional fund managers in charge of the fund(s)). An alternative, which is usually employed by large private investors and pension funds, is to hold shares directly; in the institutional environment many clients who own portfolios have what are called segregated funds, as opposed to or in addition to the pooled mutual fund alternatives.

A calculation can be made to assess whether an equity is over or underpriced, compared with a long-term government bond. This is called the yield gap or Yield Ratio. It is the ratio of the dividend yield of an equity and that of the long-term bond.

Market Value of Equity Stock

In the stock market, market price per share does not correspond to the equity per share calculated in the accounting statements. Equity stock valuations, which are often much higher, are based on other considerations related to the business' operating cash flow, profits and future prospects; some factors are derived from the accounting statement.

Note that while accounting equity can potentially be negative, market price per share is never negative since equity shares represent ownership in limited liability companies. The principle of limited liability guarantees that a shareholder's losses may never exceed his investment.

Merton Model

Under the "Merton model", the value of stock equity is modeled as a call option on the value of the whole company (including the liabilities), struck at the nominal value of the liabilities; and the equity market value thus depends on the volatility of the market value of the company assets. The idea here is that, in general, equity may be viewed as a call option on the firm: since the principle of limited liability protects equity investors, shareholders would choose not to repay the firm's debt where the value of the firm is less than the value of the outstanding debt; where firm value is greater than debt value, the shareholders would choose to repay - i.e. exercise their option - and not to liquidate.

This is the first example of a "structural model", where bankruptcy is modeled using a microeconomic model of the firm's capital structure - it treats bankruptcy as a continuous probability of default, where, on the random occurrence of default, the stock price of the defaulting company is assumed to go to zero. This microeconomic approach, to some extent, allows us to answer the question "what are the economic causes of default?" (Structural models are distinct from "reduced form models" - such as Jarrow–Turnbull - where bankruptcy is modeled as a statistical process).

Equity in Real Estate

The notion of equity as it relates to real estate derives from the concept called equity of redemption. This equity is a property right valued at the difference between the market value of the property and the amount of any mortgage or other encumbrance.

THIN CAPITALISATION

A company is said to be thinly capitalised when the level of its debt is much greater than its equity capital, i.e. its gearing, or leverage, is very high. An entity's debt-to-equity funding is sometimes expressed as a ratio. For example, a gearing ratio of 1.5:1 means that for every $1 of equity the entity has $1.5 of debt.

A high gearing ratio can create problems for:

- Creditors, which bear the solvency risk of the company.
- Revenue authorities, which are concerned about excessive interest claims.

Credit Risk

If the shareholders have introduced only a nominal amount of paid-up share capital, then the company has lower financial reserves with which to meet its obligations. If all or most of the company's capital comes from debt, which (unlike equity) needs to be serviced, and ultimately repaid, it means that the providers of capital are ultimately competing with the company's trade creditors for the same capital resources.

In general, most common law countries tend not to employ thin capitalisation rules in relation to raising and maintenance of capital. However, a number of civil law jurisdictions do.

However, in almost all jurisdictions there are certain types of regulated entity which require a certain amount, or a certain proportion, of paid-up share capital to be licensed to trade. The most common examples of this are banks and insurance companies. This is because if such companies were to fail and go into liquidation the economic effect of such failures can lead to a domino effect, which can have catastrophic consequences for other businesses and, ultimately, national economies.

Tax Issues

Even where countries' corporate laws permit companies to be thinly capitalised, revenue authorities in those countries will often limit the amount that a company can claim as a tax deduction on interest, particularly when it receives loans at non-commercial rates (e.g. from connected parties). However, some countries simply disallow interest deductions above a certain level from all sources when the company is considered to be too highly geared under applicable tax regulations.

Some tax authorities limit the applicability of thin capitalisation rules to corporate groups with foreign entities to avoid "base erosion and profit shifting" to other jurisdictions. The United States "earnings stripping" rules are an example. Hong Kong protects tax revenue by prohibiting payers from claiming tax deductions for interest paid to foreign entities, thus eliminating the possibility of using thin capitalisation to shift income to a lower-tax jurisdiction.

Thin capitalisation rules determine how much of the interest paid on corporate debt is deductible for tax purposes. Such rules are of interest to private-equity firms, which use significant amounts of debt to finance leveraged buyouts, and in the context of strategic acquisitions, where the purchaser wishes to push debt into higher taxed countries with significant pre-tax income.

SHARE CAPITAL

A corporation's share capital or capital stock is the portion of a corporation's equity that has been obtained by the issue of shares in the corporation to a shareholder, usually for cash. "Share capital" may also denote the number and types of shares that compose a corporation's share structure.

In a strict accounting sense, share capital is the nominal value of issued shares (that is, the sum of their par values, as indicated on share certificates). If the allocation price of shares is greater than their par value, as in a rights issue, the shares are said to be sold at a premium (variously called share premium, additional paid-in capital or paid-in capital in excess of par). Commonly, the share capital is the total of the aforementioned nominal share capital and the premium share capital. Conversely, when shares are issued below par, they are said to be issued at a discount or part-paid.

Sometimes, shares are allocated in exchange for non-cash consideration, most commonly when corporation A acquires corporation B for shares (new shares issued by corporation A). Here the share capital is increased to the par value of the new shares, and the merger reserve is increased to the balance of the price of corporation B.

In practice, the concept of "par value" has very little meaning, since shares usually represent a residual claim; they do not endow their owners with a claim toward any fixed sum of money. In some jurisdictions, share par values have been either abolished or made optional, so a corporation can issue shares having no par value. In that case, from an accounting perspective, all of the corporation's share capital is premium.

Besides its meaning in accounting, described above, "share capital" may also describe the number and types of shares that compose a corporation's share structure. A corporation might have an "outstanding share capital" of 500,000 shares (the "structure" usage); it has received for them a total of 2 million dollars, which is the "share capital" in the balance sheet (the accounting usage).

The legal aspects of share capital are mostly dealt with in a jurisdiction's corporate law system. An example of such an issue is that when a company allocates new shares, it must do so without inequitably diluting its existing shareholders.

Legal Capital

Legal capital is a concept used in UK company law, EU company law, and various other corporate law jurisdictions to refer to the sum of assets contributed to a company by shareholders when they are issued shares. The law often requires that this capital is maintained, and that dividends are not paid when a company is not showing a profit above the level of historically recorded legal capital.

Minimum Capital

In the UK, a public limited company must have a minimum legal capital of £50,000. There is no such requirement for a private company.

Classes of Shares

The share capital may be made up of more than one class of shares. Different classes of shares include ordinary shares, preference shares, growth shares and differed shares. Shares will be a separate class if the rights attached to them differ from the rights attached to other shares in the capital of the company.

FIXED CAPITAL

In economics and accounting, fixed capital is any kind of real, physical asset that is used in the production of a product but is not used up in the production. It contrasts with circulating capital such as raw materials, operating expenses and the like. It was first theoretically analyzed in some depth by the economist David Ricardo.

Thus fixed capital is that portion of the total capital outlay that is invested in fixed assets (such as land improvements, buildings, vehicles, plant and equipment), that stay in the business almost permanently—or at the very least, for more than one accounting period. Fixed assets can be *purchased* by a business, in which case the business owns them. They can also be *leased, hired* or *rented*, if that is cheaper or more convenient, or if owning the fixed asset is practically impossible (for legal or technical reasons).

Refining the classical distinction between fixed and circulating capital in Das Kapital, Karl Marx emphasizes that the distinction is really purely relative, i.e. it refers only to the comparative rotation speeds (turnover time) of different types of physical capital assets. Fixed capital also "circulates", except that the circulation time is much longer, because a fixed asset may be held for 5, 10 or 20 years before it has yielded its value and is discarded for its salvage value. A fixed asset may also be resold and re-used, which often happens with vehicles and planes.

In national accounts, fixed capital is conventionally defined as the stock of tangible, durable fixed assets owned or used by resident enterprises for more than one year. This includes plant, machinery, vehicles and equipment, installations and physical infrastructures, the value of land improvements, and buildings.

The European system of national and regional accounts (ESA95) explicitly includes produced intangible assets (e.g. mineral exploitation, computer software, copyright protected entertainment, literary and artistics originals) within the definition of fixed assets.

Land itself is not included in the statistical concept of fixed capital, even though it is a fixed asset. The main reason is that land is not regarded as a product (a reproducible good). But the value of land improvements is included in the statistical concept of fixed capital, being regarded as the creation of value-added through production.

Estimating the Value

Attempts have been made to estimate the value of the stock of fixed capital for the whole economy using direct enterprise surveys of "book value", administrative business records, tax assessments, and data on gross fixed capital formation, price inflation and depreciation schedules. A pioneer in this area was the economist Simon Kuznets.

The so-called "perpetual inventory method" (PIM) used to estimate fixed capital stocks was invented by Raymond W. Goldsmith in 1951 and subsequently used around the world. The basic idea of the PIM method is, that one starts off from a benchmark asset figure, and adds on the net additions to fixed assets year by year (using gross fixed capital formation data), while deducting annual depreciation, all data being adjusted for price inflation using a capital expenditure price index. In this way, one obtains a time series of annual fixed capital stocks. This data series can also be modified further with various other adjustments for prices, asset lifetimes etc. (several variants of the PIM approach are nowadays used by economic historians and statisticians).

However, it is widely acknowledged that it is extremely difficult to obtain any accurate measurement of the value of fixed capital, especially because even the owner himself or herself may not know what the assets are currently "worth". What they are worth may become apparent only at the point where they are definitely sold for a price. Some valuations for fixed assets may refer to historic cost (acquisition cost) or book value, others to current replacement cost, current sale value in the market, or scrap value.

The depreciation write-off permitted for tax purposes may also diverge from so-called "economic depreciation" or "real" depreciation rates. Economic depreciation rates are calculated on the basis of the observed average market prices that depreciated assets at different ages actually sell for.

Sometimes statisticians try to estimate the average "service lives" of fixed assets as a basis for calculating depreciation and scrap values, based on the observed length of time that fixed assets are actually held and used by their owners who own the business.

Almost always, the capital stock estimate which statisticians arrive at is a theoretical estimate based on a variety of data sources, and it does not correspond to the historical cost of fixed assets nor to actual depreciation write-offs. However, it is believed to be a more accurate representation of the true value of the fixed capital stock.

Investment Risk

A business executive who invests in or accumulates fixed capital is tying up wealth in a fixed asset, hoping to make a future profit. Thus, such an investment usually implies a risk. Sometimes depreciation write-offs are also viewed partly as a compensation for this risk. Often leasing or renting a fixed asset (such as a vehicle) rather than buying it is preferred by enterprises because the cost of using it is lowered thereby, and the real owner may be able to obtain special tax advantages.

Sources of Funding for Fixed Capital Investment

An owner can obtain funding for purchase of fixed capital assets from the aptly named capital market, where loans are given on a long-term basis. Funding can also come from reserve funds, the selling of shares, and the issuing of debentures, bonds or other promissory notes.

Factors which Influence Fixed-capital Requirements

- The nature of the undertaking: The nature of the business certainly plays a role in determining fixed capital requirements. A florist, for example, needs less fixed capital than a vehicle-assembly factory.
- The size of the undertaking: A general rule applies: the bigger the business, the higher the need for fixed capital.
- The stage of development of the undertaking: The requirement of capital for a new undertaking is usually greater than that needed for an established business that has reached optimum size.

COST OF CAPITAL

The cost of capital is the cost of a company's funds (both debt and equity), or, from an investor's point of view "the required rate of return on a portfolio company's existing securities". It is used to evaluate new projects of a company. It is the minimum return that investors expect for providing capital to the company, thus setting a benchmark that a new project has to meet.

For an investment to be worthwhile, the expected return on capital has to be higher than the cost of capital. Given a number of competing investment opportunities, investors are expected to put their capital to work in order to maximize the return. In other words, the cost of capital is the rate of return that capital could be expected to earn in the best alternative investment of equivalent risk; this is the opportunity cost of capital. If a project is of similar risk to a company's average business activities it is reasonable to use the company's average cost of capital as a basis for the evaluation or cost of capital is a firm's cost of raising funds. However, for projects outside the core business of the company, the current cost of capital may not be the appropriate yardstick to use, as the risks of the businesses are not the same.

A company's securities typically include both debt and equity, one must therefore calculate both the cost of debt and the cost of equity to determine a company's cost of capital. Importantly, both cost of debt and equity must be forward looking, and reflect the expectations of risk and return in the future. This means, for instance, that the past cost of debt is not a good indicator of the actual forward looking cost of debt.

Once cost of debt and cost of equity have been determined, their blend, the weighted average cost of capital (WACC), can be calculated. This WACC can then be used as a discount rate for a project's projected free cash flows to the firm.

Example:

Suppose a company considers taking on a project or investment of some kind, for example installing a new piece of machinery in one of their factories. Installing this new machinery will cost money; paying the technicians to install the machinery, transporting the machinery, buying the parts and so on. This new machinery is also expected to generate new profit (otherwise, assuming the company is interested in profit, the company would not consider the project in the first place). So the company will finance the project with two broad categories of finance: issuing debt, by taking out a loan or other debt instrument such as a bond; and issuing equity, usually by issuing new shares.

The new debt-holders and shareholders who have decided to invest in the company to fund this new machinery will expect a return on their investment: debt-holders require interest payments and shareholders require dividends (or capital gain from selling the shares after their value increases). The idea is that some of the profit generated by this new project will be used to repay the debt and satisfy the new shareholders.

Suppose that one of the sources of finance for this new project was a bond (issued at par value) of $200,000 with an interest rate of 5%. This means that the company would issue the bond to some willing investor, who would give the $200,000 to the company which it could then use, for a specified period of time (the term of the bond) to finance its project. The company would also make regular payments to the investor of 5% of the original amount they invested ($10,000), at a yearly or monthly rate depending on the specifics of the bond (these are called coupon payments). At the end of the lifetime of the bond (when the bond matures), the company would return the $200,000 they borrowed.

Suppose the bond had a lifetime of ten years and coupon payments were made yearly. This means that the investor would receive $10,000 every year for ten years, and then finally their $200,000 back at the end of the ten years. From the investor's point of view, their investment of $200,000 would be regained at the end of the ten years (entailing zero gain or loss), but they would have *also* gained from the coupon payments; the $10,000 per year for ten years would amount to a net gain of $100,000 to the investor. This is the amount that compensates the investor for taking the risk of investing in the company (since, if it happens that the project fails completely and the company goes bankrupt, there is a chance that the investor does not get their money back).

This net gain of $100,000 was paid by the company to the investor as a reward for investing their money in the company. In essence, this is how much the company paid to borrow $200,000. It was the *cost* of raising $200,000 of new capital. So to raise $200,000 the company had to pay $100,000 out of their profits; thus we say that the *cost of debt* in this case was 50%.

Theoretically, if the company were to raise further capital by issuing more of the same bonds, the new investors would also expect a 50% return on their investment (although in practice the required return varies depending on the size of the investment, the lifetime of the loan, the risk of the project and so on).

The cost of equity follows the same principle: the investors expect a certain return from their investment, and the company must pay this amount in order for the investors to be willing to invest in the company. (Although the cost of equity is calculated differently since dividends, unlike interest payments, are not necessarily a fixed payment or a legal requirement).

Cost of Debt

When companies borrow funds from outside lenders, the interest paid on these funds is called the cost of debt. The cost of debt is computed by taking the rate on a risk-free bond whose duration matches the term structure of the corporate debt, then adding a default premium. This default premium will rise as the amount of debt increases (since, all other things being equal, the risk rises as the cost of debt rises). Since in most cases debt expense is a deductible expense, the cost of debt is computed on an after-tax basis to make it comparable with the cost of equity (earnings are taxed as well). Thus, for profitable firms, debt is discounted by the tax rate. The formula can be written as:

$$K_D = (R_f + \text{credit risk rate})(1 - T),$$

where T is the corporate tax rate and R_f is the risk free rate.

Cost of Equity

The cost of equity is *inferred* by comparing the investment to other investments (comparable) with similar risk profiles. It is commonly computed using the capital asset pricing model formula:

Cost of equity = Risk free rate of return + Premium expected for risk

Cost of equity = Risk free rate of return + Beta × (market rate of return – risk free rate of return)

where,

Beta = sensitivity to movements in the relevant market. Thus in symbols we have:

$$E_s = R_f + \beta_s(R_m - R_f)$$

where,

E_s is the expected return for a security,

R_f is the expected risk-free return in that market (government bond yield),

β_s is the sensitivity to market risk for the security,

R_m is the historical return of the stock market,

$(R_m - R_f)$ is the risk premium of market assets over risk free assets.

The risk free rate is the yield on long term bonds in the particular market, such as government bonds.

An alternative to the estimation of the required return by the capital asset pricing model as above, is the use of the Fama–French three-factor model.

Expected Return

The expected return (or required rate of return for investors) can be calculated with the "dividend capitalization model", which is:

$$K_{cs} = \frac{\text{Dividend}_{\text{Payment/Share}}(1+\text{Growth})}{\text{Price}_{\text{Market}}} + \text{Growth}_{\text{rate}}.$$

Comments:

The models state that investors will expect a return that is the risk-free return plus the security's sensitivity to market risk (β) times the market risk premium.

The risk premium varies over time and place, but in some developed countries during the twentieth century it has averaged around 5% whereas in the emerging markets, it can be as high as 7%. The equity market real capital gain return has been about the same as annual real GDP growth. The capital gains on the Dow Jones Industrial Average have been 1.6% per year over the period 1910-2005. The dividends have increased the total "real" return on average equity to the double, about 3.2%.

The sensitivity to market risk (β) is unique for each firm and depends on everything from management to its business and capital structure. This value cannot be known "ex ante" (beforehand), but can be estimated from *ex post* (past) returns and past experience with similar firms.

Cost of Retained Earnings/Cost of Internal Equity

Note that retained earnings are a component of equity, and, therefore, the cost of retained earnings (internal equity) is equal to the cost of equity as explained above. Dividends (earnings that are paid to investors and not retained) are a component of the return on capital to equity holders, and influence the cost of capital through that mechanism.

Cost of internal equity = [(next year's dividend per share/(current market price per share - flotation costs)] + growth rate of dividends)].

Weighted Average Cost of Capital

The weighted cost of capital (WACC) is used in finance to measure a firm's cost of capital. WACC is not dictated by management. Rather, it represents the minimum return that a company must earn on an existing asset base to satisfy its creditors, owners, and other providers of capital, or they will invest elsewhere.

The total capital for a firm is the value of its equity (for a firm without outstanding warrants and options, this is the same as the company's market capitalization) plus the cost of its debt (the cost of debt should be continually updated as the cost of debt changes as a result of interest rate changes). Notice that the "equity" in the debt to equity ratio is the market value of all equity, not the shareholders' equity on the balance sheet. To calculate the firm's weighted cost of capital, we must first calculate the costs of the individual financing sources: Cost of Debt, Cost of Preference Capital, and Cost of Equity Cap.

Calculation of WACC is an iterative procedure which requires estimation of the fair market value of equity capital if the company is not listed. The Adjusted Present Value method (APV) is much easier to use in this case as it separates the value of the project from the value of its financing program.

Factors that can affect Cost of Capital

Below are a list of factors that might affect the cost of capital:

Capital Structure

Because of tax advantages on debt issuance, it will be cheaper to issue debt rather than new equity (this is only true for profitable firms, tax breaks are available only to profitable firms). At some point, however, the cost of issuing new debt will be greater than the cost of issuing new equity. This is because adding debt increases the default risk - and thus the interest rate that the company must pay in order to borrow money. By utilizing too much debt in its capital structure, this increased default risk can also drive up the costs for other sources (such as retained earnings and preferred stock) as well. Management must identify the "optimal mix" of financing – the capital structure where the cost of capital is minimized so that the firm's value can be maximized.

The Thomson Financial league tables show that global debt issuance exceeds equity issuance with a 90 to 10 margin.

The structure of capital should be determined considering the weighted average cost of capital.

Accounting Information

Lambert, Leuz & Verrecchia have found that the quality of accounting information can affect a firm's cost of capital, both directly and indirectly.

Breakpoint of Marginal Cost of Capital

Modigliani–Miller theorem

If there were no tax advantages for issuing debt, and equity could be freely issued, Miller and

Modigliani showed that, under certain assumptions (no tax), the value of a levered firm and the value of an unlevered firm should be the same.

WEIGHTED AVERAGE COST OF CAPITAL

The weighted average cost of capital (WACC) is the rate that a company is expected to pay on average to all its security holders to finance its assets. The WACC is commonly referred to as the firm's cost of capital. Importantly, it is dictated by the external market and not by management. The WACC represents the minimum return that a company must earn on an existing asset base to satisfy its creditors, owners, and other providers of capital, or they will invest elsewhere.

Companies raise money from a number of sources: common stock, preferred stock, straight debt, convertible debt, exchangeable debt, warrants, options, pension liabilities, executive stock options, governmental subsidies, and so on. Different securities, which represent different sources of finance, are expected to generate different returns. The WACC is calculated taking into account the relative weights of each component of the capital structure. The more complex the company's capital structure, the more laborious it is to calculate the WACC.

Companies can use WACC to see if the investment projects available to them are worthwhile to undertake.

Calculation

In general, the WACC can be calculated with the following formula:

$$\text{WACC} \quad \frac{\sum r_i \cdot MV_i}{\sum MV}$$

where N is the number of sources of capital (securities, types of liabilities); r_i is the required rate of return for security i; and MV_i is the market value of all outstanding securities i.

In the case where the company is financed with only equity and debt, the average cost of capital is computed as follows:

$$\text{WACC} = \frac{D}{D+E} K_d + \frac{E}{D+E} K_e$$

where D is the total debt, E is the total shareholder's equity, K_d is the cost of debt, and K_e is the cost of equity. The market values of debt and equity should be used when computing the weights in the WACC formula.

Tax Effects

Tax effects can be incorporated into this formula. For example, the WACC for a company financed by one type of shares with the total market value of MV_e and cost of equity R_e and one type of bonds with the total market value of MV_d and cost of debt R_d, in a country with corporate tax rate t, is calculated as:

$$\text{WACC} = \frac{MV_e}{MV_d + MV_e} \cdot R_e + \frac{MV_d}{MV_d + MV_e} \cdot R_d \cdot (1 - t)$$

This calculation can vary significantly due to the existence of many plausible proxies for each element. As a result, a fairly wide range of values for the WACC of a given firm in a given year may appear defensible.

Components

Debt

Advantages:

- No loss of control (voting rights),
- Upper limit is placed on share of profits,
- Flotation costs are typically lower than equity,
- Interest expense is tax deductible.

Disadvantages:

- Legally obliged to make payments no matter how tight the funds on hand are,
- In the case of bonds, full face value comes due at one time,
- Taking on more debt = taking on more financial risk (more systematic risk) requiring higher cash flows.

The firm's debt component is stated as k_d and since there is a tax benefit from interest payments then the after tax WACC component is $k_d(1\text{-}T)$; where T is the tax rate.

Equity

Advantages:

- No legal obligation to pay (depends on class of shares),
- No maturity,
- Lower financial risk,
- It could be cheaper than debt, with good prospects of profitability.

Disadvantages:

- New equity dilutes current ownership share of profits and voting rights (control),
- Cost of underwriting equity is much higher than debt,
- Too much equity = target for a leveraged buy-out by another firm,
- No tax shield, dividends are not tax deductible, and may exhibit double-taxation.

3 ways of calculating KK_e:

- Capital Asset Pricing Model,
- Dividend Discount Method,
- Bond Yield Plus Risk Premium Approach.

Cost of new equity should be the adjusted cost for any underwriting fees terme flotation costs (F).

$$K_e = D_1/P_0(1\text{-}F) + g$$

where, F = flotation costs, D_1 is dividends, P_0 is price of the stock, and g is the growth rate.

Weighted average cost of capital equation:

$$WACC= (W_d)[(K_d)(1\text{-}t)]+ (W_{pf})(K_{pf})+ (W_{ce})(K_{ce}).$$

Marginal Cost of Capital Schedule

Marginal cost of capital (MCC) schedule or an investment opportunity curve is a graph that relates the firm's Weighted cost of each unit of capital to the total amount of new capital raised. The first step in preparing the MCC schedule is to rank the projects using internal rate of return (IRR). The higher the IRR the better off a project is.

CAPITAL SURPLUS

A capital surplus is the additional paid-in capital in excess of par value that an investor pays when buying shares from an issuing entity. This amount represents the difference between the market value of shares and their par value. The term is is no longer commonly used; instead, the concept is now called additional paid-in capital in the accounting literature.

Par value was originally the price at which a company's shares were initially offered for sale, so that prospective investors could be assured that the company would not issue shares at a price below the par value. However, par value is no longer required by some states; in other states, companies are allowed to set the par value at a minimal amount, such as $0.01 per share. The result is that nearly all of the price paid for a share of stock is recorded as additional paid-in capital (or capital surplus, to use the older term). If a company issues shares that have no stated par value at all, then there is no capital surplus; instead, the funds are recorded in the common stock account.

For example, if ABC Company were to sell 100 shares of its $1 par value common stock for $9 per share, it would record $100 of the $900 in total proceeds in the Common Stock account and $800 in the Additional Paid-in Capital account. In earlier days, the $800 entry to the Additional Paid-In Capital account would instead have been made to the Capital Surplus account.

Thus, if the capital surplus term were still used, a company would acquire a capital surplus by selling its stock to investors at a price above the designated par value of the stock, with the incremental amount above the par value being identified as capital surplus.

References

- What-is-financial-capital-3305825: thebalance.com, Retrieved 5 March 2019
- Godwin, Steve (April 25, 2015). Protecting Your Money in the Stock Market: It's a Herd Game!. Xlibris. ISBN 978-1503558427
- Hovakimian, A.; Opler, T.; Titman, S. (2001). "The Debt-Equity Choice". Journal of Financial and Quantitative Analysis. 36 (1): 1–24. Doi:10.2307/2676195. JSTOR 2676195
- What-is-a-capital-surplus: accountingtools.com, Retrieved 3 May 2019
- Hervé Stolowy; Michel Lebas (January 2006). Financial Accounting and Reporting: A Global Perspective. Cengage Learning EMEA. P. 42. ISBN 1-84480-250-7
- Lambert, R. , Leuz, C. And Verrecchia, R. E. (2007), Accounting Information, Disclosure, and the Cost of Capital. Journal of Accounting Research, 45: 385-420. Doi:10.1111/j.1475-679X.2007.00238.x

5

Financial Statements

The formal records of the financial activities and positions of a business, entity or person are referred to as financial statements. The four basic financial statements are balance sheet, income statement, cash flow statement and statement of changes in equity. The topics elaborated in this chapter will help in gaining a better perspective about these types of financial statements.

Financial statements are written records that convey the business activities and the financial performance of a company. Financial statements are often audited by government agencies, accountants, firms, etc. to ensure accuracy and for tax, financing, or investing purposes. Financial statements include:

- Balance sheet,
- Income statement,
- Cash flow statement.

Using Financial Statement Information

Investors and financial analysts rely on financial data to analyze the performance of a company and make predictions about its future direction of the company's stock price. One of the most important resources of reliable and audited financial data is the annual report, which contains the firm's financial statements.

The financial statements are used by investors, market analysts, and creditors to evaluate a company's financial health and earnings potential. The three major financial statement reports are the balance sheet, income statement, and statement of cash flows.

Understanding Balance Sheets

The balance sheet provides an overview of a company's assets, liabilities, and stockholders' equity as a snapshot in time. The date at the top of the balance sheet tells you when the snapshot was taken, which is generally the end of the fiscal year.

The Balance Sheet Formula

Assets=(Liabilities+Owner's Equity)

The balance sheet totals will be calculated already, but here's how you identify them.

- Locate total assets on the balance sheet for the period.
- Total all liabilities, which should be a separate listing on the balance sheet.
- Locate total shareholder's equity and add the number to total liabilities.
- Total assets should equal the total of liabilities and total equity.

Data From the Balance Sheet

The balance sheet identifies how assets are funded, either with liabilities, such as debt, or stockholders' equity, such as retained earnings and additional paid-in capital. Assets are listed on the balance sheet in order of liquidity.

Liabilities are listed in the order in which they will be paid. Short-term or current liabilities are expected to be paid within the year, while long-term or noncurrent liabilities are debts expected to be paid in over one year.

Items Included in the Balance Sheet

Below are examples of items listed on the balance sheet.

Assets

- Cash and cash equivalents are liquid assets, which may include Treasury bills and certificates of deposit.
- Accounts receivables are the amount of money owed to the company by its customers for the sale of its product and service.
- Inventory.

Liabilities

- Debt including long-term debt.
- Rent, tax, and utilities.
- Wages payable.
- Dividends payable.

Shareholders' Equity

- Shareholders' equity is a company's total assets minus its total liabilities. Shareholders' equity represents the amount of money that would be returned to shareholders if all of the assets were liquidated and all of the company's debt was paid off.
- Retained earnings are part of shareholders' equity and are the percentage of net earnings that were not paid to shareholders as dividends.

Example of a Balance Sheet

Below is a portion of Exxon Mobil Corporation's (XOM) balance sheet as of September 30, 2018.

- Total assets were $354,628 (highlighted in green).
- Total liabilities were $157,797 (1st red highlighted area).
- Total equity was $196,831 (in red).
- Total liabilities and equity were $354,628, which equals the total assets for the period.

EXXON MOBIL CORPORATION CONDENSSED CONSOLIDATED BALANCE SHEET (millions of dollar)	
	Sept. 30, 2018
Assets	
Current assets	
Cash and cash equivalents	5,669
Notes and accounts receivable-net inventories	27,880
Crude oil, products and merchandise	14,617
Materials and supplies	4,144
Other Current Assets	1,665
Total current assets	53,975
Investments advances and long term receivables	40,427
Property, plant and equipment- net	249,153
Other asset, including intangibles-net	11,073
Total assets	354,628
Liabilities	
Current Liabilities	
Notes and loans payable	19,413
Accounts payable and accrued liabilities	41,417
Income taxes payable	4,161
Total current liabilities	65,288
Long-term debt	20,624
Postretirement benefits reserves	21,448
Deferred income tax liabilities	27,084
Long-term obligations to equity companies	4,625
Other long-term obligations	18,728
Total liabilities	157,797

Income Statements

Unlike the balance sheet, the income statement covers a range of time, which is a year for annual financial statements and a quarter for quarterly financial statements. The income statement provides an overview of revenues, expenses, net income and earnings per share. It usually provides two to three years of data for comparison.

Income Statement Formula and Calculation

Net Income=(Revenue–Expenses)

- Total all revenue or sales for the period.
- Total all expenses and costs of operating the business.
- Subtract total expenses from revenue to achieve net income or the profit for the period.

Data From Income Statements

An income statement is one of the three important financial statements used for reporting a company's financial performance over a specific accounting period. Also known as the profit and loss statement or the statement of revenue and expense, the income statement primarily focuses on a company's revenues and expenses during a particular period.

Once expenses are subtracted from revenues, the statement produces a company's profit figure called net income.

Types of Revenue

Operating revenue is the revenue earned by selling a company's products or services. The operating revenue for an auto manufacturer would be realized through the production and sale of autos. Operating revenue is generated from the core business activities of a company.

Non-operating revenue is the income earned from non-core business activities. These revenues fall outside the primary function of the business. Some non-operating revenue examples include:

- Interest earned on cash in the bank.
- Rental income from a property.
- Income from strategic partnerships like royalty payment receipts.
- Income from an advertisement display located on the company's property.

Other income is the revenue earned from other activities. Other income could include gains from the sale of long-term assets such as land, vehicles, or a subsidiary.

Types of Expenses

Primary expenses are incurred during the process of earning revenue from the primary activity of the business. Expenses include the cost of goods sold (COGS), selling, general and administrative expenses (SG&A), depreciation or amortization, and research and development (R&D). Typical expenses include employee wages, sales commissions, and utilities such as electricity and transportation.

Expenses that are linked to secondary activities include interest paid on loans or debt. Losses from the sale of an asset are also recorded as expenses.

The main purpose of the income statement is to convey details of profitability and the financial results of business activities. However, it can be very effective in showing whether sales or revenue is increasing when compared over multiple periods. Investors can also see how well a company's management is controlling expenses to determine whether a company's efforts in reducing the cost of sales might boost profits over time.

Example of an Income Statement

Below is a portion of Exxon Mobil Corporation's (XOM) income statement as of September 30, 2018.

- Total revenues were $76,605 for the period.
- Total costs were $67,525.
- Net income or profit was $6,240.

EXXON MOBIL CORPORATION CONDENSSED CONSOLIDATED STATEMENT OF INCOME (millions of dollar)	
	Three Months ending Sept. 30,2018
	2018
Revenues and Other Income	
Sales and other operating revenue	74,187
Income from equity affiliates	1,960
Other income	458
Total revenues and other income	76,605
Cost and other deductions	
Crude oil and product purchases	41,776
Production and manufacturing expenses	9,097
Selling, general and administrative expenses	2,892
Depreciation and depletion	4,658
Exploration expenses, including dry holes	292
Non- service pension and postretirement benefit expense	307
Interest expense	200
Other taxes and duties	8,303
Total costs and other deductions	67,525
Income before income tax	9,080
Income taxes	2,634
Net income including non-controlling interests	6,446
Net Income attribute to non-controlling interests	206
Net income attribute to ExxonMobil	6,240

Cash Flow Statement

The cash flow statement (CFS) measures how well a company generates cash to pay its debt obligations, fund its operating expenses, and fund investments. The cash flow statement complements the balance sheet and income statement.

Data From the Cash Flow Statement

The CFS allows investors to understand how a company's operations are running, where its money is coming from, and how money is being spent. The CFS also provides insight as to whether a company is on a solid financial footing.

There is no formula, per se, for calculating a cash flow statement, but instead, it contains three sections that report the cash flow for the various activities that a company has used its cash. Those three components of the CFS are listed below:

Operating Activities

The operating activities on the CFS include any sources and uses of cash from running the business and selling its products or services. Cash from operations includes any changes made in cash, accounts receivable, depreciation, inventory, and accounts payable. These transactions also include wages, income tax payments, interest payments, rent, and cash receipts from the sale of a product or service.

Investing Activities

Investing activities include any sources and uses of cash from a company's investments into the long-term future of the company. A purchase or sale of an asset, loans made to vendors or received from customers or any payments related to a merger or acquisition is included in this category.

Also, purchases of fixed assets such as property, plant, and equipment (PPE) are included in this topic. In short, changes in equipment, assets, or investments relate to cash from investing.

Financing Activities

Cash from financing activities include the sources of cash from investors or banks, as well as the uses of cash paid to shareholders. Financing activities include debt issuance, equity issuance, stock repurchases, loans, dividends paid, and repayments of debt.

The cash flow statement reconciles the income statement with the balance sheet in three major business activities.

Example of a Cash Flow Statement

Below is a portion of Exxon Mobil Corporation's (XOM) cash flow statement as of September 30, 2018. We can see the three areas of the cash flow statement and their results.

EXXON MOBIL CORPORATION CONDENSSED CONSOLIDATED STATEMENT OF INCOME (millions of dollar)	
	Nine Months ending Sept,30,2018
	2018
Cash flows from operating activities	
Net Income including non-controlling interests	15,215
Depreciation and depletion	13,717
Changes in operational working capital, excluding cash and debt	(25)
All other items-net	(1,500)
Net cash provided by operating activities	27,407
Cash flows from investing activities	
Additions to property, plant and equipment	(13,480)
Proceeds associated with sales of subsidiaries, property, plant and equipment, sales and returns of investments	3,239
Additional investment and advances	(1,113)
Other investing activities including collection of advances	492
Net cash used in investing activities	(10,862)
Cash flow from financing activities	
Additions to long-term debt	-
Additions to short-term debt	-
Reductions in short-term debt	(4,279)
` Additions/(reductions) in commercial paper, and debt with three months or less maturity (I)	1,626
Cash dividends to ExxonMobil shareholders	(10,296)
Cash dividends to non-controlling interests	(192)
Changes in non-controlling interests	(374)
Common stock acquired	(430)
Net Cash used in financing activities	(13,945)
Effect of exchange rate changes on cash	(108)
Increase/(decrease) in cash and cash equivalents	2,492
Cash and cash equivalents at beginning of period	3,177
Cash and cash equivalents at end of period	5,669

- Operating activities generated a positive cash flow of $27,407 for the period.
- Investing activities generated negative cash flow or cash outflows of -$10,862 for the period. Additions to property, plant, and equipment made up the majority of cash outflows, which means the company invested in new fixed assets.
- Financing activities generated negative cash flow or cash outflows of -$13,945 for the

period. Reductions in short-term debt and dividends paid out made up the majority of the cash outflows.

Financial Statement Limitations

Although financial statements provide a wealth of information on a company, they do have limitations. The statements are open to interpretation, and as a result, investors often draw vastly different conclusions about a company's financial performance.

For example, some investors might want stock repurchases while other investors might prefer to see that money invested in long-term assets. A company's debt level might be fine for one investor while another might have concerns about the level of debt for the company. When analyzing financial statements, it's important to compare multiple periods to determine if there are any trends as well as compare the company's results its peers in the same industry.

Understanding the Balance Sheet, Income Statement and Cash Flow Statement

Many people find it challenging to use a company's financial statements as management tools until they understand how to interpret them. Accounting data collected over time is used to prepare the three key financial statements, which includes the cash flow statement, balance sheet, and income statement, also known as the profit & loss statement.

Key Elements of a Financial Statement

The elements include:

- Cash flow statement from ongoing operations.
- Balance sheet listing company liabilities and assets.
- Income statement—also known as the profit & loss statement—showing financial performance.

Each statement takes the company's financial pulse in a different area. To show how these documents work, the following examines an actual historical balance sheet, income statement and cash flow statement of Target Corporation, shows how you can calculate some financial ratios, and a few ways to interpret the data.

Interpreting the Balance Sheet

Balance sheet information allows you to calculate several financial ratios that measure company performance. Additionally, current balance sheets often present data from at least one previous period, so you can compare how financial performance has changed.

The balance sheet presents the company's financial status as a snapshot, or at a certain point in time. For example, if the balance sheet is presented as of May 1, 2018, you would see the bank account balances from that date in the balance sheet's line item called cash, in the current assets section.

Using Target Corp. as an example here, you can analyze the data in its balance sheet by calculating some financial ratios, using the formulas as follows. Note that all figures are stated in millions of dollars.

Balance Sheet Ratios

Quick Ratio

This measures Target's ability to meet its debt obligations without selling off inventory; the higher the result, the better. It is expressed as (current assets minus inventories) divided by current liabilities. In Target's case, that is ($14,706 minus $6,254) divided by $11,117, which equals 0.76.

- Interpretation: If this number declines over time or falls short of your benchmark, you may be investing too much capital in inventory or you may have taken on too much short-term debt.

Current Ratio

This is another test of short-term liquidity, determined by dividing current assets by current liabilities. In Target's case, that is equivalent to $14,706 divided by $11,117, which equals 1.32.

- Interpretation: This number should be above 1, and it's usually a sign of strength if it exceeds 2. If this number is below 1, that means your short-term liabilities exceed your short-term assets. A liability is considered current if it is due within a year. An asset is current if it can be converted into cash within a year.

Debt-to-Equity Ratio

In brief, divide total debt by total equity. In Target's case, the denominator is termed a shareholder's investment because Target is a public company. Using Target's data, that ratio is expressed as $8,675 divided by $15,633, which equals 0.555.

- Interpretation: Long-term creditors will view this number as a measure of how aggressive your firm is. If your business is already levered up with debt, they may be reluctant to offer additional financing.

Working Capital

This refers to the cash available for daily operations. It is derived by subtracting current liabilities from current assets, which in this example is $14,706 minus $11,117, which equals $3,589.

- Interpretation: If this number is negative, that means your firm is unable to meet its current obligations. To improve this number, examine your inventory management practices; a backup of goods and the resulting loss in sales can take a toll on your business's cash resources.

Interpreting the Income Statement

Like a balance sheet, an income statement is a means for measuring a company's financial performance. Some of the ratios discussed draw data from both the income statement and the balance sheet. These examples continue using the published data from Target for the calculations. Note that all figures are presented in millions of dollars.

Gross Profit Margin

The money Target earns from selling a T-shirt, minus what it paid for that item—known as the cost of goods sold, or COGS—is called gross profit. Sales minus COGS, divided by sales, yields the gross profit margin. According to Target's income statement, that would be ($59,490 minus $39,399) divided by $59,490, which equals 0.337, or 33.7 percent.

Operating Income

This is gross profit minus operating expenses minus depreciation. It is also called EBIT (earnings before interest and taxes). Using Target's data, the formula would be expressed as $59,490 minus $39,399 minus $12,819 minus $707 minus $1,496, which equals $5,069.

Operating Profit Margin

Use the total derived in the previous step and divide it by total sales. In this case, the equation is $5,069 divided by $59,490, which equals .085, or 8.5 percent.

- Interpretation: This tally is also known as EBIT margin and is an effective way to measure operational efficiency. If you find this number to be low, either raise revenues or cut costs. It may help to analyze which of your customers are the most profitable and concentrate your efforts there.

Net Profit Margin

Net earnings divided by total revenue yields the net profit margin. In this case, $2,787 divided by $59,490, which equals .047, or 4.7 percent.

ROA

This stands for return on assets and measures how much profit a company is generating for each dollar of assets. Calculate ROA by dividing the revenue figure from the income statement by assets from the balance sheet. For Target, that equates to $59,490 divided by $14,706, which equals 4.04. In other words, for every dollar Target has in assets, it is able to generate $4.04 of revenue.

ROE

The same idea as above, but replacing assets with the equity. In this case, $59,490 divided by $15,633, which equals 3.81.

Accounts Receivable Collection

Many businesses experience a lag between the time they bill customers and when they see the revenue. This may be due to trade credit or because customers are not paying. While you can note this potential revenue in the balance sheet under accounts receivable, if you're not able to collect it, eventually your business will lack sufficient cash.

- Interpretation: To measure how many days it takes to collect all accounts receivable, use this formula: 365 (days) divided by accounts receivable turnover (total net sales divided by accounts receivable). In Target's case, that equates to 365 divided by the sum of $59,490 divided by $6,194, which equals 38. This means that, on average, it takes Target 38 days to collect on its accounts. If you find your business has a healthy balance sheet but is short on cash, increase collection on outstanding accounts.

Interpreting the Cash Flow Statement

The cash flow statement discloses how a company raised money and how it spent those funds during a given period. It is also an analytical tool, measuring an enterprise's ability to cover its expenses in the near term. Generally speaking, if a company is consistently bringing in more cash than it spends, that company is considered to be of good value.

A cash flow statement is divided into three parts: operations, investing and financing. The following is an analysis of a real-world cash flow statement belonging to Target Corp. Note that all figures are stated in millions of dollars.

Cash From Operations

This is cash that was generated over the year from the company's core business transactions. Note how the statement starts with net earnings and works backward, adding in depreciation and subtracting out inventory and accounts receivable. In simple terms, this is earnings before interest and taxes (EBIT) plus depreciation minus taxes.

- Interpretation: This may serve as a better indicator than earnings since noncash earnings can't be used to pay off bills.

Cash From Investing

Some businesses will invest outside their core operations or acquire new companies to expand their reach.

- Interpretation: This portion of the cash flow statement accounts for cash used to make new investments, as well as proceeds gained from previous investments. In Target's case, this number in 2006 was ($4,693), which shows the company spent significant cash investing in projects it hopes will lead to future growth.

Cash From Financing

This last section refers to the movement of cash from financing activities. Two common financing activities are taking on a loan or issuing stock to new investors. Dividends to current investors also fit in here. Again, Target reports a negative number for 2006, ($1,004). But this should not be misconstrued: The company paid off $1,155 of its previous debt, paid out $380 in dividends and repurchased $901 of company stock.

- Interpretation: Investors will like these last two items, since they reap the dividends, and it signals that Target is confident in its stock performance and wants to keep it for the company's gain. A simple formula for this topic: cash from issuing stock minus dividends paid, minus cash used to acquire stock.

The final step in analyzing cash flow is to add the cash balances from the reporting year and the previous year; in Target's case, that's ($835) plus $1,648, which equals $813. Even though Target ran a negative cash balance for both years, it still has an overall positive cash balance due to its high cash surplus in 2004.

CASH FLOW STATEMENT

In financial accounting, a cash flow statement, also known as statement of cash flows, is a financial statement that shows how changes in balance sheet accounts and income affect cash and cash equivalents, and breaks the analysis down to operating, investing, and financing activities. Essentially, the cash flow statement is concerned with the flow of cash in and out of the business. As an analytical tool, the statement of cash flows is useful in determining the short-term viability of a company, particularly its ability to pay bills. International Accounting Standard 7 (IAS 7), is the International Accounting Standard that deals with cash flow statements.

People and groups interested in cash flow statements include:

- Accounting personnel, who need to know whether the organization will be able to cover payroll and other immediate expenses.
- Potential lenders or creditors, who want a clear picture of a company's ability to repay.
- Potential investors, who need to judge whether the company is financially sound.
- Potential employees or contractors, who need to know whether the company will be able to afford compensation.
- Company Directors, who are responsible for governance of the company, and are responsible for ensuring that the company doesn't trade while insolvent.
- Shareholders of the business.

Statement of Cash Flow - Simple Example for the period 1 Jan 2006 to 31 Dec 2006	
Cash flow from operations	$4,000
Cash flow from investing	($1,000)
Cash flow from financing	($2,000)
Net cash flow	$1,000
Parentheses indicate negative values	

The cash flow statement was previously known as the flow of funds statement. The cash flow statement reflects a firm's liquidity.

The statement of financial position is a snapshot of a firm's financial resources and obligations at a single point in time, and the income statement summarizes a firm's financial transactions over an interval of time. These two financial statements reflect the accrual basis accounting used by firms to match revenues with the expenses associated with generating those revenues. The cash flow statement includes only inflows and outflows of cash and cash equivalents; it excludes transactions that do not directly affect cash receipts and payments. These non-cash transactions include depreciation or write-offs on bad debts or credit losses to name a few. The cash flow statement is a cash basis report on three types of financial activities: operating activities, investing activities, and financing activities. Non-cash activities are usually reported in footnotes.

The cash flow statement is intended to:

- Provide information on a firm's liquidity and solvency and its ability to change cash flows in future circumstances.
- Provide additional information for evaluating changes in assets, liabilities and equity.
- Improve the comparability of different firms' operating performance by eliminating the effects of different accounting methods.
- Indicate the amount, timing and probability of future cash flows.

The cash flow statement has been adopted as a standard financial statement because it eliminates allocations, which might be derived from different accounting methods, such as various timeframes for depreciating fixed assets.

Cash basis financial statements were very common before accrual basis financial statements. The "flow of funds" statements of the past were cash flow statements.

In 1863, the Dowlais Iron Company had recovered from a business slump, but had no cash to invest for a new blast furnace, despite having made a profit. To explain why there were no funds to invest, the manager made a new financial statement that was called a *comparison balance sheet*, which showed that the company was holding too much inventory. This new financial statement was the genesis of the cash flow statement that is used today.

In the United States in 1973, the Financial Accounting Standards Board (FASB) defined rules that made it mandatory under Generally Accepted Accounting Principles (US GAAP) to report sources and uses of funds, but the definition of "funds" was not clear. Net working capital might be cash or might be the difference between current assets and current liabilities. From the late 1970 to the mid-1980s, the FASB discussed the usefulness of predicting future cash flows. In 1987, FASB Statement No. 95 (FAS 95) mandated that firms provide cash flow statements. In 1992, the International Accounting Standards Board issued International Accounting Standard 7 (IAS 7), Cash Flow Statement, which became effective in 1994, mandating that firms provide cash flow statements.

US GAAP and IAS 7 rules for cash flow statements are similar, but some of the differences are:

- IAS 7 requires that the cash flow statement include changes in both cash and cash equivalents. US GAAP permits using cash alone or cash and cash equivalents.

- IAS 7 permits bank borrowings (overdraft) in certain countries to be included in cash equivalents rather than being considered a part of financing activities.
- IAS 7 allows interest paid to be included in operating activities or financing activities. US GAAP requires that interest paid be included in operating activities.
- US GAAP (FAS 95) requires that when the direct method is used to present the operating activities of the cash flow statement, a supplemental schedule must also present a cash flow statement using the indirect method. The IASC strongly recommends the direct method but allows either method. The IASC considers the indirect method less clear to users of financial statements. Cash flow statements are most commonly prepared using the indirect method, which is not especially useful in projecting future cash flows.

Cash Flow Activities

The cash flow statement is partitioned into three segments, namely:

- Cash flow resulting from operating activities.
- Cash flow resulting from investing activities.
- Cash flow resulting from financing activities.

The money coming into the business is called cash inflow, and money going out from the business is called cash outflow.

Operating Activities

Operating activities include the production, sales and delivery of the company's product as well as collecting payment from its customers. This could include purchasing raw materials, building inventory, advertising, and shipping the product.

Under IAS 7, operating cash flows include:

- Receipts for the sale of loans, debt or equity instruments in a trading portfolio.
- Interest received on loans.
- Payments to suppliers for goods and services.
- Payments to employees or on behalf of employees.
- Interest payments (alternatively, this can be reported under financing activities in ias 7).
- Buying Merchandise.

Items which are added back to [or subtracted from, as appropriate] the net income figure (which is found on the Income Statement) to arrive at cash flows from operations generally include:

- Depreciation (loss of tangible asset value over time).
- Deferred tax.

- Amortization (loss of intangible asset value over time).
- Any gains or losses associated with the sale of a non-current asset, because associated cash flows do not belong in the operating section (unrealized gains/losses are also added back from the income statement).
- Dividends received general reserves.

Investing Activities

Examples of Investing activities are:

- Purchase or Sale of an asset (assets can be land, building, equipment, marketable securities, etc.).
- Loans made to suppliers or received from customers.
- Payments related to mergers and acquisition.

Financing Activities

Financing activities include the inflow of cash from investors such as banks and shareholders, as well as the outflow of cash to shareholders as dividends as the company generates income. Other activities which impact the long-term liabilities and equity of the company are also listed in the financing activities section of the cash flow statement.

Under IAS 7:

- Payments of dividends.
- Payments for repurchase of company shares.
- For non-profit organizations, receipts of donor-restricted cash that is limited to long-term purposes.

Items under the financing activities section include:

- Dividends paid.
- Sale or repurchase of the company's stock.
- Net borrowings.
- Repayment of debt principal, including capital leases.

Disclosure of Non-cash Activities

Under IAS 7, non-cash investing and financing activities are disclosed in footnotes to the financial statements. Under US General Accepted Accounting Principles (GAAP), non-cash activities may be disclosed in a footnote or within the cash flow statement itself. Non-cash financing activities may include:

- Leasing to purchase an asset.

- Converting debt to equity.
- Exchanging non-cash assets or liabilities for other non-cash assets or liabilities.
- Issuing share.
- Payment of dividend taxes in exchange for assets.

Preparation Methods

The direct method of preparing a cash flow statement results in a more easily understood report. The indirect method is almost universally used, because FAS 95 requires a supplementary report similar to the indirect method if a company chooses to use the direct method.

Direct Method

The direct method for creating a cash flow statement reports major classes of gross cash receipts and payments. Under IAS 7, dividends received may be reported under operating activities or under investing activities. If taxes paid are directly linked to operating activities, they are reported under operating activities; if the taxes are directly linked to investing activities or financing activities, they are reported under investing or financing activities. Generally Accepted Accounting Principles (GAAP) vary from International Financial Reporting Standards in that under GAAP rules, dividends received from a company's investing activities is reported as an "operating activity," not an "investing activity."

Sample cash flow statement using the direct method:

Cash flows from (used in) operating activities		
Cash receipts from customers	9,500	
Cash paid to suppliers and employees	(2,000)	
Cash generated from operations (sum)	7,500	
Interest paid	(2,000)	
Income taxes paid	(3,000)	
Net cash flows from operating activities		2,500
Cash flows from (used in) investing activities		
Proceeds from the sale of equipment	7,500	
Dividends received	3,000	
Net cash flows from investing activities		10,500
Cash flows from (used in) financing activities		
Dividends paid	(2,500)	
Net cash flows used in financing activities		(2,500)
Net increase in cash and cash equivalents		10,500
Cash and cash equivalents, beginning of year		1,000
Cash and cash equivalents, end of year		$11,500

Indirect Method

The indirect method uses net-income as a starting point, makes adjustments for all transactions for non-cash items, then adjusts from all cash-based transactions. An increase in an asset account is subtracted from net income, and an increase in a liability account is added back to net income. This method converts accrual-basis net income (or loss) into cash flow by using a series of additions and deductions.

Rules (Operating Activities)

To Find Cash Flows from Operating Activities using the Balance Sheet and Net Income	
For Increases in	Net Inc Adj
Current Assets (Non-Cash)	Decrease
Current Liabilities	Increase
For All Non-Cash...	
*Expenses (Decreases in Fixed Assets)	Increase
*Non-cash expenses must be added back to NI. Such expenses may be represented on the balance sheet as decreases in long term asset accounts. Thus decreases in fixed assets increase NI.	

The following rules can be followed to calculate Cash Flows from Operating Activities when given only a two-year comparative balance sheet and the Net Income figure. Cash Flows from Operating Activities can be found by adjusting Net Income relative to the change in beginning and ending balances of Current Assets, Current Liabilities, and sometimes Long Term Assets. When comparing the change in long term assets over a year, the accountant must be certain that these changes were caused entirely by their devaluation rather than purchases or sales (i.e. they must be operating items not providing or using cash) or if they are non-operating items.

- Decrease in non-cash current assets are added to net income.
- Increase in non-cash current asset are subtracted from net income.
- Increase in current liabilities are added to net income.
- Decrease in current liabilities are subtracted from net income.
- Expenses with no cash outflows are added back to net income (depreciation and amortization expense are the only operating items that have no effect on cash flows in the period).
- Revenues with no cash inflows are subtracted from net income.
- Non operating losses are added back to net income.
- Non operating gains are subtracted from net income.

The intricacies of this procedure might be seen as,

$$\text{Net Cash Flows from Operating Activities} = \text{Net Income} + \text{Rule Items}$$

For example, consider a company that has a net income of $100 this year, and its A/R increased by

$25 since the beginning of the year. If the balances of all other current assets, long term assets and current liabilities did not change over the year, the cash flows could be determined by the rules above as $100 – $25 = Cash Flows from Operating Activities = $75. The logic is that, if the company made $100 that year (net income), and they are using the accrual accounting system (not cash based) then any income they generated that year which has not yet been paid for in cash should be subtracted from the net income figure in order to find cash flows from operating activities. And the increase in A/R meant that $25 of sales occurred on credit and have not yet been paid for in cash.

In the case of finding Cash Flows when there is a change in a fixed asset account, say the Buildings and Equipment account decreases, the change is added back to Net Income. The reasoning behind this is that because Net Income is calculated by, Net Income = Rev - Cogs - Depreciation Exp - Other Exp then the Net Income figure will be decreased by the building's depreciation that year. This depreciation is not associated with an exchange of cash, therefore the depreciation is added back into net income to remove the non-cash activity.

Rules (Financing Activities)

Finding the Cash Flows from Financing Activities is much more intuitive and needs little explanation. Generally, the things to account for are financing activities:

- Include as outflows, reductions of long term notes payable (as would represent the cash repayment of debt on the balance sheet).
- Or as inflows, the issuance of new notes payable.
- Include as outflows, all dividends paid by the entity to outside parties.
- Or as inflows, dividend payments received from outside parties.
- Include as outflows, the purchase of notes stocks or bonds.
- Or as inflows, the receipt of payments on such financing vehicles.

In the case of more advanced accounting situations, such as when dealing with subsidiaries, the accountant must:

- Exclude intra-company dividend payments.
- Exclude intra-company bond interest.

A traditional equation for this might look something like,

$$\begin{aligned}\text{Net Cash Flows from} &= \left[\text{Dividends received from } 3^{\text{rd}} \text{ parties}\right] - \left[\text{Dividends paid to } 3^{\text{rd}} \text{ parties}\right] \\ \text{Financing Activities} &- [\text{Dividends paid to NCI but not intracompany dividend payments}].\end{aligned}$$

BALANCE SHEET

The balance sheet is one of the three fundamental financial statements and is key to both financial modeling and accounting. The balance sheet displays the company's total assets, and how these assets are financed, through either debt or equity. It can also be referred to as a statement of net worth, or a statement of financial position. The balance sheet is based on the fundamental equation: Assets = Liabilities + Equity.

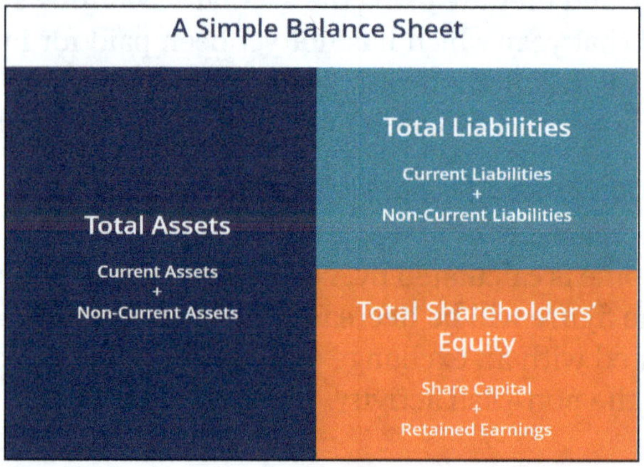

As such, the balance sheet is divided into two sides (or sections). The left side of the balance sheet outlines all a company's assets. On the right side, the balance sheet outlines the companies liabilities and shareholders' equity. On either side, the main line items are generally classified by liquidity. More liquid accounts like Inventory, Cash, and Trades Payables are placed before illiquid accounts such as Plant, Property, and Equipment (PP&E) and Long-Term Debt. The assets and liabilities are also separated into two categories: current asset/liabilities and non-current (long-term) assets/liabilities.

Balance Sheet Example

Below is an example of Amazon's 2017 balance sheet taken from CFI's Amazon Case Study Course. As you will see, it starts with current assets, then non-current assets and total assets. Below that is liabilities and stockholders' equity which includes current liabilities, non-current liabilities, and finally shareholders' equity.

CONSOLIDATED BALANCE SHEETS (in millions except per share data)		
	December 31,	
ASSETS		
Current assets:		
Cash and cash equivalents	$ 19,334	$ 20,522
Marketable securities	6,647	10,464
Inventories	11,461	16,047
Accounts receivable, net and other	8,339	13,164
Total current assets	45,781	60,197
Property and equipment, net	29,114	48,886
Goodwill	3,784	13,350
Other assets	4,723	8,897
Total assets	$83,402	$ 131,310

LIABILITIES AND DTOCKHOLDERS' EQUITY		
Current liabilities:		
Accounts payable	$ 25,309	$34,616
Accrued expenses and other	13,739	18,170
Unearned revenue	4,768	5,097
Total current liabilities	43,816	57,883
Long-term debt	7,694	24,743
Other long- term liabilities	12,607	20,975
Commitments and contingencies (Note 7)		
Stock holders' equity		
Preferred stock, $0.01 par value		
Authorised shares—500		
Issued and outstanding shares—none	-	-
Outstanding Shares – 477 and 484	5	5
Treasury stock, at cost	(1,837)	(1,837)
Additional paid-in capital	17,186	21,389
Accumulated other comprehensive loss	(985)	(484)
Retained earnings	4,916	8,636
Total stockholders' equity	19,285	27,709
Total liabilities and stockholders' equity	$ 83,402	$ 131,310

How the Balance Sheet is Structured

Balance sheets, like all financial statements, will have minor differences between organizations and industries. However, there are several "buckets" and line items that are almost always included in common balance sheets. We briefly go through commonly found line items under Current Assets, Long-Term Assets, Current Liabilities, Long-Term Liabilities, and Equity.

Current Assets

Cash and Equivalents

The most liquid of all assets, cash, appears on the first line of the balance sheet. Cash Equivalents are also lumped under this line item and include assets that have short-term maturities under three months or assets that the company can liquidate on short notice, such as marketable securities. Companies will generally disclose what equivalents it includes in the footnotes to the balance sheet.

Accounts Receivable

This account includes the balance of all sales revenue still on credit, net of any allowances for doubtful accounts (which generates a bad debt expense). As companies recover accounts receivables, this account decreases and cash increases by the same amount.

Inventory

Inventory includes amounts for raw materials, work-in-progress goods, and finished goods. The company uses this account when it reports sales of goods, generally under cost of goods sold in the income statement.

Non-current Assets

Plant, Property and Equipment (PP&E)

Property, Plant, and Equipment (also known as PP&E) capture the company's tangible fixed assets. This line item is noted net of depreciation. Some companies will class out their PP&E by the different types of assets, such as Land, Building, and various types of Equipment. All PP&E is depreciable except for Land.

Intangible Assets

This line item will include all of the companies intangible fixed assets, which may or may not be identifiable. Identifiable intangible assets include patents, licenses, and secret formulas. Unidentifiable intangible assets include brand and goodwill.

Current Liabilities

Accounts Payable

Accounts Payables, or AP, is the amount a company owes suppliers for items or services purchased on credit. As the company pays off their AP, it decreases along with an equal amount decrease to the cash account.

Current Debt/Notes Payable

Includes non-AP obligations that are due within one year time or within one operating cycle for the company (whichever is longest). Notes payable may also have a long-term version, which includes notes with a maturity of more than one year.

Current Portion of Long-term Debt

This account may or may not be lumped together with the above account, Current Debt. While they may seem similar, the current portion of long-term debt is specifically the portion due within this year of a piece of debt that has a maturity of more than one year. For example, if a company takes on a bank loan to be paid off in 5-years, this account will include the portion of that loan due in the next year.

Non-current Liabilities

Bonds Payable

This account includes the amortized amount of any bonds the company has issued.

Long-term Debt

This account includes the total amount of long-term debt (Excluding the current portion, if that account is present under current liabilities). This account is derived from the debt schedule, which outlines all the companies outstanding debt, the interest expense and the principal repayment for every period.

Shareholders' Equity

Share Capital

This is the value of funds that shareholders have invested in the company. When a company is first formed, shareholders will typically put in cash. For example, an investor starts a company and seeds it with $10M. Cash (an asset) rises by $10M, and Share Capital (an equity account) rises by $10M, balancing out the balance sheet.

Retained Earnings

This is the total amount of net income the company decides to keep. Every period, a company may pay out dividends from its net income. Any amount remaining (or exceeding) is added to (deducted from) retained earnings.

How is the Balance Sheet used in Financial Modeling?

This statement is a great way to analyze a company's financial position. An analyst can generally use the balance sheet to calculate a lot of financial ratios that can determine how well a company is performing, how liquid or solvent a company is, and how efficient it is.

Changes in balance sheet accounts are also used to calculate cash flow in the cash flow statement. For example, a positive change in plant, property, and equipment is equal to capital expenditure minus depreciation expense. If depreciation expense is known, capital expenditure can be calculated and included as a cash outflow under cash flow from investing in the cash flow statement.

	Historical Results					Forecast Period			
Financial Model	2014	2015	2016	2017	2018	2019	2020	2021	2022
Balance Sheets									
Assets									
Cash	81,210	83,715	1,11,069	1,39,550	1,59,474	1,82,573	1,90,511	2,24,399	2,61,248
Accounts receivables	5,904	6,567	7,117	7,539	8,179	8,997	9,896	10,758	11,650
Inventory	9,601	9,825	10,531	11,342	15,267	19,343	24,191	26,894	29,772
Current Assets	96,715	1,00,107	1,28,717	1,58,430	1,82,920	2,10,913	2,24,599	2,62,051	3,02,670
Property & Equipment	42,350	40,145	38,602	37,521	45,017	51,013	55,811	59,649	62,719
Goodwill									
Total Assets	1,39,065	1,40,252	1,67,319	1,95,951	2,27,937	2,61,927	2,80,410	3,21,700	3,65,389
Liabilities									
Short Term Debt									
Accounts Payable	4,800	4912	5,265	5,671	7,061	7,952	8,951	9,951	11,016

Current Liabilities	4,800	4912	5,265	5,671	7,061	7,952	8,951	9,951	11,016
Long Term Debt	50,000	30,000	30,000	30,000	30,000	30,000	10,000	10,000	10,000
Total Liabilities	54,800	34,912	35,265	35,671	37,061	37,952	18,951	19,951	21,016
Shareholder's Equity									
Equity Capital	70,000	70,000	70,000	70,000	70,000	70,000	70,000	70,000	70,000
Retained Earnings	14,265	35,340	62,053	90,280	1,20,876	1,53,974	1,91,459	2,31,749	2,74,373
Shareholder's Equity	84,265	1,05,340	1,32,053	1,60,280	1,90,876	2,23,974	2,61,459	3,01,749	3,44,373
Total Liabilities & Shareholder's Equity	1,39,065	1,40,252	1,67,319	1,95,951	2,27,937	2,61,927	2,80,410	3,21,700	3,65,389

Importance of the Balance Sheet

The balance sheet is a very important financial statement for many reasons. It can be looked at on its own, and in conjunction with other statements like the income statement and cash flow statement to get a full picture of a company's health.

4 important takeaways include:

1. Liquidity – Comparing a company's current assets to its current liabilities provides a picture of liquidity. Current assets should be greater than current liabilities so the company can cover its short-term obligations. The Current Ratio and Quick Ratio are examples of liquidity financial metrics.
2. Leverage – Looking at how a company is financed indicates how much leverage it has, which in turn indicates how much financial risk the company is taking. Comparing debt to equity and debt to total capital are common ways of assessing leverage on the balance sheet.
3. Efficiency – By using the income statement in connection with the balance sheet it's possible to assess how efficiently a company uses its assets. For example, dividing revenue into fixed assets produces the Asset Turnover Ratio to indicate how efficiently the company turns assets into revenue. Additionally, the working capital cycle shows how well a company manages its cash in the short term.
4. Rates of Return – The balance sheet can be used to evaluate how well a company generates returns. For example, dividing net income into shareholders' equity produces Return on Equity (ROE), and dividing net income into total assets produces Return on Assets (ROA), and dividing net income into debt plus equity results in Return on Invested Capital (ROIC).

INCOME STATEMENT

An income statement or profit and loss account (also referred to as a profit and loss statement (P&L), statement of profit or loss, revenue statement, statement of financial performance, earnings statement, statement of earnings, operating statement, or statement of operations) is one of the financial statements of a company and shows the company's revenues and expenses during a particular period.

It indicates how the revenues (also known as the *"top line"*) are transformed into the net income or net profit (the result after all revenues and expenses have been accounted for). The purpose of the income statement is to show managers and investors whether the company made money (profit) or lost money (loss) during the period being reported.

An income statement represents a period of time (as does the cash flow statement). This contrasts with the balance sheet, which represents a single moment in time.

Charitable organizations that are required to publish financial statements do not produce an income statement. Instead, they produce a similar statement that reflects funding sources compared against program expenses, administrative costs, and other operating commitments. This statement is commonly referred to as the statement of activities. Revenues and expenses are further categorized in the statement of activities by the donor restrictions on the funds received and expended.

The income statement can be prepared in one of two methods. The Single Step income statement totals revenues and subtracts expenses to find the bottom line. The Multi-Step income statement takes several steps to find the bottom line: starting with the gross profit, then calculating operating expenses. Then when deducted from the gross profit, yields income from operations.

Adding to income from operations is the difference of other revenues and other expenses. When combined with income from operations, this yields income before taxes. The final step is to deduct taxes, which finally produces the net income for the period measured.

Usefulness and Limitations of Income Statement

Income statements may help investors and creditors determine the past financial performance of the enterprise, predict the future performance, and assess the capability of generating future cash flows using the report of income and expenses.

However, information of an income statement has several limitations:

- Items that might be relevant but cannot be reliably measured are not reported (*e.g.*, brand recognition and loyalty).
- Some numbers depend on accounting methods used (*e.g.*, using FIFO or LIFO accounting to measure inventory level).
- Some numbers depend on judgments and estimates (*e.g.*, depreciation expense depends on estimated useful life and salvage value).

```
                    - INCOME STATEMENT GREENHARBOR LLC -
                    For the year ended DECEMBER 31 2010

                                                    €          €
                                                  Debit      Credit

Revenues
GROSS REVENUES (including INTEREST income)                   296,397
                                                            --------

Expenses:
```

ADVERTISING	6,300	
BANK & CREDIT CARD FEES	144	
BOOKKEEPING	2,350	
SUBCONTRACTORS	88,000	
ENTERTAINMENT	5,550	
INSURANCE	750	
LEGAL & PROFESSIONAL SERVICES	1,575	
LICENSES	632	
PRINTING, POSTAGE & STATIONERY	320	
RENT	13,000	
MATERIALS	74,400	
TELEPHONE	1,000	
UTILITIES	1,491	

TOTAL EXPENSES		(195,512)

NET INCOME		100,885

Guidelines for statements of comprehensive income and income statements of business entities are formulated by the International Accounting Standards Board and numerous country-specific organizations, for example the FASB in the U.S.

Names and usage of different accounts in the income statement depend on the type of organization, industry practices and the requirements of different jurisdictions.

If applicable to the business, summary values for the following items should be included in the income statement:

Operating Section

- Revenue - Cash inflows or other enhancements of assets (including accounts receivable) of an entity during a period from delivering or producing goods, rendering services, or other activities that constitute the entity's ongoing major operations. It is usually presented as sales minus sales discounts, returns, and allowances. Every time a business sells a product or performs a service, it obtains revenue. This often is referred to as gross revenue or sales revenue.
- Expenses - Cash outflows or other using-up of assets or incurrence of liabilities (including accounts payable) during a period from delivering or producing goods, rendering services, or carrying out other activities that constitute the entity's ongoing major operations.
    - Cost of Goods Sold (COGS)/Cost of Sales - Represents the direct costs attributable to goods produced and sold by a business (manufacturing or merchandizing). It includes material costs, direct labour, and overhead costs (as in absorption costing), and excludes operating costs (period costs) such as selling, administrative, advertising or R&D, etc.

- Selling, General and Administrative expenses (SG&A or SGA) - Consist of the combined payroll costs. SGA is usually understood as a major portion of non-production related costs, in contrast to production costs such as direct labour.
    - Selling expenses - Represent expenses needed to sell products e.g., salaries of sales people, commissions and travel expenses, advertising, freight, shipping, depreciation of sales store buildings and equipment, etc.
    - General and Administrative (G&A) expenses - Represent expenses to manage the business (salaries of officers/executives, legal and professional fees, utilities, insurance, depreciation of office building and equipment, office rents, office supplies, etc.
- Depreciation/Amortization - The charge with respect to fixed assets/intangible assets that have been capitalised on the balance sheet for a specific (accounting) period. It is a systematic and rational allocation of cost rather than the recognition of market value decrement.
- Research & Development (R&D) expenses - Represent expenses included in research and development.

Expenses recognised in the income statement should be analysed either by nature (raw materials, transport costs, staffing costs, depreciation, employee benefit etc.) or by function (cost of sales, selling, administrative, etc.). If an entity categorises by function, then additional information on the nature of expenses, at least, – depreciation, amortisation and employee benefits expense – must be disclosed. The major exclusive of costs of goods sold, are classified as operating expenses. These represent the resources expended, except for inventory purchases, in generating the revenue for the period. Expenses often are divided into two broad sub classicifications selling expenses and administrative expenses.

Non-operating Section

- Other revenues or gains - Revenues and gains from other than primary business activities (e.g., rent, income from patents, goodwill). It also includes unusual gains that are either unusual or infrequent, but not both (e.g., gain from sale of securities or gain from disposal of fixed assets).
- Other expenses or losses - Expenses or losses not related to primary business operations, (e.g., foreign exchange loss).
- Finance costs - Costs of borrowing from various creditors (e.g., interest expenses, bank charges).
- Income tax expense - Sum of the amount of tax payable to tax authorities in the current reporting period (current tax liabilities/tax payable) and the amount of deferred tax liabilities (or assets).

Irregular Items

They are reported separately because this way users can better predict future cash flows - irregular items most likely will not recur. These are reported net of taxes.

- Discontinued operations is the most common type of irregular items. Shifting business locations, stopping production temporarily, or changes due to technological improvement do not qualify as discontinued operations. Discontinued operations *must* be shown separately.

Cumulative effect of changes in accounting policies (principles) is the difference between the book value of the affected assets (or liabilities) under the old policy (principle) and what the book value would have been if the new principle had been applied in the prior periods. For example, valuation of inventories using LIFO instead of weighted average method. The changes should be applied retrospectively and shown as adjustments to the *beginning* balance of affected components in Equity. All comparative financial statements should be restated.

However, changes in estimates (e.g., estimated useful life of a fixed asset) only requires prospective changes.

No items may be presented in the income statement as extraordinary items under IFRS regulations, but are permissible under US GAAP. Extraordinary items are both unusual (abnormal) and infrequent, for example, unexpected natural disaster, expropriation, prohibitions under new regulations. Natural disaster might not qualify depending on location (e.g., frost damage would not qualify in Canada but would in the tropics).

Additional items may be needed to fairly present the entity's results of operations.

Disclosures

Certain items must be disclosed separately in the notes (or the statement of comprehensive income), if material, including:

- Write-downs of inventories to net realisable value or of property, plant and equipment to recoverable amount, as well as *reversals* of such write-downs.
- Restructurings of the activities of an entity and *reversals* of any provisions for the costs of restructuring.
- Disposals of items of property, plant and equipment.
- Disposals of investments.
- Discontinued operations.
- Litigation settlements.
- Other reversals of provisions.

Earnings Per Share

Because of its importance, earnings per share (EPS) are required to be disclosed on the face of the income statement. A company which reports any of the irregular items must also report EPS for these items either in the statement or in the notes.

$$\text{Earnings per share} = \frac{\text{Net income} - \text{Preferred stock dividends}}{\text{Weighted average of common stock shares outstanding}}$$

There are two forms of EPS reported:

- Basic: In this case "weighted average of shares outstanding" includes only actual stocks outstanding.
- Diluted: In this case "weighted average of shares outstanding" is calculated as if all stock options, warrants, convertible bonds, and other securities that could be transformed into shares are transformed. This increases the number of shares and so EPS decreases. Diluted EPS is considered to be a more reliable way to measure EPS.

Bottom Line

"Bottom line" is the net income that is calculated after subtracting the expenses from revenue. Since this forms the last line of the income statement, it is informally called "bottom line." It is important to investors as it represents the profit for the year attributable to the shareholders.

After revision to IAS 1 in 2003, the Standard is now using profit or loss for the year rather than *net profit or loss* or *net income* as the descriptive term for the bottom line of the income statement.

Requirements of IFRS

On 6 September 2007, the International Accounting Standards Board issued a revised IAS 1: Presentation of Financial Statements, which is effective for annual periods beginning on or after 1 January 2009.

A business entity adopting IFRS must include:

- A Statement of comprehensive income or
- Two separate statements comprising:
    - An income statement displaying components of profit or loss.
    - A statement of comprehensive income that begins with profit or loss (bottom line of the income statement) and displays the items of other comprehensive income for the reporting period.

All non-owner changes in equity (i.e., *comprehensive income*) shall be presented in either in the statement of comprehensive income (or in a separate income statement and a statement of comprehensive income). Components of comprehensive income may not be presented in the statement of changes in equity.

Comprehensive income for a period includes profit or loss (net income) for that period and other comprehensive income recognised in that period.

All items of income and expense recognised in a period must be included in profit or loss unless a Standard or an Interpretation requires otherwise. Some IFRSs require or permit that some components to be excluded from profit or loss and instead to be included in other comprehensive income.

Items and Disclosures

The statement of comprehensive income should include:

- Revenue.
- Finance costs (including interest expenses).
- Share of the profit or loss of associates and joint ventures accounted for using the equity method.
- Tax expense.
- A *single* amount comprising the total of (1) the *post-tax* profit or loss of *discontinued operations* and (2) the *post-tax* gain or loss recognised on the disposal of the assets or disposal group(s) constituting the *discontinued operation.*
- Profit or loss.
- Each component of other comprehensive income classified by nature.
- Share of the other comprehensive income of associates and joint ventures accounted for using the equity method.
- Total comprehensive income.

The following items must also be disclosed in the statement of comprehensive income as allocations for the period:

- Profit or loss for the period attributable to non-controlling interests and owners of the parent.
- Total comprehensive income attributable to non-controlling interests and owners of the parent.

No items may be presented in the statement of comprehensive income (or in the income statement, if separately presented) or in the notes as extraordinary items.

STATEMENT OF CHANGES IN EQUITY

A Statement of changes in equity and similarly the statement of changes in owner's equity for a sole trader, statement of changes in partners' equity for a partnership, statement of changes in Shareholders' equity for a Company or statement of changes in Taxpayers' equity for Government financial statements is one of the four basic financial statements.

The statement explains the changes in a company's Share Capital, accumulated reserves and retained earnings over the reporting period. It breaks down changes in the owners' interest in the organization, and in the application of retained profit or surplus from one accounting period to the next. Line items typically include profits or losses from operations, dividends paid, issue or redemption of shares, revaluation reserve and any other items charged or credited to accumulated other comprehensive income. It also includes the Non-Controlling Interest attributable to other individuals and organisations.

The statement is expected under the generally accepted accounting principles and explains the owners' equity shown on the balance sheet, where:

Owners' equity = Assets – Liabilities

In the United States this is called a *statement of retained earnings* and it is required under the U.S. Generally Accepted Accounting Principles (U.S. GAAP) whenever comparative balance sheets and income statements are presented. It may appear in the balance sheet, in a combined income statement and changes in retained earnings statement, or as a separate schedule.

Therefore, the statement of retained earnings uses information from the income statement and provides information to the balance sheet.

Retained earnings are part of the balance sheet (another basic financial statement) under "stockholders equity (shareholders' equity)" and is mostly affected by net income earned during a period of time by the company less any dividends paid to the company's owners/stockholders. The retained earnings account on the balance sheet is said to represent an "accumulation of earnings" since net profits and losses are added/subtracted from the account from period to period.

Retained Earnings are part of the "Statement of Changes in Equity". The general equation can be expressed as following:

Ending Retained Earnings = Beginning Retained Earnings – Dividends Paid + Net Income.

This equation is necessary to use to find the Profit Before Tax to use in the Cash Flow Statement under Operating Activities when using the indirect method. This is used whenever a comprehensive income statement is not given but only the balance sheet is given.

Requirements of IFRS

IAS 1 requires a business entity to present a separate statement of changes in equity (SOCE) as one of the components of financial statements.

The statement shall show:

- Total comprehensive income for the period, showing separately amounts attributable to owners of the parent and to non-controlling interests.
- The effects of retrospective application, when applicable, for each component.
- Reconciliations between the carrying amounts at the *beginning* and the *end* of the period for each component of equity, separately disclosing:
  - Profit or loss.
  - Each item of other comprehensive income.

  - Transactions with owners, showing separately contributions by and distributions to owners and changes in ownership interests in subsidiaries that do not result in a loss of control.

However, the amount of dividends recognised as distributions, and the related amount per share, *may* be presented in the notes instead of presenting in the statement of changes in equity.

For small and medium enterprises (SMEs), the statement of changes in equity should show all changes in equity including:

- Total comprehensive income.
- Owners' investments.
- Dividends.
- Owners' withdrawals of capital.
- Treasury share transactions.

They can omit the statement of changes in equity if the entity has no owner investments or withdrawals other than dividends, and elects to present a combined statement of comprehensive income and retained earnings.

TRADING STATEMENT

The trading statement is an expanded version of sales portion of the Income statement. The trading statement's main objective is to determine sales, cost of sales and gross profit. The trading statement forms part of effective bookkeeping within the accounting discipline.

Primary Formula

Sales - Cost of Sales = Gross Profit.

Cost of Sales

The main parts of a cost of sales calculation consists of:

- Opening inventories (The amount of inventories that the entity has on hand from the previous year).
- + Purchases (The amount of inventories that the entity purchases over the course of the year).
- = Goods available for sale (Opening inventories + Purchases +/- other items).
- - Closing inventories (Inventory on hand at the end of the year).

Example: A business entity purchases £10400 worth of equipment in order to construct computers. During the financial year, £1400 worth of equipment is returned to the entity by its customers as the equipment was determined to be faulty. The previous financial year, the entity had £3000 worth of equipment left over. The entity makes use of a trucking company to deliver all of its goods. The trucking company charges the entity £120 for the year to deliver the equipment. The entity sold £14500 worth of items during the year to various customers. The entity checked its inventory stock levels at the end of the year and determined that there was £2000 worth of inventories left over.

Solution: Sales calculation:

Sales = Sales for the year - Returns in (Goods that were returned to the entity during the course of the year),

Sales = £14500 - £1400,

Sales = £13100.

Cost of sales calculation:

Cost of sales	£
Opening inventories	£3000
+ Purchases	£10400
+ Freight (in)	£120
= Goods available for sale	£13520
- Closing inventories	(£2000)

Therefore, Cost of sales = Goods available for sale - Closing inventory,

Cost of sales = £13520 - £2000,

Cost of sales = £11520,

Gross profit calculation: Gross profit = Sales - Cost of sales,

Gross profit = £13100 - £11520,

Gross profit = £1580.

Ratio Calculation

Often, information in the trading statement is left out and it is up to the bookkeeper to determine the missing value. This is a very popular bookkeeping examination type question. The best way to go about solving the unknown variable being either sales, cost of sales or gross profit is to make use of a ratio calculation.

Want/Have Method

Using the example above, we can clearly determine all three variables (sales, cost of sales and gross profit) as all of the information is provided in the question. If for instance the question did not stipulate both the sales and the cost of sales figures though the gross profit figure was given, a ratio calculation can then be performed.

For a ratio calculation, the question will have additional information regarding the mark-up percentages of the sales, cost of sales and gross profit.

AUDITOR'S REPORT

The auditor's report is a disclaimer thereof, issued by either an internal auditor or an independent external auditor as a result of an internal or external audit, as an assurance service in order for the user to make decisions based on the results of the audit.

An auditor's report is considered an essential tool when reporting financial information to users, particularly in business. Since many third-party users prefer, or even require financial information to be certified by an independent external auditor, many audiotapes rely on auditor reports to certify their information in order to attract investors, obtain loans, and improve public appearance. Some have even stated that financial information without an auditor's report is "essentially worthless" for investing purposes.

Auditor's Report on Financial Statements

It is important to note that auditor reports on financial statements are neither evaluations nor any other similar determination used to evaluate entities in order to make a decision. The report is only an opinion on whether the information presented is correct and free from material misstatements, whereas all other determinations are left for the user to decide.

There are four common types of auditor's reports, each one presenting a different situation encountered during the auditor's work. The four reports are as follows:

Unqualified Opinion

An opinion is said to be unqualified when he or she does not have any significant reservation in respect of matters contained in the Financial Statements. The most frequent type of report is referred to as the "Unqualified Opinion", and is regarded by many as the equivalent of a "clean bill of health" to a patient, which has led many to call it the "Clean Opinion", but in reality it is not a clean bill of health, because the Auditor can only provide reasonable assurance regarding the Financial Statements, not the health of the company itself, or the integrity of company records not part of the foundation of the Financial Statements. This type of report is issued by an auditor when the financial statements are free of material misstatements and are presented fairly in accordance with the Generally Accepted Accounting Principles (GAAP), which in other words means that the company's financial condition, position, and operations are fairly presented in the financial statements. It is the best type of report an auditee may receive from an external auditor.

An Unqualified Opinion indicates the following:

1. The Financial Statements have been prepared using the Generally Accepted Accounting Principles which have been consistently applied.
2. The Financial Statements comply with relevant statutory requirements and regulations.

3. There is adequate disclosure of all material matters relevant to the proper presentation of the financial information subject to statutory requirements, where applicable.

4. Any changes in the accounting principles or in the method of their application and the effects there of have been properly determined and disclosed in the Financial Statements.

The report consists of a title and header, a main body, the auditor's signature and address, and the report's issuance date. US auditing standards require that the title includes "independent" to convey to the user that the report was unbiased in all respects. Traditionally, the main body of the unqualified report consists of three main paragraphs, each with distinct standard wording and individual purpose. Nonetheless, certain auditors (including PricewaterhouseCoopers) have since modified the arrangement of the main body (but not the wording) in order to differentiate themselves from other audit firms, even though such modification is contrary to the clarified US AICPA standards on auditing.

The first paragraph (commonly referred to as the introductory paragraph) .states the audit work performed and identifies the responsibilities of the auditor and the auditee in relation to the financial statements. The second paragraph (commonly referred to as the scope paragraph) details the scope of audit work, provides a general description of the nature of the work, examples of procedures performed, and any limitations the audit faced based on the nature of the work. This paragraph also states that the audit was performed in accordance with the country's prevailing generally accepted auditing standards and regulations. The third paragraph (commonly referred to as the opinion paragraph) simply states the auditor's opinion on the financial statements and whether they are in accordance with generally accepted accounting principles.

The following is an example of a standard unqualified auditor's report on financial statements as it is used in most countries, using the name ABC Company as an auditee's name. Note that this report is acceptable only for periods ending before December 15, 2012:

Independent Auditor's Report

Board of Directors, Stockholders, Owners, and Management of
ABC Company, Inc.
123 Main St.
Anytown, Any Country

We have audited the accompanying balance sheet of ABC Company, Inc. (the "Company") as of December 31, 20XX and the related statements of income, retained earnings, and cash flows for the year then ended. These financial statements are the responsibility of the Company's management. Our responsibility is to express an opinion on these financial statements based on our audit.

We conducted our audit in accordance with auditing standards generally accepted in (the country where the report is issued). Those standards require that we plan and perform the audit to obtain reasonable assurance about whether the financial statements are free of material misstatement. An audit includes examining, on a test basis, evidence supporting the amounts and disclosures in the financial statements. An audit also includes assessing the accounting principles used and significant estimates made by management, as well as evaluating the overall financial statement presentation. We believe that our audit provides a reasonable basis for our opinion.

In our opinion, the financial statements referred to above present fairly, in all material respects, the financial position of the Company as of December 31, 20XX, and the results of its operations and its cash flows for the year then ended in accordance with generally accepted accounting principles in (the country where the report is issued).

AUDITOR'S SIGNATURE
Auditor's name and address

Date = Last day of any significant field work
This date should not be dated earlier than when the auditor has sufficient audit evidence to support the opinion.

Recently modifications have been made by the PCAOB to the opinion in the independent auditors report. These changes can be attributed to the introduction of SAS No. 122 and SAS No. 123. For periods ending after December 15, 2012, the following is an example of a standard unqualified auditor's report on financial statements as it is used in most countries, using the name ABC Company, which was incorporated in California, as an auditee's name.

Independent Auditor's Report

Board of Directors, Stockholders, Owners, and Management of
ABC Company, Inc.
123 Main St.
Anytown, Any Country

We have audited the accompanying financial statements of ABC Company, Inc. (a California corporation), which comprise the balance sheet as of December 31, 20XX, and the related statements of income, retained earnings, and cash flows for the year then ended, and the related notes to the financial statements.

Management's Responsibility for the Financial Statements

Management is responsible for the preparation and fair presentation of these consolidated financial statements in accordance with U.S. generally accepted accounting principles; this includes the design, implementation, and maintenance of internal control relevant to the preparation and fair presentation of consolidated financial statements that are free from material misstatement, whether due to fraud or error.

Auditor's Responsibility

Our responsibility is to express an opinion on these consolidated financial statements based on our audit. We conducted our audit in accordance with U.S. generally accepted auditing standards. Those standards require that we plan and perform the audit to obtain reasonable assurance about whether the consolidated financial statements are free from material misstatement.

An audit involves performing procedures to obtain audit evidence about the amounts and disclosures in the consolidated financial statements. The procedures selected depend on the auditors' judgment, including the assessment of the risks of material misstatement of the consolidated financial statements, whether due to fraud or error. In making those risk assessments, the auditor considers internal control relevant to the entity's preparation and fair presentation of the consolidated financial statements in order to design audit procedures that are appropriate in the circumstances, but not for the purpose of expressing an opinion on the effectiveness of the entity's internal control. Accordingly, we express no such opinion. An audit also includes evaluating the appropriateness of accounting policies used and the reasonableness of significant accounting estimates made by management, as well as evaluating the overall presentation of the consolidated financial statements.

We believe that the audit evidence we have obtained is sufficient and appropriate to provide a basis for our audit opinion.

Opinion

In our opinion, the financial statements referred to above present fairly, in all material respects, the financial position of ABC Company, Inc. as of December 31, 20XX, and the results of its operations and its cash flows for the year then ended in accordance with U.S. generally accepted accounting principles.

Auditor's signature.

Auditor's name and address.

Date = Last day of any significant field wor.

This date should not be dated earlier than when the auditor has sufficient audit evidence to support the opinion.

Qualified Opinion Report

Qualified report is given by the auditor in either of these two cases:

- When the financial statements are materially misstated due to misstatement in one particular account balance, class of transaction or disclosure that does not have pervasive effect on the financial statements.
- When the auditor is unable to obtain audit evidence regarding particular account balance, class of transaction or disclosure that does not have pervasive effect on the financial statements.

The report is mostly like a Clear Opinion Report and only includes a paragraph viz. Basis for Qualification after Scope paragraph and before Opinion paragraph. Opinion paragraph in addition to its standard wording includes "except for the matter described in Basis for Qualification paragraph the financial statements give true and fair view."

A Qualified Opinion report is issued when the auditor encountered one of the two types of situations which do not comply with generally accepted accounting principles, however the rest of the financial statements are fairly presented. This type of opinion is very similar to an unqualified or "clean opinion", but the report states that the financial statements are fairly presented with a certain exception which is otherwise misstated. The two types of situations which would cause an auditor to issue this opinion over the Unqualified opinion are:

- Single deviation from GAAP – This type of qualification occurs when one or more areas of the financial statements do not conform with GAAP (e.g. are misstated), but do not affect the rest of the financial statements from being fairly presented when taken as a whole. Examples of this include a company dedicated to a retail business that did not correctly calculate the depreciation expense of its building. Even if this expense is considered material, since the rest of the financial statements do conform with gaap, then the auditor qualifies the opinion by describing the depreciation misstatement in the report and continues to issue a clean opinion on the rest of the financial statements.
- Limitation of scope – This Type of qualification occurs when the auditor could not audit one or more areas of the financial statements, and although they could not be verified, the rest of the financial statements were audited and they conform to GAAP. Examples of this include an auditor not being able to observe and test a company's inventory of goods. If the auditor audited the rest of the financial statements and is reasonably sure that they conform with GAAP, then the auditor simply states that the financial statements are fairly presented, with the exception of the inventory which could not be audited.

The wording of the qualified report is very similar to the Unqualified opinion, but an explanatory paragraph is added to explain the reasons for the qualification after the scope paragraph but before the opinion paragraph. The introductory paragraph is left exactly the same as in the unqualified opinion, while the scope and the opinion paragraphs receive a slight modification in line with the qualification in the explanatory paragraph.

The scope paragraph is edited to include the following phrase in the first sentence, so that the user may be immediately aware of the qualification. This placement also informs the user that, except for the qualification, the rest of the audit was performed without qualifications.

The opinion paragraph is also edited to include an additional phrase in the first sentence, so that the user is reminded that the auditor's opinion explicitly excludes the qualification expressed. Depending on the type of qualification, the phrase is edited to either state the qualification and the adjustments needed to correct it, or state the scope limitation and that adjustments could have but not necessarily been required in order to correct it.

For a qualification arising from a deviation from GAAP, the following phrase is added to the opinion paragraph:

> "In our opinion, except for the effects of the Company's incorrect determination of depreciation expense, the financial statement referred to in the first paragraph presents fairly, in all material respects, the financial position of".

For a qualification arising from a scope of limitation, the following phrase is added to the opinion paragraph:

> "In our opinion, except for the effects of such adjustments, if any, as might have been

determined to be necessary had we been able to perform proper tests and procedures on the Company's inventory, the financial statement referred to in the first paragraph presents fairly, in all material respects, the financial position of".

Adverse Opinion Report

An Adverse Opinion Report is issued on the financial statements of a company when the financial statements are materially misstated and such misstatements have pervasive effect on the financial statements.

An Adverse Opinion is issued when the auditor determines that the financial statements of an auditee are materially misstated and, when considered as a whole, do not conform with GAAP. It is considered the opposite of an unqualified or clean opinion, essentially stating that the information contained is materially incorrect, unreliable, and inaccurate in order to assess the auditee's financial position and results of operations. Investors, lending institutions, and governments very rarely accept an auditee's financial statements if the auditor issued an adverse opinion, and usually request the auditee to correct the financial statements and obtain another audit report.

Generally, an adverse opinion is only given if the financial statements pervasively differ from GAAP. An example of such a situation would be failure of a company to consolidate a material subsidiary.

The wording of the adverse report is similar to the qualified report. The scope paragraph is modified accordingly and an explanatory paragraph is added to explain the reason for the adverse opinion after the scope paragraph but before the opinion paragraph. However, the most significant change in the adverse report from the qualified report is in the opinion paragraph, where the auditor clearly states that the financial statements are not in accordance with GAAP, which means that they, as a whole, are unreliable, inaccurate, and do not present a fair view of the auditee's position and operations.

> "In our opinion, because of the situations mentioned above (in the explanatory paragraph), the financial statements referred to in the first paragraph do not present fairly, in all material respects, the financial position of".

Disclaimer of Opinion Report

A Disclaimer of Opinion is issued in either of the following cases:

- When the auditor is not independent or when there is conflict of interest.
- When the limitation on scope is imposed by client, as a result the auditor is unable to obtain sufficient appropriate audit evidence.
- When there are significant uncertainties in the business of client.

The audit report changes significantly when there is Disclaimer of opinion. An additional paragraph "Basis for Disclaimer" is added in audit report which is placed after Scope paragraph and before Opinion paragraph. In Scope paragraph the wording changes to "We were engaged to audit the financial statements of XYZ Co. Ltd." from "We have audited the financial statements of XYZ Co. Ltd." In Opinion paragraph wording changes to "We do not express an opinion on the financial statements of XYZ Co. Ltd. due to situations explained in Basis for Disclaimer paragraph".

A Disclaimer of Opinion, commonly referred to simply as a Disclaimer, is issued when the auditor could not form and consequently refuses to present an opinion on the financial statements. This type of report is issued when the auditor tried to audit an entity but could not complete the work due to various reasons and does not issue an opinion. The disclaimer of opinion report can be traced back to 1949, when the Statement on Auditing Procedure No. 23: Recommendation Made To Clarify Accountant's Representations When Opinion Is Not Expressed was published in order to provide guidance to auditors in presenting a disclaimer.

Statements on Auditing Standards (SAS) provide certain situations where a disclaimer of opinion may be appropriate:

- A lack of independence, or material conflicts of interest, exist between the auditor and the auditee.
- There are significant scope limitations, whether intentional or not, which hinder the auditor's work in obtaining evidence and performing procedures.
- There is a substantial doubt about the auditee's ability to continue as a going concern or, in other words, continue operating.
- There are significant uncertainties within the auditee.

Although this type of opinion is rarely used, the most common examples where disclaimers are issued include audits where the auditee willfully hides or refuses to provide evidence and information to the auditor in significant areas of the financial statements, where the auditee is facing significant legal and litigation issues in which the outcome is uncertain (usually government investigations), and where the auditee has going concern issues (the auditee may not continue operating in the near future). Investors, lending institutions, and governments typically reject an auditee's financial statements if the auditor disclaimed an opinion, and will request the auditee to correct the situations the auditor mentioned and obtain another audit report.

A disclaimer of opinion differs substantially from the rest of the auditor's reports because it provides very little information regarding the audit itself, and includes an explanatory paragraph stating the reasons for the disclaimer. Although the report still contains the letterhead, the auditee's name and address, the auditor's signature and address, and the report's issuance date, every other paragraph is modified extensively, and the scope paragraph is entirely omitted since the auditor is basically stating that an audit could not be realized.

In the introductory paragraph, the first phrase changes from "We have audited" to "We were engaged to audit" in order to let the user know that the auditee commissioned an audit, but does not mention that the auditor necessarily completed the audit. Additionally, since the audit was not completely and adequately performed, the auditor refuses to accept any responsibility by omitting the last sentence of the paragraph. The scope paragraph is omitted in its entirety since, effectively, no audit was performed. Similar to the qualified and the adverse opinions, the auditor must briefly discuss the situations for the disclaimer in an explanatory paragraph. Finally, the opinion paragraph changes completely, stating that an opinion could not be formed and is not expressed because of the situations mentioned in the previous paragraphs.

The following is a draft of the three main paragraphs of a disclaimer of opinion because of inadequate accounting records of an auditee, which is considered a significant scope of limitation:

We were engaged to audit the accompanying balance sheet of ABC Company, Inc. (the "Company") as of December 31, 20XX and the related statements of income and cash flows for the year then ended. These financial statements are the responsibility of the Company's management.

The Company does not maintain adequate accounting records to provide sufficient information for the preparation of the basic financial statements. The Company's accounting records do not constitute a double-entry system which can produce financial statements.

Because of the significance of the matters discussed in the preceding paragraphs, the scope of our work was not sufficient to enable us to express, and we do not express, an opinion of the financial statements referred to in the first paragraph.

Auditor's Report on Internal Controls of Public Companies

Following the enactment of the Sarbanes-Oxley Act of 2002, the Public Company Accounting Oversight Board (PCAOB) was established in order to monitor, regulate, inspect, and discipline audit and public accounting firms of public companies. The PCAOB Auditing Standards No. 2 now requires auditors of public companies to include an additional disclosure in the opinion report regarding the auditee's internal controls, and to opine about the company's and auditor's assessment on the company's internal controls over financial reporting. These new requirements are commonly referred to as the COSO Opinion.

The auditor's report is modified to include all necessary disclosures by either presenting the report subsequent to the report on the financial statements, or combining both reports into one auditor's report. The following is an example of the former version of adding a separate report immediately after the auditor's report on financial statements.

Internal Control over Financial Reporting

We have also audited management's assessment, included in the accompanying Management's Annual Report on Internal Control Over Financial Reporting, that the Company maintained effective internal control over financial reporting as of December 31, 20XX, based on criteria established in Internal Control—Integrated Framework issued by the Committee of Sponsoring Organizations of the Treadway Commission ("COSO").The Company's management is responsible for maintaining effective internal control over financial reporting and for its assessment of the effectiveness of internal control over financial reporting. Our responsibility is to express an opinion on management's assessment and on the effectiveness of the Company's internal control over financial reporting based on our audit.We conducted our audits in accordance with the standards of the Public Company Accounting Oversight Board (United States). Those standards require that we plan and perform the audit to obtain reasonable assurance about whether effective internal control over financial reporting was maintained in all material respects. Our audit of internal control over financial reporting included obtaining an understanding of internal control over financial reporting, evaluating management's assessment, testing and evaluating the design and operating effectiveness of internal control, and performing such other procedures as we considered necessary in the circumstances. We believe that our audit provides a reasonable basis for our opinion.

A company's internal control over financial reporting is a process designed to provide reasonable assurance regarding the reliability of financial reporting and the preparation of financial statements for external purposes in accordance with generally accepted accounting principles. A company's internal control over financial reporting includes those policies and procedures that (1) pertain to the maintenance of records that, in reasonable detail, accurately and fairly reflect the transactions and dispositions of the assets of the company; (2) provide reasonable assurance that transactions are recorded as necessary to permit preparation of financial statements in accordance with generally accepted accounting principles, and that receipts and expenditures of the company are being made only in accordance with authorizations of management and directors of the company; and (3) provide reasonable assurance regarding prevention or timely detection of unauthorized acquisition, use, or disposition of the company's assets that could have a material effect on the financial statements.

Because of its inherent limitations, internal control over financial reporting may not prevent or detect misstatements. Also, projections of any evaluation of effectiveness to future periods are subject to the risk that controls may become inadequate because of changes in conditions, or that the degree of compliance with the policies or procedures may deteriorate.

In our opinion, management's assessment that ABC Company maintained effective internal control over financial reporting as of December 31, 20XX, is fairly stated, in all material respects, based on criteria established in Internal Control—Integrated Framework issued by COSO. Furthermore, in our opinion, ABC Company maintained, in all material respects, effective internal control over financial reporting as of December 31, 20XX, based on criteria established in Internal Control—Integrated Framework issued by COSO.

Going Concern

Going concern is a term which means that an entity will continue to operate in the near future which is generally more than next 12 months, so long as it generates or obtains enough resources to operate. If the auditee is not a going concern, it means that the entity might not be able to sustain itself within the next twelve months. Auditors are required to consider the going concern of an auditee before issuing a report. If the auditee is a going concern, the auditor does not modify his/her report in any way. However, if the auditor considers that the auditee is not a going concern, or will not be a going concern in the near future, then the auditor is required to include an explanatory paragraph before the opinion paragraph or following the opinion papragraph, in the audit report explaining the situation, which is commonly referred to as the going concern disclosure. Such an opinion is called an "unqualified modified opinion".

Unfortunately, many auditors are increasingly reluctant to include this disclosure in their opinions, since it is considered a "self-fulfilling prophecy" by some. This is because a disclosure for a lack of going concern is viewed negatively by investors, lending institutions, and credit agencies, and therefore reduces the chance that the auditee may obtain the capital or borrowing it needs to survive once the disclosure is made. If this situation occurs, the auditee is more likely to stop being a going concern while the auditor loses potential future audit engagements, and so the auditor may be pressured to avoid including a going concern disclosure. In a study performed on 2001 bankruptcies, nearly half (48%) of selected public companies who faced bankruptcy in 2001 did not have a "going concern disclosure" in the previous auditor's reports. Additionally, 12 of the 20 largest bankruptcies in U.S. history occurred between 2001 and 2002 and none of them had a "going concern disclosure" in their previous auditor's report.

As for the actual wording of the auditor's report, when a lack of going concern is determined by the auditor, the disclosure paragraph should state the situation, state the auditor's determination, and state the auditee's plan to correct the situation. The disclosure paragraph should immediately follow the opinion paragraph.

The following is the most widely used format of the paragraph which, in this case, deals with a company that has recurring losses:

The accompanying financial statements have been prepared assuming that the Company will continue as a going concern. As discussed in Note (X) to the financial statements, the Company has suffered recurring losses and has a net capital deficiency. These conditions raise substantial doubt about its ability to continue as a going concern. Management's plans in regard to these matters are also described in Note (X). The financial statements do not include any adjustments relating to the recoverability and classification of asset carrying amounts or the amount and classification of liabilities that might result should the Company be unable to continue as a going concern.

Other Explanatory Information and Paragraphs

Although the auditor reports mentioned above are the standard reports for financial statement audits, the auditor may add additional information to the report if it is deemed necessary without changing the overall opinion of the report. Usually, this additional information is included after the opinion paragraph, although some situations require that the additional information be included in paragraphs before the opinion paragraph. The most frequent paragraphs include:

- Limiting distribution of the report – In some occasions, the audit report is restricted to a specified user and the auditor includes this restriction in the report, such as a report for financial statements made in cash basis which are prepared for tax purposes only, financial statements for a wholly owned subsidiary whose sole user of its financial statements is its parent company, etc.
- Additional or supplemental information – Certain auditees include additional and supplemental information with their financial statements which is not directly related to the financial statements. Examples due to size, time, location, and technical constraints. When the main auditor has to rely on another auditor's work, the main auditor may either accept responsibility for the component's information and not modify the audit report, or may choose to disclaim the audit on the specific component, stating that the main auditor did not audit the component, that another auditor audited the component, that the component's audited information is therefore the responsibility of another auditor, and that the main auditor is simply including it in the original auditee's information. If used, this disclaimer is usually included in the introductory paragraph.

Auditor's Reports on Financial Statements in Different Countries

The auditor's report usually does not vary from country to country, although some countries do require either additional or less wording. In the United States, auditors are required to include in the scope paragraphs a phrase stating that they conducted their audit "in accordance with generally accepted auditing standards in the United States of America", and, in the opinion paragraph, state whether the financial statements are presented "in conformity with generally accepted accounting principles in the United States of America". Some countries, such as the Philippines, use similar reports to those issued in the United States, with the exception that second paragraph would state that the audit was conducted in accordance with Philippine Standards on Auditing, and that the financial statements are in accordance with Philippine Financial Reporting Standards.

XBRL ASSURANCE

XBRL assurance is the auditor's opinion on whether a financial statement or other business report published in XBRL, is relevant, accurate, complete, and fairly presented. An XBRL report is an electronic file and called instance in XBRL terminology.

IFAC and other accounting organizations are discussing the topic to decide on a common approach and XBRL auditing standards. The auditor may give assurance to an XBRL financial statement, an XBRL business report and XBRL real-time reporting (often referred to as continuous reporting). The short term focus is on XBRL financial statements and regulatory reports, while the future focus is expected to be more on real-time reporting.

Digital Reporting Process

An XBRL report is part of a digital reporting supply chain. The auditor should not focus only on the reliability of the report itself. It is better to focus on the whole supply chain including the communication over a network of the report. The auditor needs to check if the report that has been sent (and received) is complete and in time.

In assessing the XBRL reporting process the auditor can use a reference model in which the layering of the whole digital reporting supply chain is reflected. The auditor performs an audit on every layer of the digital reporting supply chain, with assistance of experts and use of software tools on specific areas. A known example of a reference model is the OSI model. The use of a more comprehensive and detailed reference model by the auditor seems logical.

Model

XBRL assurance is a container concept which covers multiple types of XBRL reports, audits, audit reports and related topics. In order for the auditor to be able to give the assurance, several aspects need to be clear:

- The identification of the audit object.
- The XBRL audit objectives, XBRL auditing standards and audit approach that fit with the XBRL audit object.
- Content of the audit report, the text including the auditor's opinion.

- How to keep the (unbreakable) link between the (electronic) audit object and the audit report with use of the auditor's (electronic) signature.

With XBRL assurance the auditor needs to distinguish between primary and secondary audit objects:

- The primary audit object is the XBRL file (instance) containing the data. The auditor may give assurance to an XBRL financial statement, an XBRL report or XBRL real-time reporting.
- The secondary audit objects containing metadata that play a role in the XBRL reporting chain:
  - The XBRL taxonomy, in three different instances:
    - Reporting on the basis of a standard taxonomy.
    - Reporting on the basis of a custom taxonomy.
    - Reporting on the basis of a combination: both standard base-taxonomy and custom extension-taxonomy.
  - Presentation- or rendering metadata may come in different forms: stylesheet (XSLT), inline XBRL, XBRL rendering linkbase or proprietary software.

The term standard taxonomy is here used in the context of clear ownership. A standard taxonomy is owned by an authoritative body and responsibility for the quality is taken by the owner. Obvious taxonomy owners are governments, regulators and standard setters. Ownership can be linked with creation, maintenance, publication and certification of the taxonomy. A custom taxonomy is not owned by an authoritative body.

Base-taxonomy and extension-taxonomy refer to the XBRL mechanism where an extension-taxonomy refers to -or imports- a base-taxonomy to expand the available reporting concepts and their relations.

XBRL assurance can be described using following model:

Primary audit object	XBRL financial statement	XBRL report /filing	Real time reporting
Aspect			
Audit objectives, auditing standards and audit approach			
Audit report (text) including the auditor's opinion			
Link between audit report and audit object and auditor's signature			

Audit Objectives and Approach

The following, mainly XBRL specific reporting steps serve as a basis for the audit approach. The auditor checks that:

- The right standard (base) taxonomy has been used.
- The custom (extension) taxonomy is complete, correct and accurate.

- The sourcedata used for reporting is reliable.
- The correct and complete mapping (or tagging) of sourcedata to taxonomy elements has occurred.
- The XBRL report (instance) is technically correct and validates with the taxonomy.
- The sending of the XBRL reporting was complete, accurate and timely.

The distinction between a standard (base) taxonomy and a custom (extension) taxonomy is important for the auditor. A standard taxonomy is normally owned, created and published by the government or regulator. It is the responsibility of the government or regulator to create a taxonomy that is correct. The quality of a standard taxonomy is fixed input for the auditor. The auditor just needs to check -with help of software tools- that the right taxonomy is used. With a custom (extension) taxonomy this is not the case. The auditor needs to validate the custom (extension) taxonomy, a secondary audit object. He needs to perform an audit to check if this taxonomy complies with regulations and if it is accurate and complete.

A significant difference with paper based assurance is the concept of material misstatement. Material misstatement concerns the accuracy of the audit opinion on a financial statement or filing as a whole. An XBRL report contains a collection of individually identifiable business facts. The facts are building blocks of an XBRL report. Material misstatement in an XBRL report concerns the individually identifiable business facts.

Audit Report

The most common audit report in the world is an external auditor's report on an auditee's financial statements and its accompanying notes. XBRL assurance covers different audit reports depending on the primary and secondary audit objects.

To let the auditor to give an opinion on fair view is not obvious. An XBRL report (instance) contains little presentation metadata. More presentation metadata is needed to present the XBRL report in a human readable manner.

The auditor opts for an approach whereby the current audit object (a paper based report) will be cut in two new audit objects, each with its own audit report and opinion. The primary audit object is the instance containing all the business facts. The secondary audit object contains the presentation or rendering metadata.

The split in primary and secondary audit objects with different audit reports (and opinions) is necessary to prevent any confusion about the assurance the auditor adds to the XBRL financial statement instance or any other XBRL report without presentation in a human readable form.

One approach to this is to have different auditor opinions on the primary audit object and the secondary object that combined make clear the XBRL report provides a fair view.

Electronic Signature

This aspect covers the unbreakable linkage of the audit report and auditor's signature to the (primary or secondary) audit object. Both the primary and the secondary audit objects are electronic files which can be altered without leaving a trace. All this means that the auditor must use techniques like encryption and electronic signatures, ensuring that his opinion actually came from him and is permanently linked to the audited XBRL audit object without any unauthorized changes.

Other Aspects

The XBRL standard has the ability to define business rules. These business rules can be found in different places in the XBRL taxonomy, that is in datatypes or linkbases. Application of these business rules will contribute to the reliability of the XBRL report. The business rules can be used by the reporting company, the taxonomy author or the auditor.

PnL EXPLAINED

PnL Explained also called P&L Explain, P&L Attribution or Profit and Loss Explained is a type of report commonly used by traders, especially derivatives (swaps and options) traders and produced by Product control, that attributes or *explains* the daily fluctuation in the value of a portfolio of trades to the root causes of the changes.

P&L is the day-over-day change in the value of a portfolio of trades typically calculated using the following formula: PnL = Value today - Value from Prior Day.

Report

A PnL Explained Report will usually contain one row per trade or group of trades and will have at a minimum these columns:

- Column 1: PnL - This is the PnL as calculated outside of the PnL Explained report.
- Column 2: PnL Explained - This is the sum of the explanatory columns.
- Column 3: PnL Unexplained - This is calculated as PnL - PnL Explained (i.e., Column 1 - Column 2).
- Column 4: Impact of Time - This is the PnL due to the change in time.
- Column 5: Impact of Prices - This is the PnL, i.e., the change in the value of a portfolio due to changes in commodity or equity/stock prices.
- Column 6: Impact of Interest Rates - This is the PnL due to changes in interest rates.
- Column 7: Impact of Volatility - This is the PnL due to changes in volatilities. Volatilities are used to value Option (finance) (i.e., calls and puts).
- Column 8: Impact of New Trades - PnL from trades done on the current day.
- Column 9: Impact of Cancellation/Amendment - PnL from trades cancelled or changed on the current day.

Methodologies

There are two methodologies for calculating Pnl Explained, the 'sensitivities' method and the 're-valuation' method.

Sensitivities Method

The Sensitivities Method involves first calculating option sensitivities known as the Greeks because of the common practice of representing the sensitivities using Greek letters. For example, the delta of an option is the value an option changes due to a $1 move in the underlying commodity or equity/stock. To calculate 'Impact of Prices' the formula is: Impact of Prices = Option Delta * Price Move; so if the price moves $100 and the option's delta is 0.05% then the 'Impact of Prices' is $0.05. To generalize, then, for example to yield curves:

Impact of Prices = Position Sensitivity * Move in the variable in question.

Revaluation Method

The Revaluation Method recalculates the value of a trade based on the current and the prior day's prices. The formula for Impact of Prices using the Revaluation Method is:

- Impact of Prices = (Trade Value using Today's Prices) - (Trade Value using Prior Day's Prices).

  for some small value assets such as loose tools.

- Depreciation = value at the beginning of the year (opening balance) + purchases in the year - value at the end of the year (closing balance).

PnL Unexplained

PnL unexplained is a critical metric that regulators and product control within a bank alike pay attention to.

PnL Attribution is used to test the hypothesis that the risk factors identified for a risky position are sufficient to materially explain the value change expected from the risky position;. Such that if position sensitivities to those risk factors are calculated, then the value change observed over a day can be attributed to the market price change of those risk factors, with the magnitude of the estimated as a sum product of the risk factor sensitivities and the corresponding daily risk factor price change.

Any residual P&L left unexplained (PnL Unexplained) would be expected to be small IF the identified risk factors are indeed sufficient to materially explain the expected value change of the position AND if the models used to calculate sensitivities to these risk factors are correct. PnL Unexplained is thus a critical metric that when large may highlight instances where the risk factors classified for a risky position are incomplete or the models used for sensitivities calculations are incorrect or inconsistent.

SINGLE ENTRY SYSTEM

A single entry system records a transaction with a single entry and only maintains one side of every transaction. It is the oldest method of recording financial transactions and is less popular than the double entry system and is mainly used for entries recorded in the income statement. This term is used to describe the problems associated with the accounts from an incomplete transaction and is popularly called as 'Preparation of accounts from incomplete records'.

The core information involves cash receipts and cash disbursements rather than asset and liability records. The primary form is the cash book which is an expanded form of the check register. This mainly has columns which record particular sources and uses of cash, and starts with the opening balance and ends with closing balance. The single entry system is mainly used in the manual process of accounting and by small firms who do not have the financial capability and resources that are necessary for a full-fledged accounting system. Mainly all the computerized accounting systems use double entry accounting.

Below is the example format of single entry system of accounting.

#	Date	Particulars	Revenue	Expenses	Inventory	Payroll
		Balance Forward	$20,000	$5,000	$ 7,000	$3,000
1000	Jul-18	Wages				$1,500
1001	Jul-19	Utilities		$200		
1002	Jul-20	Deposit	$15,000			
1003	Jul-21	Goods			$2,000	
		Ending Balance	$35,000	$5,200	$9,000	$4,500

This is an inaccurate and unscientific way of recording transactions where there is no linkage among the transactions or the available information. There is no record of real and personal accounts and the cash book mixes up the business and personal transactions.

Types of Single Entry Accounting System

Pure Single Entry

In this, no information is available of sales, purchases and cash and bank balances only personal accounts are considered. This method cannot be used in the practical world since it does not provide any information regarding cash or the daily transactions.

Simple Single Entry

This account is kept on the basis of double entry system but only two accounts are considered, i.e the personal and the cash account. Entries are made only from these accounts and no other account is considered.

Quasi Single Entry

In this type of accounting apart from the personal and cash accounts, other subsidiary accounts are also maintained. The main ones being sales, purchases accounts, and bill books. Discounts are also recorded in the personal account. Other vital information like wages, rent, salaries is also available. This method is adopted as a substitute to double entry accounting system.

On a whole, by looking at the types we can determine that the single entry accounting system can be defined as the system which is a mixture of Single-entry double entry and no entry.

Advantages of using Single Entry System Accounting

- It is comparatively simple and easy to implement.
- No professionals are required, resources with a basic understanding of accounting or business can perform single entry system.
- This type of accounting suits small firms which are at starting stage and startups.
- Income and expense are accounted on a daily basis.
- Only limited accounts are opened since all the transactions related to personal account are recorded relating in personal and real accounts.
- As mentioned in the previous point, that limited accounts are opened and the books are limited, expenses to maintain these accounts are also limited.
- The single entry system is purely based on the income statement hence, it becomes easier to determine the profit and loss.

Please note that Profits under this system can only be an estimate and therefore cannot necessarily be true and correct.

Problems Associated with Single Entry System in Accounting

Assets

In terms of keeping recording or tracking, single entry system does not track assets. Thus, it makes it easier for them to be lost or stolen.

Audited Statements

The double entry system is necessary for auditing financial statements, necessary for checks and balances of each account. It is impossible to audit statements in a single entry system. Even if one wants to do it they will have to convert the single entry to double entries and balance it for auditing.

Increased Risk of Errors

In this system, there is no check for other account and cannot be balanced. This makes it more difficult to keep a check or find missing entries and track errors.

Performance Analysis

Financial position cannot be determined since there is no proper balance sheet maintained and also due to the limited information. It makes it difficult for the management to analyze its performance and estimate future metrics.

Incomplete Records

This system only focuses mainly only on those transactions which involve business or transactions with external parties and ignores the other vital transactions that may be necessary to determine the financial position of the company and should have a place in the financial statements.

Accuracy

Arithmetical accuracy cannot be achieved since this system does not prepare a trial balance.

Difference between Single Entry and Double Entry Accounting System

The Major Differences in Single Entry Accounting and Double Entry Accounting System:

- Single entry system can be defined as a system where only one aspect of each transaction is maintained i.e either debit or credit, on the contrary in double method accounting system both these transactions are recorded.
- Single entry transaction is simple and does not require detailed knowledge in accounts whereas double entry transaction requires expertise.
- Incomplete records are maintained in single entry system while double entry captures both the sides and records.
- Single entry system maintains cash accounts and personal accounts while double entry system maintains all kind of account ie real, nominal and personal.
- Since small firms do not have the financial capabilities and resources single entry accounting is suitable on the contrary for large firms it is necessary to have a double entry accounting system.
- Frauds and errors are easier to identify in double entry accounting system than in single entry system.
- As compared with the double entry system, single entry system has no standardization and there is no uniformity between the different businesses following the same method. Each business maintains accounts as per its convenience and requirements.

DOUBLE ENTRY SYSTEM

Double-entry bookkeeping, in accounting, is a system of bookkeeping so named because every entry to an account requires a corresponding and opposite entry to a different account. The double-entry has two equal and corresponding sides known as debit and credit. The left-hand side is debit and right-hand side is credit. For instance, recording a sale of $100 might require two entries: a debit of $100 to an account named "Cash" and a credit of $100 to an account named "Revenue."

The accounting equation:

$$\text{Assets} = \text{Equity} + \text{Liabilities}$$

is an error detection tool; if at any point the sum of debits for all accounts does not equal the corresponding sum of credits for all accounts, an error has occurred. However, satisfying the equation does not guarantee that there are no errors; the ledger may still "balance" even if the wrong ledger accounts have been debited or credited.

Accounting Entries

In the double-entry accounting system, at least two accounting entries are required to record each financial transaction. These entries may occur in asset, liability, equity, expense, or revenue accounts. Recording of a debit amount to one or more accounts and an equal credit amount to one or more accounts results in total debits being equal to total credits for all accounts in the general ledger. If the accounting entries are recorded without error, the aggregate balance of all accounts having *Debit* balances will be equal to the aggregate balance of all accounts having *Credit* balances. Accounting entries that debit and credit related accounts typically include the same date and identifying code in both accounts, so that in case of error, each debit and credit can be traced back to a journal and transaction source document, thus preserving an audit trail. The accounting entries are recorded in the "Books of Accounts". Regardless of which accounts and how many are impacted by a given transaction, the fundamental accounting equation of *assets equal liabilities plus capital* will hold.

Approaches

There are two different ways to memorize the effects of debits and credits on accounts in the double-entry system of bookkeeping. They are the Traditional Approach and the Accounting Equation Approach. Irrespective of the approach used, the effect on the books of accounts remains the same, with two aspects (debit and credit) in each of the transactions.

Traditional Approach

Following the Traditional Approach (also called the British Approach) accounts are classified as real, personal, and nominal accounts. Real accounts are accounts relating to assets and liabilities including the capital account of the owners. Personal accounts are accounts relating to persons or organisations with whom the business has transactions and will mainly consist of accounts of debtors and creditors. Nominal accounts are revenue, expenses, gains, and losses. Transactions are entered in the books of accounts by applying the following golden rules of accounting:

- Real account: Debit what comes in and credit what goes out.
- Personal account: Debit the receiver and credit the giver.
- Nominal account: Debit all expenses & losses and credit all incomes & gains.

Accounting Equation Approach

This approach is also called the American approach. Under this approach transactions are recorded based on the accounting equation, i.e., Assets = Liabilities + Capital. The accounting equation is a statement of equality between the debits and the credits. The rules of debit and credit depend on the nature of an account. For the purpose of the accounting equation approach, all the accounts are classified into the following five types: assets, liabilities, income/revenues, expenses, or capital gains/losses.

If there is an increase or decrease in a set of accounts, there will be equal decrease or increase in another set of accounts. Accordingly, the following rules of debit and credit hold for the various categories of accounts:

- Assets Accounts: debit entry represents an increase in assets and a credit entry represents a decrease in assets.
- Capital Account: credit entry represents an increase in capital and a debit entry represents a decrease in capital.
- Liabilities Accounts: credit entry represents an increase in liabilities and a debit entry represents a decrease in liabilities.
- Revenues or Incomes Accounts: credit entry represents an increase in incomes and gains, and debit entry represents a decrease in incomes and gains.
- Expenses or Losses Accounts: debit entry represents an increase in expenses and losses, and credit entry represents a decrease in expenses and losses.

These five rules help learning about accounting entries and also are comparable with traditional (British) accounting rules.

Books of Accounts

Each financial transaction is recorded in at least two different nominal ledger accounts within the financial accounting system, so that the total debits equals the total credits in the general ledger, i.e. the accounts balance. This is a partial check that each and every transaction has been correctly recorded. The transaction is recorded as a "debit entry" (Dr) in one account, and a "credit entry" (Cr) in a second account. The debit entry will be recorded on the debit side (left-hand side) of a general ledger account, and the credit entry will be recorded on the credit side (right-hand side) of a general ledger account. If the total of the entries on the debit side of one account is greater than the total on the credit side of the same nominal account, that account is said to have a debit balance.

Double entry is used only in nominal ledgers. It is not used in daybooks (journals), which normally do not form part of the nominal ledger system. The information from the daybooks will be used in the nominal ledger and it is the nominal ledgers that will ensure the integrity of the resulting financial information created from the daybooks (provided that the information recorded in the daybooks is correct).

The reason for this is to limit the number of entries in the nominal ledger: entries in the daybooks can be totalled before they are entered in the nominal ledger. If there are only a relatively small number of transactions it may be simpler instead to treat the daybooks as an integral part of the nominal ledger and thus of the double-entry system.

However, as can be seen from the examples of daybooks shown below, it is still necessary to check, within each daybook, that the postings from the daybook balance.

The double entry system uses nominal ledger accounts. From these nominal ledger accounts a trial balance can be created. The trial balance lists all the nominal ledger account balances. The list is split into two columns, with debit balances placed in the left hand column and credit balances placed in the right hand column. Another column will contain the name of the nominal ledger account describing what each value is for. The total of the debit column must equal the total of the credit column.

Debits and Credits

Double-entry bookkeeping is governed by the accounting equation. If revenue equals expenses, the following (basic) equation must be true:

Assets = Liabilities + Equity

For the accounts to remain in balance, a change in one account must be matched with a change in another account. These changes are made by debits and credits to the accounts. Note that the usage of these terms in accounting is not identical to their everyday usage. Whether one uses a debit or credit to increase or decrease an account depends on the normal balance of the account. Assets, Expenses, and Drawings accounts (on the left side of the equation) have a normal balance of *debit*. Liability, Revenue, and Capital accounts (on the right side of the equation) have a normal balance of *credit*. On a general ledger, debits are recorded on the left side and credits on the right side for each account. Since the accounts must always balance, for each transaction there will be a debit made to one or several accounts and a credit made to one or several accounts. The sum of all debits made in each day's transactions must equal the sum of all credits in those transactions. After a series of transactions, therefore, the sum of all the accounts with a debit balance will equal the sum of all the accounts with a credit balance.

Debits and credits are numbers recorded as follows:

- Debits are recorded on the left side of a ledger account, a.k.a. T account. Debits increase balances in asset accounts and expense accounts and decrease balances in liability accounts, revenue accounts, and capital accounts.
- Credits are recorded on the right side of a T account in a ledger. Credits increase balances in liability accounts, revenue accounts, and capital accounts, and decrease balances in asset accounts and expense accounts.
- Debit accounts are asset and expense accounts that usually have debit balances, i.e. the total debits usually exceed the total credits in each debit account.
- Credit accounts are revenue (income, gains) accounts and liability accounts that usually have credit balances.

	Debit	Credit
Asset	Increase	Decrease
Liability	Decrease	Increase

Income (revenue)	Decrease	Increase
Expense	Increase	Decrease
Capital	Decrease	Increase

The mnemonic DEADCLIC is used to help remember the effect of debit or credit transactions on the relevant accounts. DEAD: Debit to increase Expense, Asset and Drawing accounts and CLIC: Credit to increase Liability, Income and Capital accounts.

The account types are related as follows:

> Current equity = sum of equity changes across time (increases on the left side are debits, and increases on the right side are credits, and vice versa for decreases).
>
> Current equity = Assets - Liabilities.
>
> Sum of equity changes across time = owner's investment (Capital above) + Revenues - Expenses.

Advantages of Double Entry System

Although no one knows when double-entry accounting first emerged, but Italian mathematician and Franciscan friar Luca Pacioli wrote the first codified system describing the technique in the late 1400s. This publication led to the expansion and adoption of double-entry accounting as a standard business practice, leading to today's Generally Accepted Accounting Principles (GAAP) in the United States and in the International Financial Reporting System (IFRS) used by the rest of the world. The advantages of the double-entry accounting system are based on the way it reveals recording errors, giving clues about the types of errors, as well as clearly illustrating that errors are present. The importance of the double-entry system is so significant that most common accounting software packages include double-entry structure into their software architecture.

One of the merits of the double-entry system is that any transaction has two equal and opposite effects on business finances. For example, let's say that a company buys a machine to manufacture a product that it sells. The purchase of the machine reduces the amount of cash the company has while simultaneously increasing the value of the company's assets. Therefore, recording the transaction requires a debit, or reduction, in a cash account while also requiring a credit, or increase, in a capital account. With every transaction recorded as both a debit and a credit in the general ledger, the totals of each should always balance. When there is a value difference between debits and credits, it indicates a recording error. If you must list two advantages of double-entry accounting over single-entry methods, these advantages are:

- Double-entry accounting helps guarantee accurate financial records by revealing data entry errors.
- Double-entry accounting provides a complete record of financial transactions for a business.

Other Merits of the Double-entry System

Other advantages include the ability to compare financial activity in a meaningful way between periods, such as month-to-month or year-to-year. This leads to reliable financial information upon which accurate financial reports can be based. This permits comparison between businesses in terms of financial reporting, even when the businesses aren't in the same industry or sector. Shareholders, investors and financiers typically place a high priority in financial reports prepared with standard accounting techniques, including double-entry accounting systems. Using a standard double-entry bookkeeping system may also save you money in administrative costs. Double-entry is the common language of accountants, so financial records in this format may make your accountant's job easier and more affordable.

INCOMPLETE RECORDS SYSTEM

There can be two ways of maintaining the accounting records, one is the double entry system and another is the single entry system. The records maintained according to the single entry system are known as Incomplete Records. Usually, small firms like grocery shops, general stores, food joints, etc. keep their books on the single entry system.

In the Double entry system we keep the books on the basis of the Dual Aspect Concept i.e. every debit has a respective credit. The firms that do not keep their accounting books as per this system follow the single entry system. Under the single entry system, a firm maintains only cash account and the accounts of the debtors and the creditors properly.

It does not maintain the accounts of expenses, incomes, assets, and liabilities properly. Hence, as the information provided by these records is incomplete, they are known as Incomplete Records.

Reasons for Incompleteness

The proprietor may keep the accounting records on the basis of single entry due to the following reasons:

- He has no knowledge or lack of knowledge about the accounting principles and concepts.
- The double entry system is comparatively an expensive way of maintaining the financial accounts. The accountants may charge a handsome amount as fees.

- Maintaining incomplete records consumes less time.
- It is more convenient to maintain records as per the single entry system.

Limitations of Incomplete Records

Though maintaining Incomplete Records is easier but it is not a systematic method of maintaining accounts. Its limitations are as follows:

- We cannot prepare a Trial Balance to ensure the accuracy of the accounts in the absence of the double entry system.
- It fails to ascertain the accurate financial results of the organization.
- Investigation and examination of the profitability, solvency, and liquidity are difficult. Hence, the outsiders and banks may not lend money for the expansion of the business.
- In case of loss by fire or theft claiming the insurance amount causes great difficulty due to incomplete records and missing information.
- Also, convincing the income tax authorities about the computed income is difficult in the absence of proper accounting.

REVENUE INCOME

In accounting, revenue is the income that a business has from its normal business activities, usually from the sale of goods and services to customers. Revenue is also referred to as sales or turnover. Some companies receive revenue from interest, royalties, or other fees. Revenue may refer to business income in general, or it may refer to the amount, in a monetary unit, earned during a period of time, as in "Last year, Company X had revenue of $42 million". Profits or net income generally imply total revenue minus total expenses in a given period. In accounting, in the balance statement it is a subsection of the Equity section and revenue increases equity, it is often referred to as the "top line" due to its position on the income statement at the very top. This is to be contrasted with the "bottom line" which denotes net income (gross revenues minus total expenses).

For non-profit organizations, annual revenue may be referred to as gross receipts. This revenue includes donations from individuals and corporations, support from government agencies, income from activities related to the organization's mission, and income from fundraising activities, membership dues, and financial securities such as stocks, bonds or investment funds.

In general usage, revenue is income received by an organization in the form of cash or cash equivalents. Sales revenue or revenues is income received from selling goods or services over a period of time. Tax revenue is income that a government receives from taxpayers.

In more formal usage, revenue is a calculation or estimation of periodic income based on a particular standard accounting practice or the rules established by a government or government agency. Two common accounting methods, cash basis accounting and accrual basis accounting, do not use the same process for measuring revenue. Corporations that offer shares for sale to the public are usually required by law to report revenue based on generally accepted accounting principles or International Financial Reporting Standards.

In a double-entry bookkeeping system, revenue accounts are general ledger accounts that are summarized periodically under the heading Revenue or Revenues on an income statement. Revenue account names describe the type of revenue, such as "Repair service revenue", "Rent revenue earned" or "Sales".

Business Revenue

Money income from activities that is ordinary for a particular corporation, company, partnership, or sole-proprietorship. For some businesses, such as manufacturing or grocery, most revenue is from the sale of goods. Service businesses such as law firms and barber shops receive most of their revenue from rendering services. Lending businesses such as car rentals and banks receive most of their revenue from fees and interest generated by lending assets to other organizations or individuals.

Revenues from a business's primary activities are reported as sales, sales revenue or net sales. This includes product returns and discounts for early payment of invoices. Most businesses also have revenue that is incidental to the business's primary activities, such as interest earned on deposits in a demand account. This is included in revenue but not included in net sales. Sales revenue does not include sales tax collected by the business.

Other revenue (a.k.a. non-operating revenue) is revenue from peripheral (non-core) operations. For example, a company that manufactures and sells automobiles would record the revenue from the sale of an automobile as "regular" revenue. If that same company also rented a portion of one of its buildings, it would record that revenue as "other revenue" and disclose it separately on its income statement to show that it is from something other than its core operations. The combination of all the revenue generating systems of a business is called its revenue model.

Financial Statement Analysis

Revenue is a crucial part of financial statement analysis. The company's performance is measured to the extent to which its asset inflows (revenues) compare with its asset outflows (expenses). Net income is the result of this equation, but revenue typically enjoys equal attention during a standard earnings call. If a company displays solid "top-line growth", analysts could view the period's performance as positive even if earnings growth, or "bottom-line growth" is stagnant. Conversely, high net income growth would be tainted if a company failed to produce significant revenue growth. Consistent revenue growth, if accompanied by net income growth, contributes to the value of an enterprise and therefore the stock price.

Revenue is used as an indication of earnings quality. There are several financial ratios attached to it:

- The most important being gross margin and profit margin. Also, companies use revenue to determine bad debt expense using the income statement method.
- Price/Sales is sometimes used as a substitute for a Price to earnings ratio when earnings

are negative and the P/E is meaningless. Though a company may have negative earnings, it almost always has positive revenue.

- Gross Margin is a calculation of revenue less cost of goods sold, and is used to determine how well sales cover direct variable costs relating to the production of goods.
- Net income/sales, or profit margin, is calculated by investors to determine how efficiently a company turns revenues into profits.

Government Revenue

Government revenue includes all amounts of money (i.e., taxes and fees) received from sources outside the government entity. Large governments usually have an agency or department responsible for collecting government revenue from companies and individuals.

Government revenue may also include reserve bank currency which is printed. This is recorded as an advance to the retail bank together with a corresponding currency in circulation expense entry, that is, the income derived from the Official Cash rate payable by the retail banks for instruments such as 90-day bills. There is a question as to whether using generic business-based accounting standards can give a fair and accurate picture of government accounts, in that with a monetary policy statement to the reserve bank directing a positive inflation rate, the expense provision for the return of currency to the reserve bank is largely symbolic, such that to totally cancel the currency in circulation provision, all currency would have to be returned to the reserve bank and cancelled.

Association Non-dues Revenue

Association non-dues revenue is revenue generated through means besides association membership fees. This revenue can be found through means of sponsorships, donations or outsourcing the association's digital media outlets.

Accounting Terms

Net sales = gross sales – (customer discounts, returns, and allowances).

Gross profit = net sales – cost of goods sold.

Operating profit = gross profit – total operating expenses.

Net profit = operating profit – taxes – interest.

Net profit = net sales – cost of goods sold – operating expense – taxes – interest.

REVENUE EXPENDITURE

A revenue expenditure, also called an income statement expenditure, is a cost related to assets that are not capitalized because they will not provide a financial benefit in future periods. In other words, revenue expenditures are extra expenses incurred because of an asset, but they don't add any additional value to the asset or increase its useful life or productivity.

These expenses are not added to the book value of the asset because they don't provide any future benefit. Remember, the definition of an asset is a resource that provides a future benefit. These expenditures don't provide a benefit, so they are expensed and reported on the income statement instead of being capitalized and reported on the balance sheet.

Example:

An example of a revenue expenditure is an additional cost attached to a fixed asset like a piece of machinery. Some machines need to be cleaned and lubricated regularly. These costs don't really add any value to the machine. They are just necessary to keep the equipment running.

Another example of a non-value adding cost is painting. Over time machines like lathes and drill presses tend to rust and corrode. In order to keep them operational, managers usually schedule them to be disassembled, sandblasted, repainted, and assembled. The entire process doesn't add any value to the machine. It just maintains its integrity and keeps it from rusting away.

These revenue expenditures are in sharp contrast to betterments. Betterments are expenses that actually improve the performance or useful life of the asset. They not only keep the asset operational; they extend the operational life. Betterments are usually capitalized and added to the asset cost on the balance sheet. These improvements are then depreciated over time instead of being expensed immediately like revenue expenditures.

References

- Interpreting-the-cash-flow-statement-1200760: thebalancesmb.com, Retrieved 23 February 2019
- Bodie, Zane; Alex Kane; Alan J. Marcus (2004). Essentials of Investments, 5th ed. Mcgraw-Hill Irwin. P. 455. ISBN 0-07-251077-3
- Balance-sheet, accounting, knowledge, resources: corporatefinanceinstitute.com, Retrieved 22 May 2019
- "Is this the most influential work in the history of capitalism?". Bbc.com. 23 October 2017. Retrieved 23 October 2017
- Warren, Carl (2008). Survey of Accounting. Cincinnati: South-Western College Pub. Pp. 128–132. ISBN 978-0-324-65826-2
- Single-entry-system-in-accounting: wallstreetmojo.com, Retrieved 2 June 2019
- Benefits-doubleentry-accounting-23836: chron.com, Retrieved 13 March 2019
- Meaning-reasons-incompleteness-its-limitations, accounts-from-incomplete-records, accountancy, guides: toppr.com, Retrieved 29 June 2019
- Revenue-expenditures, accounting-dictionary: myaccountingcourse.com, Retrieved 30 January 2019

6

Financial Statement Analysis

The process of analyzing and reviewing an organization's financial statements in order to make better economic decisions for earning income in future is referred to as financial statement analysis. The most common methods of financial statement analysis are horizontal analysis and vertical analysis. This chapter has been carefully written to provide an easy understanding of these methods of financial statement analysis.

The term 'financial analysis', also known as analysis and interpretation of financial statements', refers to the process of determining financial strengths and weaknesses of the firm by establishing strategic relationship between the items of the balance sheet, profit and loss account and other operative data.

"Analyzing financial statements," according to Metcalf and Titard, "is a process of evaluating the relationship between component parts of a financial statement to obtain a better understanding of a firm's position and performance."

"Financial statement analysis is largely a study of relationship among the various financial factors in a business as disclosed by a single set-of statements and a study of the trend of these factors as shown in a series of statements."

The purpose of financial analysis is to diagnose the information contained in financial statements so as to judge the profitability and financial soundness of the firm. Just like a doctor examines his patient by recording his body temperature, blood pressure, etc. before making his conclusion regarding the illness and before giving his treatment, a financial analyst analysis the financial statements with various tools of analysis before commenting upon the financial health or weaknesses of an enterprise.

The analysis and interpretation of financial statements is essential to bring out the mystery behind the figures in financial statements. Financial statements analysis is an attempt to determine the significance and meaning of the financial statement data so that forecast may be made of the future earnings, ability to pay interest and debt maturities (both current and long-term) and profitability of a sound dividend policy.

The term 'financial statement analysis' includes both 'analysis', and 'interpretation'. A distinction should, therefore, be made between the two terms. While the term 'analysis' is used to mean the simplification of financial data by methodical classification of the data given in the financial statements, 'interpretation' means, 'explaining the meaning and significance of the data so simplified.'

However, both' analysis and interpretation' are interlinked and complimentary to each other Analysis is useless without interpretation and interpretation without analysis is difficult or even impossible.

Most of the authors have used the term 'analysis' only to cover the meanings of both analysis and interpretation as the objective of analysis is to study the relationship between various items of financial statements by interpretation. We have also used the term Financial statement Analysis or simply 'Financial Analysis' to cover the meaning of both analysis and interpretation.

Objectives and Importance of Financial Statement Analysis

The primary objective of financial statement analysis is to understand and diagnose the information contained in financial statement with a view to judge the profitability and financial soundness of the firm, and to make forecast about future prospects of the firm. The purpose of analysis depends upon the person interested in such analysis and his object.

However, the following purposes or objectives of financial statements analysis may be stated to bring out the significance of such analysis:

1. To assess the earning capacity or profitability of the firm.
2. To assess the operational efficiency and managerial effectiveness.
3. To assess the short term as well as long term solvency position of the firm.
4. To identify the reasons for change in profitability and financial position of the firm.
5. To make inter-firm comparison.
6. To make forecasts about future prospects of the firm.
7. To assess the progress of the firm over a period of time.
8. To help in decision making and control.
9. To guide or determine the dividend action.
10. To provide important information for granting credit.

Parties Interested in Financial Analysis

The following parties are interested in the analysis of financial statements:

1. Investors or potential investors.
2. Management.
3. Creditors or suppliers.
4. Bankers and financial institutions.
5. Employees.

6. Government.
7. Trade associations.
8. Stock exchanges.
9. Economists and researchers.
10. Taxation authorities

Limitations of Financial Statement Analysis

Financial analysis is a powerful mechanism of determining financial strengths and weaknesses of a firm. But, the analysis is based on the information available in the financial statements. Thus, the financial analysis suffers from serious inherent limitations of financial statements.

The financial analyst has also to be careful about the impact of price level changes, window-dressing of financial statements, changes in accounting policies of a firm, accounting concepts and conventions, and personal judgment, etc.

Some of the important limitations of financial analysis are, however, summed up as below:

1. It is only a study of interim reports.
2. Financial analysis is based upon only monetary information and non-monetary factors are ignored.
3. It does not consider changes in price levels.
4. As the financial statements are prepared on the basis of a going concern, it does not give exact position. Thus accounting concepts and conventions cause a serious limitation to financial analysis.
5. Changes in accounting procedure by a firm may often make financial analysis misleading.
6. Analysis is only a means and not an end in itself. The analyst has to make interpretation and draw his own conclusions. Different people may interpret the same analysis in different ways.

Requisites of Financial Statement Analysis

Knowledge of Accounting

The analyst should have a sound knowledge in accounting, its principles, concepts, conventions. Otherwise he will not be able to analyse the financial statements in details. Moreover, practical application of accounting knowledge is absolutely required in order to accomplish his objectives.

Objective of the Analysis/Study

The analyst must be clear about the objective or purpose of the analysis. Usually, he is entrusted to do so for his client. Naturally, he should know his client and his requirements. Accordingly, he will analyse the financial statements for collecting such information which are desired by his clients.

Techniques of Analysis

The analyst must select the appropriate techniques for the purpose of analysis. He may apply a particular technique in one place whereas a different technique in other places.

Rearrangement/Regrouping of Financial Data

The analyst must rearrange or regroup the primary data collected by him from financial statements for the purpose of his needs and uses of financial statements. For example, if he wants to know the working capital position he must know the total current assets and total current liabilities position from the data contained in financial statements.

Determination of the Extent of Analysis

The analyst must determine first the extent of his analysis which will facilitate him to make plans for his work and also to prepare a schedule of work for the study.

Study of External and Internal Environment

The analyst should be well acquainted with the external as well as the internal environment which is faced by the firms; e.g. competitors, attitude of the creditors and debtors etc. Similarly, he must study the internal environment of the company also, e.g. structural changes, employee morale etc. which will practically help him to study and analyse the financial statements and to prepare a report.

Interpretation of Findings

The analyst must interpreted his findings in a lucid style in simple form which is easily understandable by the common users of financial statements.

Submission of Report

After proper interpretation he must prepare a report on the basis of his findings and submit the same to his client for taking decisions on future courses of action.

HORIZONTAL ANALYSIS

Horizontal analysis is used in financial statement analysis to compare historical data, such as ratios, or line items, over a number of accounting periods. Horizontal analysis can either use absolute comparisons or percentage comparisons, where the numbers in each succeeding period are expressed as a percentage of the amount in the baseline year, with the baseline amount being listed as 100%. This is also known as base-year analysis.

How Horizontal Analysis is Used

Generally accepted accounting principles (GAAP) are based on consistency and comparability of financial statements. Consistency is the ability to accurately review one company's financial statements over a period of time because accounting methods and applications remain constant. Comparability is the ability to review side-by-side two or more different companies' financials. Horizontal analysis not only improves the review of a company's consistency over time directly, but it also improves comparability of growth in a company to that of its competitors as well.

Horizontal analysis allows investors and analysts to see what has been driving a company's financial performance over a number of years, as well as to spot trends and growth patterns such as seasonality. It enables analysts to assess relative changes in different line items over time, and project them into the future. By looking at the income statement, balance sheet, and cash flow statement over time, one can create a complete picture of operational results, and see what has been driving a company's performance and whether it is operating efficiently and profitably.

The analysis of critical measures of business performance, such as profit margins, inventory turnover, and return on equity, can detect emerging problems and strengths. For example, earnings per share (EPS) may have been rising because the cost of goods sold (COGS) have been falling, or because sales have been growing strongly. And coverage ratios, like the cash flow-to-debt ratio and the interest coverage ratio can reveal whether a company can service its debt through sufficient liquidity. Horizontal analysis also makes it easier to compare growth rates and profitability among multiple companies.

Example of Horizontal Analysis

Horizontal analysis typically shows the changes from the base period in dollar and percentage. For example, when someone says that revenues have increased by 10% this past quarter, that person is using horizontal analysis. The percentage change is calculated by first dividing the dollar change between the comparison year and the base year by the line item value in the base year, then multiplying the quotient by 100.

For example, assume an investor wishes to invest in company XYZ. The investor may wish to determine how the company grew over the past year. Assume that in company XYZ's base year, it reported net income of $10 million and retained earnings of $50 million. In the current year, company XYZ reported net income of $20 million and retained earnings of $52 million. Consequently, it has an increase of $10 million in its net income and $2 million in its retained earnings year over year. Therefore, company ABC's net income grew by 100% (($20 million - $10 million) / $10 million * 100) year over year, while its retained earnings only grew by 4% (($52 million - $50 million) / $50 million * 100).

Criticism of Horizontal Analysis

Depending on which accounting period an analyst starts from and how many accounting periods are chosen, the current period can be made to appear unusually good or bad. For example, the current period's profits may appear excellent when only compared with those of the previous quarter, but are actually quite poor if compared to the results for the same quarter in the preceding year.

A common problem with horizontal analysis is that the aggregation of information in the financial statements may have changed over time, so that revenues, expenses, assets, or liabilities may shift between different accounts and therefore appear to cause variances when comparing account balances from one period to the next. Indeed, sometimes companies change the way they break down their business segments, in order to make the horizontal analysis of growth and profitability trends more difficult to detect. Accurate analysis can be affected by one-off events and accounting charges.

Vertical Analysis vs. Horizontal Analysis

While horizontal analysis looks changes in the dollar amounts in a company's financial statements over time, vertical analysis looks at each line item as a percentage of a base figure within the current period. Thus, line items on an income statement can be stated as a percentage of gross sales, while line items on a balance sheet can be stated as a percentage of total assets or liabilities, and vertical analysis of a cash flow statement shows each cash inflow or outflow as a percentage of the total cash inflows. Vertical analysis is also known as common size financial statement analysis.

VERTICAL ANALYSIS

Vertical analysis is a method of financial statement analysis in which each line item is listed as a percentage of a base figure within the statement. Thus, line items on an income statement can be stated as a percentage of gross sales, while line items on a balance sheet can be stated as a percentage of total assets or liabilities, and vertical analysis of a cash flow statement shows each cash inflow or outflow as a percentage of the total cash inflows.

How Vertical Analysis Works

Vertical analysis makes it much easier to compare the financial statements of one company with another, and across industries. This is because one can see the relative proportions of account balances. It also makes it easier to compare previous periods for time series analysis, in which quarterly and annual figures are compared over a number of years, in order to gain a picture of whether performance metrics are improving or deteriorating.

For example, by showing the various expense line items in the income statement as a percentage of sales, one can see how these are contributing to profit margins and whether profitability is improving over time. It thus becomes easier to compare the profitability of a company with its peers.

Financial statements that include vertical analysis clearly show line item percentages in a separate column. These types of financial statements, including detailed vertical analysis, are also known as common-size financial statements and are used by many companies to provide greater detail on a company's financial position. Common-size financial statements often incorporate comparative financial statements that include columns comparing each line item to a previously reported period.

Example of Vertical Analysis

For example, suppose XYZ Corporation has gross sales of $5 million and cost of goods sold of $1 million and general and administrative expenses of $2 million and a 25% tax rate, its income statement will look like this if vertical analysis is used.

Sales	5,000,000	100%
Cost of goods sold	1,000,000	20%
Gross profit	4,000,000	80%
General and Administrative Expenses	2,000,000	40%
Operating Income	2,000,000	40%
Taxes (%25)	500,000	10%
Net income	1,500,000	30%

Vertical vs. Horizontal Analysis

Another form of financial statement analysis used in ratio analysis is horizontal analysis or trend analysis. This is where ratios or line items in a company's financial statements are compared over a certain period of time by choosing one year's worth of entries as a baseline, while every other year represents percentage differences in terms of changes to that baseline.

For example, the amount of cash reported on the balance sheet on December 31 of 2018, 2017, 2016, 2015, and 2014 will be expressed as a percentage of the December 31, 2014, amount. Instead of dollar amounts, you might see 141, 135, 126, 118, and 100.

This shows that the amount of cash at the end of 2018 is 141% of the amount it was at the end of 2014. By doing the same analysis for each item on the balance sheet and income statement, one can see how each item has changed in relationship to the other items.

RATIO ANALYSIS

Ratio analysis is a quantitative method of gaining insight into a company's liquidity, operational efficiency, and profitability by comparing information contained in its financial statements. Ratio analysis is a cornerstone of fundamental analysis.

Outside analysts use several types of ratios to assess companies, while corporate insiders rely on them less because of their access to more detailed operational data about a company.

When investors and analysts talk about fundamental or quantitative analysis, they are usually referring to ratio analysis. Ratio analysis involves evaluating the performance and financial health of a company by using data from the current and historical financial statements.

The data retrieved from the statements is used to compare a company's performance over time to assess whether the company is improving or deteriorating, to compare a company's financial standing with the industry average, or to compare a company to one or more other companies operating in its sector to see how the company stacks up.

Ratio analysis can be used to establish a trend line for one company's results over a large number of financial reporting periods. This can highlight company changes that would not be evident if looking at a given ratio that represents just one point in time.

Comparing a company to its peers or its industry averages is another useful application for ratio analysis. Calculating one ratio for competitors in a given industry and comparing across the set of companies can reveal both positive and negative information.

Since companies in the same industry typically have similar capital structures and investment in fixed assets, their ratios should be substantially the same. Different ratio results could mean that one firm has a potential issue and is underperforming the competition, but they could also mean that a certain company is much better at generating profits than its peers. Many analysts use ratios to review sectors, looking for the most and least valuable companies in the group.

Examples of Ratio Analysis Categories

Most investors are familiar with a few key ratios, particularly the ones that are relatively easy to calculate and interpret. Some of these ratios include the current ratio, return on equity (ROE), the debt-equity (D/E) ratio, the dividend payout ratio, and the price/earnings (P/E) ratio. While there are numerous financial ratios, they can be categorized into six main groups based on the type of analysis they provide.

Liquidity Ratios

Liquidity ratios measure a company's ability to pay off its short-term debts as they come due using the company's current or quick assets. Liquidity ratios include the current ratio, quick ratio, and working capital ratio.

Solvency Ratios

Also called financial leverage ratios, solvency ratios compare a company's debt levels with its assets, equity, and earnings to evaluate whether a company can stay afloat in the long-term by paying its long-term debt and interest on the debt. Examples of solvency ratios include debt-equity ratio, debt-assets ratio, and interest coverage ratio.

Profitability Ratios

These ratios show how well a company can generate profits from its operations. Profit margin, return on assets, return on equity, return on capital employed, and gross margin ratio are all examples of profitability ratios.

Efficiency Ratios

Also called activity ratios, efficiency ratios evaluate how well a company uses its assets and liabilities to generate sales and maximize profits. Key efficiency ratios are the asset turnover ratio, inventory turnover, and days' sales in inventory.

Coverage Ratios

These ratios measure a company's ability to make the interest payments and other obligations associated with its debts. The times interest earned ratio and the debt-service coverage ratio are both examples of coverage ratios.

Market Prospect Ratios

These are the most commonly used ratios in fundamental analysis and include dividend yield, P/E ratio, earnings per share, and dividend payout ratio. Investors use these ratios to determine what they may receive in earnings from their investments and to predict what the trend of a stock will be in the future.

For example, if the average P/E ratio of all companies in the S&P 500 index is 20, with the majority of companies having a P/E between 15 and 25, a stock with a P/E ratio of 7 would be considered undervalued, while one with a P/E of 50 would be considered overvalued. The former may trend upwards in the future, while the latter will trend downwards until it matches with its intrinsic value.

Examples of Ratio Analysis in Use

Ratio analysis can provide an early warning of potential improvement or deterioration in a company's financial situation or performance. Analysts engage in extensive number-crunching of the financial data in a company's quarterly financial reports for any such hints.

Successful companies generally have solid ratios in all areas, and any hints of weakness in one area may spark a significant sell-off of the stock. Certain ratios are closely scrutinized because of their relevance to a certain sector, such as inventory turnover for the retail sector and days sales outstanding (DSOs) for technology companies.

Using any ratio in any of the categories listed above should only be considered as a starting point. Further analysis using additional ratios and qualitative analysis should be incorporated to effectively analyze a company's overall financial position.

Ratios are usually only comparable across companies in the same sector, since an acceptable ratio in one industry may be regarded as too high to too low in another. For example, companies in sectors such as utilities typically have a high debt-equity ratio which is normal for its industry, while a similar ratio for a technology company may be regarded as unsustainably high.

PROFITABILITY ANALYSIS

Profitability analysis is a component of enterprise resource planning (ERP) that allows administrators to forecast the profitability of a proposal or optimize the profitability of an existing project. Profitability analysis can anticipate sales and profit potential specific to aspects of the market such as customer age groups, geographic regions, or product types.

Profitability analysis can help key personnel in an enterprise to:

- Identify the most and least profitable clients.
- Identify the most and least profitable products or services.
- Discover which sources of information offer the most reliable facts.
- Optimize responses to changing customer needs.

- Evolve the product mix to maximize profits in the medium and long term.
- Isolate and remedy the causes of decreasing profit margins.

TREND ANALYSIS

Trend Analysis is a statistical technique that tries to determine future movements of a given variable by analyzing historical trends. In other words, it is a method that aims to predict future behaviors by examining past ones.

Trend analysis is a technique employed by technical analyst in the financial industry to predict the future movements of a given asset. They employ historical data to determine the direction of the trend. The goal of this procedure is to identify attractive investment opportunities that are currently showing an upward trend; and of course, to identify downtrends too, so investors can get out before losing money.

Perhaps one of the disadvantages of trend analysis is that past behavior is not always consistent in the future, in other words, whatever the price of a given security did in the past is not necessary an indication of what it will do in the future because there are a lot of other significant elements that come into play when it comes to determining the value a financial security.

Example:

Mr. Nolan is a Financial Analyst at Duck Financial LLC. He is currently analyzing the historical stock data of a company called Black Sea Petroleum LLC. The company's stock price has been increasing on a daily basis for the last 7 days, by 0.02% a day. Mr. Nolan determined that this is an uptrend, since in the past, whenever the company has had this increases the uptrend has endured for more than 3 months.

This is an example of how trend analysis work. By analyzing the historical behavior of the stock the analyst can gather evidence to issue an opinion and to predict future movements of the stock price. By doing this, an investor can make the decision of investing in Black Sea Petroleum LLC stocks because there's a potential gain in the transaction, according to the analyst opinion.

PURPOSES AND SIGNIFICANCE OF FINANCIAL STATEMENT ANALYSIS

Solvency

Solvency is the ability of a company to meet its long-term debts and financial obligations. Solvency is essential to staying in business as it demonstrates a company's ability to continue operations into the foreseeable future. While a company also needs liquidity to thrive and pay off its short-term obligations, such short-term liquidity should not be confused with solvency. A company that is insolvent will often enter bankruptcy.

How Solvency Works

Solvency directly relates to the ability of an individual or business to pay their long-term debts including any associated interest. To be considered solvent, the value of an entity's assets, whether in reference to a company or an individual, must be greater than the sum of its debt obligations. Various mathematical calculations can be performed to help determine the solvency of a business or individual.

Certain events can create a risk to an entity's solvency. In the case of business, the pending expiration of a patent may pose risks to solvency as it will allow competitors to produce the product in question and it results in a loss of associated royalty payments. Further, changes in certain regulations that directly impact a company's ability to continue business operations can pose an additional risk. Both businesses and individuals may experience solvency issues should a large judgment be ordered against them after a lawsuit.

Special Considerations: Solvency Ratios

Investors can use ratios to analyze a company's solvency. The interest coverage ratio divides operating income by interest expense to show a company's ability to pay the interest on its debt, with a higher result indicating greater solvency. The debt-to-assets ratio divides a company's debt by the value of its assets to show whether a company has taken on too much debt, with a lower result indicating greater solvency. Equity ratios demonstrate the amount of funds that remain after the value of the assets, offset by the outstanding debt, is divided among eligible investors.

Solvency ratios vary by industry, so it is important to understand what constitutes a good ratio for the company before drawing conclusions from the ratio calculations. Ratios that suggest lower solvency than the industry average may suggest financial problems are on the horizon.

Solvency versus Liquidity

While solvency represents a company's ability to meet long-term obligations, liquidity represents a company's ability to meet its short-term obligations. In order for funds to be considered liquid, they must be either immediately accessible or easily converted into usable funds. Cash is considered the most liquid payment vehicle. A company that lacks liquidity can be forced to enter bankruptcy even if solvent if it cannot convert its assets into funds that can be used to meet financial obligations.

Inter-firm Comparision

Meaning of Inter-firm Comparison

Inter-firm comparison is the technique which studies the performances, efficiencies, costs and profits of various concerns in an industry with the help of exchange of information in order to have a relative comparison.

It involves the process by bringing together a number of identical firms and collecting their business figures and statistics through a neutral organisation in which the participating firms repose their full confidence.

The firms are carefully screened and put into different size groups, their figures examined from a close range, comparative performance of each firm of the group drawn up showing the strong and weak points of its operations, and finally the reports are published without disclosing their identity, but using only codes and expressed in terms of certain well established ratios and percentages.

The figures under comparison may relate to (i) the financial results viz., the position of assets, liabilities, profit, capital employed, etc. expressed in terms of financial ratios; (ii) cost structure of the products viz., material cost, labour cost, overhead etc. expressed in terms of cost ratios; (iii) physical and operational performance such as output or operation per man hour, expressed in terms of productivity ratios and percentages, and so on.

The main objectives of inter-firm comparison are:

1. To know one's weak points in comparison with other firms and to improve the efficiency in future.
2. To locate the spots of in-economies so that action may be taken to effect economy by eliminating such sources of in-economies.
3. To know whether the profits of the firm are adequate and further to improve profitability position by comparing its profits with the member firms.
4. To enable the member units to standardise various functions so that wastage can be minimised.

Need for Inter-firm Comparison

Progressive management, the world over has always asked itself the question—how is my company performing in comparison to that of others? The published trading and profit and loss accounts and the balance sheets along-with the annual reports provide scanty data for purposeful study and assessment of the performance of a company.

The figures available from these reports just indicate, in a general way, the profitability, stability, solvency and growth of an organisation, but they do not throw light on whether a company has really made the optimum use of all the available resources in men, materials etc.

The answer, however, depends fully on the availability of more detailed data, and the possibility of comparison with the competitive units in the same line of manufacture.

It is the inter-firm comparison that provides the management with a vivid comparative picture of how its operating performance, financial results, and product cost structure compare with those of other firms of similar size, nature, industry or trade.

Requirements (Pre-Requisites) of an Inter-Firm Comparison Scheme. The following are the main requirements while installing a scheme of inter-firm comparison:

Adaption of Uniform Costing

There must be a sound system of uniform costing in the firm where inter-firm comparison scheme is to be implemented. A uniform manual should also be prepared and distributed among the member units to enable the function of the system efficiently.

Organisation Responsible

An organisation must be established to run the system efficiently and for better results firms of different sizes in an industry should become member of the organization. In industrially advanced countries independent agencies such as British Centre for Inter-firm Comparison, European Productivity Agency and U.S. Bureau of Labour Statistics are responsible for collection, coordination and presentation of information. In some cases trade associations, holding company or parent organisation are doing this work.

Information to be Collected

The nature of information to be collected from the participating firms depends upon the needs of the management, comparative importance of the information and the efficiency of the central body responsible for the collection of the information. The information to be collected must be relevant only.

Information is generally collected relating to costs and cost structure, labour or machine efficiency and utilisation, raw material consumption, wastage, inventory, return on capital employed, liquidity, reserves and appropriation of profit, methods of production, creditors and debtors, technical aspects etc.

Method of Collection and Presentation of Information

The time and the form in which the information is to be submitted by the member units must be decided in advance. The various statistical tools for the purpose of collection of data, its editing, classification, presentation, drawing conclusions and inferences can be used. Ratio analysis for measuring profitability, efficiency and productivity etc. can also be used.

Advantages of Inter-firm Comparison

Inter-firm comparison is nothing more than learning by example. It is for the management that inter-firm comparison has been evolved as a technique in industry. From the point of view of the working of a particular firm, it is at times impossible to know what is happening outside and why.

Inter-firm comparison by an expert outside body affords suitable knowledge, satisfying to a large extent this need for management to know that the competitors in the line are doing and how.

To the workers and their unions, inter-firm comparisons help to give an idea of the relative capacity of the firms in question in terms of wages and the wage scales, production bonus, increasing the possibilities of employment etc. as well as the relative efficiency of the workers in a particular firm vis-a-vis other firms in the same industry, the same area, or the same class of workers. It can help management to make effective divisions at strategic and operating levels.

The following are the main advantages of inter-firm comparison besides what have been stated in the advantages of uniform costing:

1. It encourages managerial efficiency in the organisation by pointing out the spots of inefficiencies and thus brings stability in the cost structure and presentation of information.

2. It creates cost consciousness among the participating firms and they are cautious in this respect at all levels of management.

3. It helps the member firms to reduce their costs in case their costs are more as compared to other firms.

4. It increases the productivity by locating the weaknesses and in-economies. Inter-firm comparison technique is a method of self-analysis of the business by the businessmen themselves. The management of the business on the basis of results obtained from the self-analysis is bound to react and look around for means to improve its performance or increase productivity. Inter-firm comparison will, therefore, prove as an incentive, to productivity.

5. It provides useful information to management of every member unit to make proper decisions and enable the management to continue to review the operations and policies of the business as a whole or its divisions.

6. It stimulates self-criticism by comparing its data with the other firms.

7. It enables the firms to evaluate the data relating to the operations of the competitors in order to analyse its weaknesses as compared to other firms.

8. The benefits of research is passed on to member units by the central organisation.

9. It ensures standardisation of production process.

10. It helps the government, regulatory agencies, and researchers in getting useful data and information to improve policies and conducting depth studies and research.

The utility of inter-firm comparison in these words: "It is not only useful for management, it also acts as a tool for decision making by bankers, shareholders, institutional investors, licencing authorities, price control organisations, creditors, trade unions, consumers' organisations and other social and economic interests. It is also useful in evaluating business results and return on capital invested which, in turn, helps in project appraisal and evaluation, conducting feasibility studies, capital budgeting, investment decisions etc."

Limitations of Inter-firm Comparison

The following limitations of inter-firm comparison may be noted:

1. The top management may not be convinced of the utility of inter-firm comparison because it is of the opinion that when other tools of comparison are available, this tool has no utility.

2. Mostly the member firms do not disclose the relevant data as they think it to be confidential. Thus the information supplied may not be reliable for comparison or decision making purposes.

3. There may be no cost accounting system properly executed in the concern. This will result in unreliable figures relating to the various aspects of cost and there is possibility of misleading results if decisions are taken on the basis of these figures.

4. There may not be available a suitable base for comparison purposes.
5. In such comparisons, time factor is totally ignored. The inconsistencies in financial reporting are totally ignored. No adjustments are made for changes in the prices. No attention is given to the level of technology and technological developments. Generally there is a lack of common valuation method in different units to be compared.

References

- Financial-statement-analysis-meaning-objectives-and-limitations-firm, meaning-financial-statements, financial-statements, accounting: yourarticlelibrary.com, Retrieved 14 July 2019
- Top-8-requisites-of-financial-statement-analysis, financial-statements-analysis, accounting: yourarticlelibrary.com, Retrieved 17 May, 2019
- Horizontalanalysis, terms: investopedia.com, Retrieved 19 April 2019
- Vertica-analysis, terms: investopedia.com, Retrieved 25 February 2019
- Profitability-analysis, definition: techtarget.com, Retrieved 26 July 2019
- Trend-analysis, accounting-dictionary: myaccountingcourse.com, Retrieved 6 January 2019
- Inter-firm-comparison-need-types-and-requirements, inter-firm-comparison, cost-accounting: yourarticlelibrary.com, Retrieved 29 January 2019

Permissions

All chapters in this book are published with permission under the Creative Commons Attribution Share Alike License or equivalent. Every chapter published in this book has been scrutinized by our experts. Their significance has been extensively debated. The topics covered herein carry significant information for a comprehensive understanding. They may even be implemented as practical applications or may be referred to as a beginning point for further studies.

We would like to thank the editorial team for lending their expertise to make the book truly unique. They have played a crucial role in the development of this book. Without their invaluable contributions this book wouldn't have been possible. They have made vital efforts to compile up to date information on the varied aspects of this subject to make this book a valuable addition to the collection of many professionals and students.

This book was conceptualized with the vision of imparting up-to-date and integrated information in this field. To ensure the same, a matchless editorial board was set up. Every individual on the board went through rigorous rounds of assessment to prove their worth. After which they invested a large part of their time researching and compiling the most relevant data for our readers.

The editorial board has been involved in producing this book since its inception. They have spent rigorous hours researching and exploring the diverse topics which have resulted in the successful publishing of this book. They have passed on their knowledge of decades through this book. To expedite this challenging task, the publisher supported the team at every step. A small team of assistant editors was also appointed to further simplify the editing procedure and attain best results for the readers.

Apart from the editorial board, the designing team has also invested a significant amount of their time in understanding the subject and creating the most relevant covers. They scrutinized every image to scout for the most suitable representation of the subject and create an appropriate cover for the book.

The publishing team has been an ardent support to the editorial, designing and production team. Their endless efforts to recruit the best for this project, has resulted in the accomplishment of this book. They are a veteran in the field of academics and their pool of knowledge is as vast as their experience in printing. Their expertise and guidance has proved useful at every step. Their uncompromising quality standards have made this book an exceptional effort. Their encouragement from time to time has been an inspiration for everyone.

The publisher and the editorial board hope that this book will prove to be a valuable piece of knowledge for students, practitioners and scholars across the globe.

Index

www.ingramcontent.com/pod-product-compliance
Lightning Source LLC
LaVergne TN
LVHW080908210926
848485LV00004B/618